CHARLES JOHNSON

CHARLES JOHNSON

The Novelist as Philosopher

Edited by
MARC C. CONNER AND WILLIAM R. NASH

UNIVERSITY PRESS OF MISSISSIPPI • *Jackson*

www.upress.state.ms.us

The University Press of Mississippi is a member of the Association of American University Presses.

Copyright © 2007 by University Press of Mississippi
All rights reserved
Manufactured in the United States of America

Paperback Edition 2010

Library of Congress Cataloging-in-Publication Data
Charles Johnson : the novelist as philosopher / edited by Marc C. Conner and William R. Nash. — 1st ed.
    p. cm.
    Includes bibliographical references and index.
    ISBN-13: 978-1-60473-506-2
    ISBN-10: 1-60473-506-6
    1. Johnson, Charles Richard, 1948——Criticism and interpretation. 2. Johnson, Charles Richard,
1948——Philosophy. 3. Philosophy in literature. 4. African Americans in literature. I. Conner, Marc C.,
1965– II. Nash, William R., 1964–
    PS3560.O3735Z63 2007
    813'.54—dc22
                                                                                                2006025331
British Library Cataloging-in-Publication Data available

To Matthew, Noah, and Isaac
—M C C

To Hadley
—W R N

CONTENTS

ACKNOWLEDGMENTS

This book represents several years of ongoing effort by a number of scholars who find Charles Johnson's writings particularly challenging, fascinating, and relevant to American culture at the dawn of the twenty-first century. I want to thank all the contributors to this volume, and especially my fellow editor Will Nash, for the rich conversations, conference papers, letters, and formal writings that have led to this study. I am grateful also to Charles Johnson, who has supported and generously aided our inquiries into his work. Alan Jacobs, Genelle Gertz, and Lucas Morel offered helpful comments to parts of this book, and Suzanne Keen and Jim Warren gave sound advice at every stage of the writing process. The Washington & Lee University library and administration have supported this project from start to finish. Seetha Srinivasan, Walter Biggins, and the University Press of Mississippi have been encouraging and helpful, and their good direction has helped shape this book into its final form. Finally, and of greatest importance, I thank my parents, Beverly and Terry Conner, my wife Barbara, and my three sons, Matthew, Noah, and Isaac. Like Andrew Hawkins, I have found that my dharma, such as it is, is that of the Householder, and in these good souls I am at home.

MCC

It's only fitting that in the last lap, even on this acknowledgment page, I am again indebted to Marc Conner. Throughout this process, he's had a clarity of vision and a depth of energy that have made this book possible. One of the main reasons that I took on this project was that it afforded me the chance to work with Marc—how wonderfully that has paid off. And since he's so ably thanked our co-conspirators, I'll simply add that I am grateful to them as well and note my tremendous respect for them, each and all. Finally, as in everything I do, my deepest debt and gratitude are to my family, especially Deb and Hadley. Their encouragement and perspective, their humor and their love, brighten my world, and I owe them both more than I can ever repay.

WRN

INTRODUCTION
Charles Johnson and Philosophical Black Fiction

MARC C. CONNER AND WILLIAM R. NASH

> *Perception is an act, and this observation puts the lie to that ancient stupidity*
> *that says the processes of philosophy and fiction are two different enterprises—*
> *they are sister disciplines, I would say, and unless a critic realizes this, his*
> *position is simply untenable.*
> —CHARLES JOHNSON, *Being and Race*

I

CHARLES JOHNSON AND PHILOSOPHICAL BLACK FICTION

"I am," Charles Johnson states, "first and foremost, a writer of philosophical fiction" (McWilliams, "An Interview" 275). This marriage of the art of fiction and the traditions of philosophy stands behind everything Johnson writes, from his novels to his short stories to his essays (both literary and philosophical— they are one and the same to Johnson) to his book reviews. Johnson's wide-ranging education and background have provided him with a formidable training in these disciplines: raised in the AME Church with a substantial background in Christianity and the Bible, he is also a formal student of western philosophy, holding a doctorate in phenomenology from SUNY–Stony Brook; he is also a longtime practitioner of Buddhism, as well as an accomplished martial artist in several oriental traditions and a student of Sanskrit; he began his artistic career as a cartoonist, then trained himself as a fiction writer. In all of his work, he strives to combine the crossing of worlds that has made up his own life, and indeed this constitutes his fundamental aesthetic position.[1]

Throughout all aspects of his writing, Johnson engages two philosophical domains that have long been considered separate and distinct, perhaps even irreconcilable: the traditions of western philosophy, from the pre-Socratics and Plato to Augustine and the medievalists to the existential tradition and contemporary philosophers; and the traditions of eastern philosophy, ranging from Buddhist to Hindu to Taoist thought. And Johnson then expands on this already audacious enterprise, for he works to integrate these formidable traditions with the history, culture, and literature of African-America. Such a combination is starkly original in the history of American letters. Johnson comments, "there is more engagement with philosophy—Western and Eastern—in my work than you will find anywhere in the history of black American literature," for this is the heart of his goal as a creative writer: "I wanted somehow to merge, in my own work, the black experience and about two thousand years' worth of philosophical reflection" (Nash, "A Conversation," 222, and McCullough 4–5).

Consequently, Johnson's writings participate in a specific literary category, *philosophical black fiction*—a category that Johnson himself has largely defined, if not created. It is crucial to note that for Johnson the main emphasis is on the philosophical engagement with the black experience—he strongly resists any identification with writing that focuses on the black experience from a limited, restricted, or essentialized perspective. Such a perspective is limited to a particularized notion of black being, one commonly associated with black cultural nationalism and its descendent, Afrocentrism. In this formulation, the notion of a Black Experience, a monolithic rendering of African-American life typically characterized by an emphasis on suffering and racial oppression, stands as a given. By privileging this vision of black life, writers restrict their creative possibilities and limit their readers' ability to "see darkness differently."[2]

In his early essay, "Philosophy and Black Fiction" (1980), Johnson argues that such a conception of black being proves that black artists "have frozen [their] vision in figures that caricature, at best, the complexity of [their] lives and leave the real artistic chore of interpretation unfinished" (60). He further complains that these authors "fail, fail utterly to express authentic ways of seeing (And let us assume there are, can be, authentic Black ways of seeing)." What, then, is the solution to this inauthentic, paralyzingly narrow conception of black being? In response to the impulse towards caricature, Johnson says, artists must make "genuine fiction [which offers] an efflorescence of meaning or a clarification of perception" (56). In his view, this goal is best achieved by fusing the craft of writing fiction and the subject matter of black American lives with elements of Western and Eastern philosophy that range temporally from the pre-Socratics to the twentieth century and spatially from America, Germany, and France to India, China, and Japan. By doing so, writers (especially black writers) can achieve the "liberation of perception" that will enable them to realize and represent the full scope of Black life and letters.

Johnson expands upon these points in "Whole Sight: Notes on New Black Fiction" (1984), a crucial essay that lays the foundation for many of the major points made in his longest aesthetic study, *Being and Race: Black Writing Since 1970* (1988). Borrowing a phrase from John Fowles, Johnson suggests that one achieves "whole sight" by articulating a particular perspective in one's fiction, and then expanding the "expression and vision" of that viewpoint in an effort to access the universal. For the black writer, "whole sight" might be called the epitome of seeing darkness differently, of opening oneself to the richness that black being contains and eschewing narrow notions of an authentic, monolithic Black Experience in favor of a messier, and ultimately much more interesting, representation of myriad experiences of blackness. In the process of calling for this full consideration of blackness, Johnson also suggests how contemporary African-American writers should situate themselves in relation to their predecessors. As he says, "the history of literary practice creates objective aesthetic possibilities, artistic works demanded historically by the foul-ups and partial breakthroughs in past literary art, novels and stories and poems that fill in the blanks and potholes created by the oversights and omissions of those writers (white and black) who preceded us" (86). The philosophical writer's responsibility, in short, is to build on the literary past to create a new vision for American literature in general and African-American literature specifically.[3]

Johnson continues with this theme in *Being and Race: Black Writing Since 1970*, the book-length project that includes revised versions of "Whole Sight" and "Philosophy and Black Fiction." Here Johnson suggests that black literature has traditionally circumscribed the range of experiences it creates by emphasizing the African-American community's suffering, overlooking in the process a broader spectrum of meanings black fiction could encompass. The recurrent theme of his discussion is that black literature is "about" identity, specifically a "crisis of identity" that he traces to the struggle between nineteenth-century separatists and integrationists (8). In Johnson's view, most black writers who write about a Black Experience have avoided the philosophical assessment of what identity and experience are (as concepts). Philosophical Black Fiction corrects that omission by, in Johnson's words, "opening up black literature to the same ethical, ontological, and epistemological questions—Western and Eastern—that I wrestled with as a student of philosophy" (Boccia 194). This is not to suggest that only Johnson writes or has written in this vein; indeed, his major predecessors in this tradition include W. E. B. Du Bois, Jean Toomer, and Ralph Ellison, to name but a few. Nevertheless, Johnson is arguably unique in the tradition for the extent of his fusion of Eastern and Western influences and his articulation of a systematic approach to making Philosophical Black Fiction.[4]

In Chapter Two of *Being and Race*, "Being and Fiction," Johnson argues that practitioners of this category must restructure the writing process as well as revise the end product. The first step comes when black writers resist "the uncritical accumulation of experience" as a means of expanding their range of potential subject matter. The problem with this sort of fieldwork, in Johnson's view, is that most often the people who do it have decided what they will find before they even look. Limited by preconceptions, and sorely in need of the "liberation of perception" and the "whole sight" that Johnson advocates in his essays, these writers simply use new experiences to confirm their existing beliefs and attitudes.

Johnson counters that limiting impulse by challenging writers to create universes that outstrip the restrictions of lived experience. For example, he urges black writers to imagine the world from the perspective of a fully developed white character. This action requires African-American writers to transcend the experience of the world that their racialized bodies give them and to create instead new, fictional life-worlds that expand both their and their readers' perceptions. One sees this expansion of perception in Johnson's creation of Flo Hatfield, the hedonistic white slave master in *Oxherding Tale*. As Andrew learns to see the world through Flo's eyes, he realizes that bondage to desire is not determined by race. Such a revelation—that there might have been someone on the old plantation who suffered as much or more than the slaves—is startling indeed, and flies in the face of most accepted characterizations of slave life. The same is true when Andrew says "it would have been easier to pick cotton" than to be all things—"husband, ravager, teacher, Galahad, eunuch, swashbuckler, student priest"—to Flo (61). The notion is somewhat humorous, to be sure (and Johnson throughout his career has insisted on the need to view African-American history with a sense of the comic, as well as the tragic); but the humorous view of slavery is not the main innovation here, as readers of works such as Ishmael Reed's *Flight to Canada* can attest. What is radical is that the author's freeing of his own perceptions about slavery enables him to offer up a fictional life-world that can free his readers' perceptions as well.

Johnson also complains that too often black writers accept language without challenging the attached preconceptions embedded within that language.

Speakers of a language arbitrarily assign labels to symbols based on collective experience. Those assignments "fix" language within boundaries that make innovation difficult. Instead, the writer must recognize that fiction is "the presence of others in language," an event in which "our subjectivity is merged with that of a stranger." "To read," Johnson argues, "is to inhabit the role and real place of others; to write is a stranger experience yet, for it involves a corresponding act of self-surrender such that my perceptions and experiences are allowed to coincide with those who came before me and despoiled words, shaped their sense and use" (*Being and Race* 39). Rather than accepting language as it is handed to us, what is needed, as Rudolph Byrd points out, is a liberating conception of the multiplicities of language such as the Russian theorist Mikhail Bakhtin offers. Bakhtin's concepts of the dialogic imagination and of heteroglossia, of the multiple meanings and intentions of language, offer a rich parallel to Johnson's own creative practice. As Byrd argues,

> Johnson positions himself "amidst heteroglossia." He is thus in dialogue with himself, with other writers, and with other philosophers. Each "literary-verbal performance" is an instance of self-assertion and self-definition; that is to say, each is the assertion of his own personal voice within the context of a range of literary and philosophical traditions. In positioning himself amid the rich, expressive verbal field of heteroglossia, which Bakhtin defines as "another's speech in another's language," each "literary-verbal performance" by Johnson becomes an illustration of what Bakhtin terms "double-voiced discourse." (*Charles Johnson's Novels* 17–18)[5]

Only such an understanding of language as multiple, many-voiced, and offering myriad perspectives to both writer and reader can accommodate Johnson's bold and innovative approaches to the written word.

Johnson's 1990 essay, "The Philosopher and the American Novel," describes the ways in which he has rendered his philosophical views on story-writing into his actual novels. He emphasizes here the need for new visions and directions in black fiction, and how writers could subsequently bring that awareness to fruition by writing fiction that raises fundamental ontological and philosophical questions, that seeks innovation in form through an exploration of older forms, and that above all arises from its creator's constant awareness that literary art could, through an infusion of philosophical subjects and methodologies, be more than it ever had been before. As the story of his creative evolution demonstrates, Johnson views Philosophical Fiction as "something you do," a form to be cultivated and expanded in service of the larger goal of advancing a richer, more complex vision of black experiences.

II

THINKING AND DOING: THE POLITICAL DIMENSIONS OF PHILOSOPHICAL BLACK FICTION

"The novel," Ralph Ellison once famously remarked, "is *always* a public gesture, though not necessarily a political one" (*Collected Essays* 158). In discussing Charles Johnson's stance towards the politics of literature, Ellison's words are quite useful. For despite the occasional critical view that Johnson avoids the political realm,[6] in fact his writings resolutely engage politics, but under the broader concept of *the public realm*. For Johnson, politics is one aspect of our social life, the life of the community—what he terms, following King, "an 'inescapable network of mutuality' that binds all people in a single 'garment of destiny'" ("The King We Left Behind" 198). Many aspects of his work are resolutely political—one thinks of the story "Executive Decision," or passages in *Dreamer* and *Oxherding Tale* that explicitly engage and comment upon political theory and practice, or essays such as "*The Second Front*," "Black Images and Their Global Impact," and "The King We Left Behind." Yet, like Plato, like Aristotle, like Shakyamuni Buddha, like Martin Luther King, Jr., Johnson views the domain of politics as part of, or even complementary to, metaphysics, ethics, and aesthetics. Thus, Johnson would recoil from Du Bois's provocative dictum, "all art is propaganda and ever must be. . . . I do not care a damn for any art that is not used for propaganda"; but he would enthusiastically pursue Du Bois's probing question (from the same essay), "for who shall describe beauty? What is it?" ("Criteria of Negro Art," 1000, 995). For Johnson has stated that "a love of doing art forces one to think about art, which leads to aesthetics, and that ultimately forces an artist to consider all the philosophical questions in epistemology, metaphysics, ethics, ontology, and so forth" (Myers 36). For Johnson, the pursuit of the beautiful, of the true, and of the good are common pursuits, whether one's task is the creation of art, or the creation of a more just society.

The essence of Johnson's political view is also the starting-point of his aesthetic practice, and is well described in Johnson's pregnant phrase, "the liberation of perception" ("Philosophy and Black Fiction" 84). As Ashraf Rushdy argues, the liberation of our ways of seeing the world expresses Johnson's actual political vision: "these ideas about writing as literally a freeing of perception have much to do with Johnson's political commitments" ("Properties of Desire" 96). For the heart of the political in Johnson's view is to free ourselves from the narrow, oppositional, categorized modes of thought that generate such repugnant social actions as tyranny, fascism, racism, sexism, oppression, and hatred. It is not that Johnson eschews political thought and action—quite the contrary. Rather, he insists that "effective social change requires effort on two 'fronts,' one directed externally to eliminate injustice in the political realm, the other directed inwardly toward refining our character and cultural values" ("The King We Left Behind" 199). To operate on only one of either of these fronts is to cripple our efforts in both. To Johnson, this is the tragedy of our failure to attend to King's teachings: "In the vacuum left by King no spokesman has emerged to electrify us with the tough-minded message that segregation and separatism, whether they arise from black or white communities, cripple our potential as social beings" ("The King We Left Behind" 194).

Consequently, while Johnson certainly remains steadfast in his efforts on the first front—all of his writings work resolutely towards righting injustice both individually and politically—his main impetus is without question the fate and character of the individual. This forms the basis of his developing critique of African-American culture over the past thirty years: "Between my generation and that of so many of the children I've seen there has been no transmission of the triumphs, personal and political, that strengthened Black Americans for centuries, allowing our predecessors to overcome staggering obstacles in the pre–civil rights era and raise strong, resourceful sons and daughters—like King and countless others before him" ("The King We Left Behind" 198). The failure of American culture, of whatever race, has been to forget the essence of King's teachings.[7] Hence Johnson devotes much of *Dreamer* to expressing the King whom he describes as "our most prominent moral philosopher of the second half of the twentieth century" ("The King We Need" 42). When Chaym Smith investigates King's life and teachings, he comes to understand the three principles that underlie Johnson's own "political" (that is, philosophical) vision:

> First, the deeper meaning of nonviolence, not merely as a strategy for protest, but as a Way, a daily praxis men must strive to translate into each and every one of their deeds . . . so that in its fullness King's moral stance implied noninjury to everything that exists. Second, *agape*, the ability to

love something not for what it presently was . . . but for what it could be, a teleological love that recognized everything as process, not product, and saw beneath the surface to a thing's potentiality. And last, the fact of integration as the life's blood of Being itself. (108)[8]

Dreamer seeks to proffer a philosophical vision of "two fronts" that will replace the bankrupt doctrines of separatism, identity politics, and racialism that Johnson sees as crippling real social growth in America. Not only through its depiction of King, but also in its presentations of positive familial models of self-reliance and responsibility (particularly to children), *Dreamer* generates a series of representations of the moral life that Johnson sees as the best solution to the divisions that cripple America today. These representations can be viewed simultaneously as "the author's social-activist response" to Johnson's guiding question—"How shall I live?" (Nash 177)—and also as a series of philosophical positions that lead to the liberation of the individual from all that constrains and limits her perception of self and world.[9] Indeed, for Johnson this is not merely a political nor a philosophical teaching, but an aesthetic one as well. He claims that the essential requirement for the artist is to forget "heavily conditioned seeing, this calcification of perception . . . we might well call this retraining of the eye the artist's equivalent to the phenomenological *epoche*, or 'bracketing' of all presuppositions in order to seize a fresh, original vision" (*Being and Race* 5).

Clearly Johnson's emphasis on philosophy cannot be separated from the multiple political implications of his writings—nor would he wish it to be so, for the thrust of his philosophy contains a political liberation and, as William Gleason argues in his essay in this volume, an injunction to "go there" into the messy, complicated, profoundly human world of the social domain. However, he would resist any effort by readers or critics to reduce his writings to the merely political—for Johnson, as for Ellison, the political follows from, rather than guides, the writing. This forms the basis for Johnson's rejection of the major premises of the Black Aesthetic (and indeed any creative writing that rests upon a foundation of racial difference).[10] He has commented that the Black Aesthetic "is an inversion of black typifications derived from earlier white stereotypes" (*Being and Race* 19), that it depends fundamentally on "the ethical dualism which has—over long centuries of Western cultural development—made white 'good' and black 'evil.'" This history of western dualisms—"the dialectic of matter and mind, subject and object . . . running the length of Western intellectual history, beginning with Plato's world of flux and world of forms" ("Phenomenology of the Black Body" 110–11)—is embodied in Johnson's fiction in the sinister, charismatic figure of Captain Falcon in *Middle Passage*, who speaks eloquently of the power to enslave that dualistic thinking offers:

> "Conflict," says he, "is what it means to be conscious. Dualism is a bloody structure of the mind. Subject and object, perceiver and perceived, self and other—these ancient twins are built into mind like the stem-piece of a merchantman. We cannot think without them, sir. And what, pray, kin such a thing mean? Only this, Mr. Calhoun: They are signs of a transcendental Fault, a deep crack in consciousness itself. Mind was made for murder. Slavery, if you think this through, forcing yourself not to flinch, is the social correlate of a deeper, ontic wound." (97–98)

If there is a *philosophical* "villain" in Johnson's thought, it is dualism—and it is no accident that the *political* villain in his work is the offspring of dualism: fear, hatred, slavery, murder.[11] Johnson's ongoing argument is that we must address this philosophical problem if we hope to ameliorate our political ills; but focusing solely on those political ills is comparable to treating symptoms, not causes.

Johnson never sentimentalizes or softens the harsh realities of the African-American experience: "The black experience in America," he writes, "like the teachings of Shakyamuni Buddha, begins with suffering" (*Turning* 46). But he insists that this is fundamentally a philosophical problem, one that can only be overcome by transcending all dualistic definitions of self and world—including that most cherished of western illusions, according to Johnson, "the belief in an enduring 'personal identity,' an 'I' endlessly called upon to prove its worth and deny its inferiority in a world that so often mirrors back only negative images of the black self":

> The emphasis in Buddhist teachings on letting go of the fabricated, false sense of self positions issues of race as foremost among samsaric illusions, along with all the essentialist conceptions of difference that have caused so much human suffering and mischief since the eighteenth century. It frees one from dualist models of epistemology that partition experience into separate, boxlike compartments of Mind and Body, Self and Other, Matter and Spirit—these divisions, one sees, are ontologically the correlates of racial divisions found in South African apartheid and American segregation and are just as pernicious. (*Turning* 54)

In place of this illusion of self and other, Johnson proffers King's "dream of the 'beloved community,' " in which all barriers are dissolved. As Johnson advances the notion of this beloved community in *Dreamer*, he invokes Buddhist monk and peace activist Thich Nhat Hanh. Nhat Hanh, whom King knew and admired, advocates awareness of all individuals' "interbeing," a term that resonates with King's famous assertion that we are all bound in a "web of mutuality." Nhat Hanh applies that consciousness of our interbeing in a quest for peace and social justice that has come to be known as "engaged Buddhism." This notion of fusing the Buddhist recognition of identity as illusion with a committed struggle for social justice pervades Johnson's work, especially his recent essays "Accepting the Invitation" and "A Sangha by Another Name" (*Turning* 42–57); indeed, "engaged Buddhsim" becomes a perfect medium for Johnson to fuse his political and philosophical interests and thereby to avoid the sort of mental dualism he deplores.[12]

In sum, Johnson employs philosophy, in the broadest sense, to understand and address the deepest social and spiritual challenges faced by humankind. Although at times scholars tend to collapse Johnson's philosophical teachings into a rough combining of east and west, in fact his thought is far more complex—certain elements of so-called western thought he rejects outright, whereas others he holds to rigorously; and he also selects carefully the elements of eastern thought that he will emphasize.[13] Johnson himself calls for "the revitalizing influence of cross-cultural fertilization" in black fiction "to move closer to the objective of *whole sight*" ("Whole Sight" 88), and this notion of "cross-cultural fertilization" of east and west is a rich metaphor for understanding Johnson's complex philosophical thought.[14] He draws upon multiple elements from both western and eastern philosophy in his effort to construct what Rudolph Byrd terms an "American palimpsest" of fiction, philosophy, and culture.[15] To best understand the literary and cultural implications of this practice, one must consider the specific philosophical texts and traditions to which Johnson is indebted, drawing upon (and ultimately combining) both the western and the eastern traditions of philosophical inquiry.

III

CHARLES JOHNSON AND WESTERN PHILOSOPHICAL TRADITIONS

Johnson has long been intimately engaged with the very roots of western philosophical thought: the pre-Socratic philosophers, those Greek thinkers who preceded the great age of Socrates, Plato, and Aristotle by several generations. These enigmatic figures, whose work generally survives only in provocative fragments, appear in his writings in fascinating ways—such as Andrew's reference to the teachings of Xenophon early in *Oxherding Tale* (12), and Rutherford's aside in *Middle Passage* about "the ancient philosopher Thales" and his belief "that the analogue for life was water, the formless, omnific sea" (4). But a more fundamental engagement occurs in Johnson's frequent returns to the opposition between Parmenides and Heraclitus, an opposition between stasis and flux, permanence and change. Heraclitus is the great exponent of both constant change and overarching unity—two principles that Johnson will insist upon: "all things are in flux," Heraclitus writes, and "listening not to me but to the Logos it is wise to agree that all things are one" (Kirk 185–86, 187). Heraclitus's most famous pronouncement insists upon this fundamental principle of constant change: "Upon those that step into the same rivers different and different waters flow . . . They scatter and . . . gather . . . come together and flow away . . . approach and depart" (195). But Parmenides, writing perhaps a generation after Heraclitus, emphasizes rather the permanent and the unchanging: "Remaining the same and in the same place it lies on its own and thus fixed it will remain" (251). Parmenides concludes that the creation is fixed, complete, and static: "what is exists completely and changelessly—it is never in process of coming to be" (252–53).

For Johnson, the heart of this fundamental opposition is the issue of identity. Parmenidean thought implies a fixed, unchanging, essential self, whereas Heraclitean thought suggests that identity is process, transformation, ceaseless change—the view that Johnson strongly favors. He has stated, "the self is one of those objects we talk about without having fully examined it. For me, if there's any way to talk about it, it's as a verb and not a noun. It's a process but not a product, and never is a product, unless it's dead" (Little, "An Interview" 100). Thus in *Middle Passage*, Rutherford subtly criticizes Squibb's desire for a single, unchanging female companion, for such an understanding of another self refuses the self's changing nature: "It seemed so Sisyphean, this endless seeking of a single woman's love . . . because they would change, grow old, and he'd again be on a quixotic, Parmenidean quest for beauty beyond the reach of Becoming" (39). Rutherford's distrust of this quest for the unchanging is confirmed in the example of the Allmuseri and the concept of identity that they impart to him: "Stupidly, I had seen their lives and culture as timeless product, as a finished thing, pure essence or Parmenidean meaning I envied and wanted to embrace, when the truth was that they were process and Heraclitean change, like any men, not fixed but evolving and as vulnerable to metamorphosis as the body of the boy we'd thrown overboard" (124). This insistence on Hereclitean change over Parmenidean stasis forms the very bedrock of Johnson's philosophical teaching. As he describes this principle in his novels, "the people who survive—this is probably true of everything I write—are the ones who are capable of change. . . . The characters who don't survive largely are those who cannot change. The nouns die in my books and the verbs go on. I think life is a process, more process than product" (Blue 137). Hence Johnson asserts in *Being and Race*, "we find meaning in flux, on the side of Heraclitus (change) and not Parmenides (stasis)" (11). It is important to note that Johnson is suggesting here a larger critique of a major strand of western philosophy: its tendency towards essentialism and dualism. His critique is not unlike the response of existentialism in the early twentieth century to Cartesian rationalism and its descendants. Throughout his writings, Johnson works to re-read western philosophy, emphasizing the elements that are in accord with his larger philosophical vision.

Intriguingly, when it comes to the more famous successors to the pre-Socratics, Plato and Aristotle, Johnson's engagement is much diminished. This is not surprising: for Plato's adherence to rationalism and idealism, and Aristotle's adherence to empiricism and realism, are neither particularly sympathetic to Johnson's own thought. After the pre-Socratics, Johnson draws primarily upon the medieval mystics and the phenomenological/existential traditions, with a sprinkling of American Transcendentalism and Pragmatism as well. However, there are elements of Platonic thought that he does bring into his writing. In a provocative early interview, Johnson states that he favors Plato's commitment to "universals," as opposed to the extreme subjectivism of Protagoras that Plato was combating. The Protagorean idea that "everybody had his own subjective truth" is unacceptable to Johnson, for it implies "a world in which there was no shared meaning at all." The argument of *The Republic*, Johnson claims, is that "the universal basically means shared meaning, at least in phenomenological terms." The contemporary importance of this bears upon the assault in recent decades against "universals," something that Johnson rejects: "What that assault comes down to is arguing that since Europeans created these ideas, they apply only to them. But if we do not have universals as I've described them, what we have is subjectivism, and we fall finally into solipsism" (Bosche 89). Johnson never abandons his commitment to what Husserl terms "the life-world" and the relations between human beings, just as he never allows the individual to be subsumed by types or general definitions—points that are essential for understanding how his philosophy bears upon his politics.[16]

What Johnson most admires in Plato and Aristotle is how each embodies the ideal of the philosopher-writer. "Some of my favorite writers among philosophers," Johnson has stated, "were also very literary people," and foremost among these philosopher-writers he places Plato: "Traditionally, you look at Plato, who writes dialogues, which are both a philosophical form and also a dramatic form" (Mudede 237). And when pressed to name "the 'dead' writers you most admire," Johnson replies, "Start with Homer and Plato" (Boccia 199). When Johnson says that "philosophers are writers" (McWilliams 237), he means this in a very technically precise way: philosophers, like storytellers, construct versions of what might be.[17] "How," he asks, "can *any* character be called 'realistic' when, as Aristotle (and Gass) and others have pointed out for two thousand years in the West, words and things belong to separate ontological orders?" There is no absolute realism, no exact rendering of the world as it is; rather, we create descriptions, and "whatever descriptions we make are, as Plato might put it, at best a 'likely story' " (Whalen-Bridge, "Shoulder" 304). Similarly, when Johnson refers to Aristotle, it is generally the Aristotle of *The Poetics*—the philosopher as storyteller—with his rigorous attention to "the dramatic structure of stories" (McWilliams, "An Interview" 291).[18]

For Johnson, the study of theology and the study of philosophy are inseparable, and so the great Christian tradition of Augustine, Aquinas, and the medieval mystic theologians occupies a central place in his thought. Johnson's first novel opens with an epigraph from St. Augustine: *Fides ergo est, quod non vides credere*—"Therefore, faith is to believe what you don't see." Similarly, *Oxherding Tale* opens with Augustine's words: *Noli foras ire, in te redit, in interiore homine habitat veritas*—"do not go abroad. Return within yourself. In the inward man dwells truth." And *Middle Passage* offers its first epigraph from Aquinas: *Homo est quo dammodo omnia*—"In a certain way, man is all things."[19] Finally, in *Dreamer* we open with the words of Meister Eckhart, greatest of the speculative mystics of the middle ages, who theorized about the union between the individual soul and God: "The Pauper has to die before the Prince can be born." In each of these cases, the epigraph from the medieval Christian tradition is the first epigraph, preceding other quotations generally from the traditions of eastern philosophy. Johnson seems to suggest that the first word, if not necessarily the last, in his fiction emerges from western medieval theology. What might this imply?

One answer is surely that in Johnson's view that theological/philosophical tradition has much in common with the eastern philosophical tradition that his work engages so thoroughly. That is, Johnson wants to show how Augustine and Aquinas, Eckhart and Anselm, are similar to the wisdom that he will explore in the Oxherding Pictures, the Vedas, the Upanishads, the Tao Te Ching. As Johnson puts it in his lecture to the Harvard Divinity School, he seeks "a potentially powerful bridge for opening an inter-faith dialogue between these two religions [Christianity and Buddhism] which so often have been seen in opposition . . . to show a little of how each complements the other" ("Tillich"). Johnson demonstrates this mingling of Christian and Buddhist in a pivotal scene from *Dreamer*, where he rewrites King's "kitchen conversion" experience to serve new philosophical/theological ends. In the historical kitchen conversion, which occurred during the heat of the Montgomery bus boycott of 1955, King experienced an awakening of his faith, a transformation from an intellectual commitment to the freedom struggle to a profound sense that the Christian God was calling him to this work. In *Dreamer*, King reflects on his "kitchen conversion" in terms that suggest Buddhist enlightenment and the realization of himself as no-self:

> *His fingers tightened round his empty cup until it shattered, obliterating inside and out. . . . His gaze drifted to the fragments of the cup that was no longer a cup. But where had the "cup" gone? . . . Then it came quietly, unbidden. He was traveling light again, for the long, lurid dream of multiplicity and separateness, the very belief in an "I" that suffered and strained to affect the world, dissolved, and for the first time he felt like a dreamer gently roused from sleep and forgetfulness. Awake, he saw he was not the doer. How could he have ever believed otherwise? (82)*

Freed by his recognition of his connection to all other sentient beings, Johnson's King moves forward to the great work that awaits and on towards the *"fuller, deeper, and more perfectly realized broken heart"* that awaits him at the end of his Way (225). In carrying out this design, Johnson demonstrates both his fluency with Eastern and Western traditions and his strong sense that a life well-lived admits, perhaps even demands, the amalgamation of various paths to spiritual, mental, and physical liberation.

Such overlappings between western and eastern thought could be cited in much more detail, for this is one of the major impulses of Johnson's fiction.[20] Johnson argues throughout his work that at the very heart of all philosophical inquiry, one fundamental issue resides: the question of the self, and the self's relation to the creation—whether by this we mean God, or the cosmos, or the human world. Johnson has stated that "if the principal novels and stories in my body of work have a central theme it is the investigation of the nature of the self and personal identity" (Boccia 200). Throughout *Being and Race* Johnson articulates this fundamental issue that "in words we find the living presence of others," for "fiction—indeed, all art—points to others with whom the writer argues about what *is*. He cannot begin *ex nihilo*" (*Being and Race* 5). This view of the communal element of fiction arises from Johnson's fundamental philosophical position, following Merleau-Ponty's definition of writing as "'the trespass of oneself upon the other and of the other upon me'" (38–39). Thus in both the medieval western tradition, and in the other philosophical traditions upon which Johnson draws, he focuses upon this central issue of self-identity and the self's relation to the larger world.

This is, of course, why Johnson is drawn primarily to the complex tradition of phenomenology. Johnson's involvement with phenomenology and existentialism, beginning with his dissertation at Stony Brook, has been remarked upon by virtually every Johnson scholar.[21] He prefaces *Being and Race* (the book that began as the dissertation) by acknowledging his fundamental indebtedness to Husserl, Heidegger, Sartre, and Merleau-Ponty, and asserts that his own "quirky variations on phenomenology" all derive from the "philosophy of experience" emphasized in this tradition. There are many important elements in Johnson's work that show the "cross-cultural fertilization" between phenomenology and African-American experience. But surely the most significant is that of "the phenomenological *epoche*," what Johnson understands as the "'bracketing' of all presuppositions in order to seize a fresh, original vision" (*Being and Race* 5). In this experiential moment, all preconceptions fall to the wayside—our conceptions of gender, race, nationality, origin, political conviction, et cetera—and one is left with the moment of perception and, crucially, the necessity to interpret that perception. As Johnson states, "phenomenology is basically forgetting what you think the human figure looks like and looking at the human figure in front of you. . . . You have to divest yourself of the prejudices, the comfortable preconceptions about what you're dealing with" (O'Connell 30).[22]

This is absolutely central to Johnson's aesthetic philosophy, his insistence upon "the enormous role played by imagination and language and cultural conditioning in our perception," as opposed to the mistaken idea that "meaning is *given* directly to us with little or no shaping necessary from our side." For in truth "great literature resolves these problems of viewpoint and epistemology by emphasizing the fact that literary art is at its best when it is a sumptuous act of imagination, invention, and interpretation" (*Being and Race* 30–31).

He insists that perception is not something that happens to us, a passive experience, but rather "perception is an act, and this observation puts the lie to that ancient stupidity that says the processes of philosophy and fiction are two different enterprises—they are sister disciplines, I would say, and unless a critic realizes this, his position is simply untenable" (32). In other words, to perceive, to philosophize, and to create artistically are essentially the same action, and they depend on the ability to shed our pre-judgments and see the world anew.

This is, again, both a philosophical and a deeply political concept for Johnson, for in the *epoche* the perception is liberated from the constraints of prejudice that create such vexed social and political suffering. Hence Johnson explains this theory in opposition to the ideologies of Afrocentrism, Negritude, and the Black Aesthetic, all of which bring to bear certain preconceptions to our experience prior to that experience. Johnson argues, "obviously, it cannot be through such ideologies that genuine creative work is achieved. Rather, all presuppositions, all theories, must be suspended before experience and meaning can be brought forth in black literary art" (*Being and Race* 29). His argument in such essays as "Whole Sight," "Philosophy and Black Fiction," and "A Phenomenology of the Black Body" is that African-American Experience far exceeds what its literary representations have so far allowed, precisely because those representations generally begin with preconceptions and structured categories that preclude genuine vision and original expression: "The point . . . is that our experience as Black men and women completely outstrips our perception—Black life is ambiguous, and a kaleidoscope of meanings rich, multisided, and what the authentic Black writer does is despoil meanings to pin down the freshest interpretation given to him. This is genuine fiction. It is also hermeneutic philosophy" ("Philosophy and Black Fiction" 82). Thus Johnson praises, throughout his writings, those African-American writers who he thinks have achieved this freshness and originality of vision: Ellison, Toomer, and Du Bois, most frequently, and Wright and Morrison, on occasion.

Finally, mention must be made of one other major philosophical figure who, like Johnson himself, works to join multiple philosophical and religious traditions to form a harmonious whole: Ralph Waldo Emerson, whom Johnson has identified as his "spiritual brother."[23] Recognizing Emerson's debt to Heraclitus's notion of life as process, Johnson finds echoes of the Transcendentalist's thought in Du Bois, Toomer, and Ellison (the "other" Ralph Waldo, whose father later claimed that he named his son for the literary giant because he was "raising this boy up to be a poet"[Jackson, 1]). Johnson's fascination with Emerson and transcendentalism also indicates where his particular literary-philosophical project fits in the national literary tradition. Like Emerson, and like Ellison, Johnson is fascinated with the nature of American identity and how this identity fits with the larger philosophical problems of the nature of the self and the individual's responsibility to the larger surrounding world. Indeed, a truly expansive—a "whole sight"—view of "philosophical black fiction" might include Emerson as an early practitioner, certainly a key influence.

IV

CHARLES JOHNSON AND EASTERN PHILOSOPHICAL TRADITIONS

Johnson is unique among African-American writers in his uses of and immersion in numerous eastern philosophical movements and traditions. Throughout his novels, he draws freely upon Hinduism, Taoism, and particularly Zen Buddhism to give structure and meaning to his characters' quests and challenges. Each Johnson scholar has devoted significant space to delineating Johnson's engagements with eastern philosophy (indeed, this ground is much more clearly defined than is Johnson's engagement with western philosophical traditions).[24] The traditions of Buddhism constitute the single major intellectual and spiritual influence on Johnson's work and life. This latter point is crucial: for Johnson's *practice* of Buddhism is as important as his reading in that broad tradition. His efforts at the application of the ideal, which reaches to the roots of the author's experience, not only inform the subject matter and the craft of his writing, but also form his personal ontological and epistemological stance.[25] Johnson has been practicing Buddhism for decades, and evidence of his devotion to this tradition is clear in every one of his novels. But Johnson recently announced a committed public activism to his Buddhism. As he told an interviewer in 2003, he has decided that "in this phase of my life, what I call Act Three, I finally had to declare myself someone devoted to the dharma . . . no longer tucking the dharma into my fiction and keeping Buddhism tucked close to my vest, but addressing it directly" (McWilliams, "An Interview" 301). Such a profession of faith suggests the need to reassess both how and why Buddhism matters so much in all of his creative output.[26]

Johnson describes his first encounter with meditation, at age fourteen, as liberating and terrifying—the former because it brought him "a feeling of inner quiet," the latter because he "was afraid [he'd] be too peaceful, too detached" from his environment if he kept up this new practice (Whalen-Bridge, "Shoulder" 307–8). Still interested in the East, but wary of excessive calm, Johnson turned his attention to the martial arts, where in the practice of kung fu and karate he found something akin to "meditation in motion," something with the power to transform the individual practitioner—a notion that he works through creatively in two of his finest short stories, "China" and "Kwoon." When, in 1982, he finally returned to and embraced sitting meditation as a crucial part of his way of being in the world, he stepped onto a path of intellectual and spiritual practice that has intensified and particularized his connection to his environment. Yet again, Johnson emphasizes that liberation is not an end in itself: "the question, I think, is what does a Buddhist do *after* awakening. . . . If he decides to stay in the world, the marketplace, in order to teach, as Shakyamuni did, or serve in some capacity, he does so—and lives daily—with nonattachment and *metta* [loving kindness towards all sentient beings]" (Whalen-Bridge, "Shoulder" 315). With the publication of *Turning the Wheel* (2003), Johnson brings decades of Buddhist practice to fruition in a collection of essays that demonstrate how his writing embodies the "engaged Buddhism" modeled by Thich Nhat Hanh.[27]

Johnson's adherence to "engaged Buddhism" demonstrates how for him, Buddhism is "something you do"—a description he has also applied to phenomenology. The resonance is unmistakably significant: Johnson sees "early Buddhism" as having "a distinctly phenomenological 'flavor'" (Whalen-Bridge, "Shoulder" 302), while at the same time he insists upon this parallel emphasis on *action*, on the application of ideas for the improvement first of the individual and then of the environment. For that reason alone, Buddhism and phenomenology represent an admirable intellectual marriage of Eastern and Western traditions, an embodiment of "whole sight" that transcends rigidly drawn lines between traditions long (mis)understood as fundamentally opposed in their respective linearity (the West) and circularity (the East). Given what we know of Johnson's aesthetic project, then, this particular fusion of East and West proves an excellent methodology for Johnson, the artist as seeker.[28]

Johnson's aim, as we have seen, is the creation of "whole sight" in fiction and its "real-world" analogue, the beloved community. In *Dreamer*, Johnson's fictional King can only press forward with his quest for social justice after the kitchen conversion that draws upon both Christian and Buddhist elements, which convinces him that the self is an illusion, that separation and otherness are agreed-upon fictions that distort reality and generate untold volumes of suffering for those pieces of the Whole (or of Emerson's Over-Soul) who embrace this pain and the concomitant isolation that it brings. Similarly, Matthew Bishop, the narrator of *Dreamer*, can only carry on King's work when he realizes the same lesson that the minister has learned about the necessity of selfless-ness; and his is a variation on a path that all of the protagonists in Johnson's fictions follow, from his first great seeker, Faith Cross, through to his most recent depiction of the young Martin Luther King, Jr., in the title story of *Dr. King's Refrigerator*.

In each case, the protagonists must overcome a dualistic sense of themselves as "othered," marked by their blackness and thereby also firmly established as victims of an unjust system that they, at least briefly, hate as much as they think it hates them. Once free of that sense of division and the desire that accompanies it, the protagonists eschew their self-conception as victims and turn instead towards a path of celebration marked by a newly discovered inner calm and a willingness to recognize their meaningful connections to others. A potent example of this would be Andrew Hawkins's moment of *moksha*, or enlightenment, when he looks on Horace Bannon's tattooed body and realizes "I was my father's father, and he my child." Freed at last from his sense of division, Andrew returns home to embrace his *svadharma* (Sanskrit for "personal responsibility") as a householder, the civically engaged, responsible member of the community who, through his love for his family, can go about the process of "rebuilding . . . the world" (176). Andrew's story demonstrates the archetypal resolution of Johnson's fictions—acknowledging, of course, that for this complex and adventurous writer, the variations that he plays on this archetypal ending in his other novels both broaden and deepen the reader's sense of these fundamental issues.

This archetypal plot structure draws upon the most profound foundation of all Buddhist practice, the Four Noble Truths:

1. *Suffering exists.*
2. *Suffering arises from attachment to desires.*
3. *Suffering ceases when attachment to desire ceases.*
4. *Freedom from suffering is possible by practicing the Eightfold Path.*

The Eightfold Path might best be understood as *praxis*, the steps by which one moves away from the isolation of individuality towards the freedom of what

Thich Nhat Hanh calls "interbeing" and what phenomenologists call "inter-subjectivity," that state of awareness of one's connection to all other sentient beings. In the simplest terms, one follows the Eightfold Path by attending to the quality and purity of one's thoughts, actions, employment—in short, one's way of being in the world. To return to Johnson's emphasis on action, the Eightfold Path is, first and foremost, "something you do," a means of living liberation that embodies "whole sight." This Path offers a profoundly power-ful tool for an author-philosopher interested in interrogating experience and in overcoming the devastating illusion of race in American life.

For all of Johnson's protagonists, the arc of their experience moves them through the first three of these states: they all know suffering, which in every case comes from some sort of desire, be it intellectual (Faith), sexual (Andrew), emotional (Rutherford), political (King), or some combination of these which bears a strong marking of racial division as well. Arguably, all of them ulti-mately mount the Eightfold Path, although readers do not see that process delineated equally clearly in the various novels—Matthew Bishop, for instance, seems much more firmly placed on the path than any of his predecessors. With these portrayals of characters that transcend suffering through their enlighten-ment, Johnson offers a lesson to his readers as well: this way is open to them if they choose it.[29]

This is not to romanticize what Johnson achieves. After all, this path is cer-tainly not easy, as the novels demonstrate. Each of Johnson's protagonists suf-fers greatly and struggles mightily on the way to enlightenment and liberation. And, in Matthew Bishop's case, one gets the sense that even after mounting the path, the Way is precarious and fraught with dangers. Nevertheless, each novel clearly sounds a hopeful note: one need not be bound to illusions and suffering in the real world any more than in Johnson's fictional life-worlds. This is the thrust of two of Johnson's most important recent essays, "Accepting the Invitation" and "A Sangha by Another Name" (both of which are collected in *Turning the Wheel*). Here the author demonstrates the particular usefulness of Buddhism to African-Americans facing the systematic racism woven firmly into the fabric of American life from our nation's first day to the present. Johnson begins "Sangha" by recognizing the truth that "the black experience in America, like the teachings of Shakyamuni Buddha, begins with suffering"; he concludes by suggesting that the Buddhist teachings may offer the best hope for survival and regeneration of black America: "For through the Dharma, the black American quest for 'freedom' realizes its profoundest, truest, and most revolutionary meaning" (*Turning*, 46, 57). Hence, Johnson moves beyond the individual liberation that Andrew Hawkins knows to something that holds liberating potential for all. In his own analogy—as in the tenth of the Ten Oxherding Pictures—the one who has awakened (the literal meaning of "Buddha") enters the market place "with bliss-bestowing hands," ready to share what he has learned and to teach others how they might learn it themselves.

Perhaps Johnson's fear of that first experience of meditation, which he once likened to "playing with a loaded pistol" ("Introduction" x), was an ideal beginning—because the time between that moment and his return to sitting meditation gave him the enriching experiences of suffering in a racialized society and of mental liberation through intensive study of Eastern and Western philosophical texts. Through his systematic study of Eastern and Western philosophy, and his growing application of Eastern principles in his life and work, Johnson has developed an increasingly harmonious philosophical, spiritual, and aesthetic practice.

These philosophical, spiritual, and aesthetic issues constitute the central focus of the nine essays that follow. We treat the entire range of Johnson's writings: each of his novels, his short fiction, the range of his non-fiction philosophical and cultural essays, his book reviews, and even several unpublished works. The essays follow the general chronology of Johnson's work, showing the development of his philosophical positions throughout his career. Linda Selzer's essay, "The Genesis of Charles Johnson's Philosophical Fiction," examines Johnson's attempt in his early short fiction to revise Western philosophy in ways that make it more responsive to the lived experience of black Americans. Selzer shows how Johnson considers certain contradictions inherent in Western rationalism, and enters into a philosophical disagreement between Kantian formalist and Schelerian nonformalist ethics—a disagreement that proves important to Johnson's own project of writing philosophically significant fiction. Gena Chandler's essay, " 'In-Itself-for-Me': Decomposition and Art in Charles Johnson's *Oxherding Tale*," approaches Johnson's self-described "platform book" from the perspective of Merleau-Ponty's fundamental premise that "man is in the world, and only in the world does he know himself" (*Phenomenology* xi). Chandler thereby focuses on motifs of decomposition in this novel, both the decomposition of actual human bodies and the decomposition of structural spaces of inquiry that challenge our very means of interpreting aesthetics. She argues that Johnson ultimately seeks to re-direct our ways of seeing artistic production, both in bodies and in works of art.

Herman Beavers's essay follows, "Bondage and Discipline: the Pedagogy of Discomfort in *The Sorcerer's Apprentice*." Beavers takes up the pedagogical practice outlined in Johnson's first story collection, the ability of Johnson's characters to loose themselves from the bondage of wanting (to be) more. Through their enactment of failed pedagogies, Johnson's characters evade the hegemony and limitations of Western concepts of selfhood, thereby achieving progress on the "Way" of enlightenment through misguidedness and incompleteness. Marc Conner, in "To Utter the Holy: The Metaphysical Romance of *Middle Passage*," then examines the ways in which Johnson moves through the modes of tragedy, comedy, and romance in his National Book Award-winning novel of 1990, *Middle Passage*. Both tragedy and comedy embody *Weltanschauungen* or world-views for Johnson that he works through in the novel both philosophically and imaginatively, using these modes to interrogate the dominant philosophical tensions of the West, from Aristotle to Nietzsche. Ultimately, Johnson finds both world-views wanting, and seeks to expand the philosophical and literary possibilities that they suggest into the transcendent domain of the encounter with the Sacred. Such a concluding vision, Conner argues, brings into relief the ways in which Johnson's metaphysics, aesthetics, ethics, and politics share a remarkable unity.

Two studies of Johnson's responses to American Pragmatism follow. William Gleason's essay, " 'Go There': The Critical Pragmatism of Charles Johnson," examines Johnson's engagement with American pragmatism that has developed in and through Johnson's numerous book reviews. Here Gleason argues that we find "a writer increasingly committed to providing philosophically consistent blueprints for reading, thinking, and living in contemporary American society." Employing the concept of the "anti-race race man" developed by Ross Posnock, Gleason argues for Johnson's "critical pragmatism," a philosophy that draws upon such cultural strains as William James, W. E. B. Du Bois, and Alain Locke. This issues in Johnson's particular version of "pluralistic democracy," which Gleason explores in both *Dreamer* and *Soulcatcher and Other Stories*. Gary Storhoff then considers Johnson's powerful interest in ethics in his essay, "Pragmatic Ethics in Charles Johnson's Fiction." Storhoff considers Johnson's corpus broadly, working through the range of his fiction to illustrate how Johnson combines Zen Buddhism and American Pragmatism in his efforts simultaneously to present pictures of ethical lives and to eschew what William James called "an ethical philosophy dogmatically made up in advance." Storhoff concludes that Johnson's overall ethical vision is broadly ecological and melioristic. This is consistent with his Buddhism, which is supported by a systematic and principled pragmatism (though as is typical for Johnson, a pragmatism treated with subtlety and qualification).

The next two essays focus on Johnson's 1998 novel, *Dreamer*—his most ambitious and complex fiction to date—in the context of Johnson's other literary and philosophical writings. In "Invisible Threads: Charles Johnson and Feminine Civility," John Whalen-Bridge uses Johnson's most recent novel as the point of entry into an assessment of Johnson's gender politics. Through an investigation of the depictions of the female not just in *Dreamer* but throughout Johnson's fictional and non-fictional corpus, Whalen-Bridge describes what he calls a "feminist evolution" in the author's work that reveals Johnson's criticisms of masculine arrogance, as well as the longstanding celebration of feminine dignity in his work. Marc Conner, in " 'At the numinous heart of being': *Dreamer* and Christian Theology," examines Johnson's uses of both "ethical and existential Christianity" in the novel and throughout Johnson's body of work. Conner argues that Johnson turns in *Dreamer* away somewhat from the eastern philosophical traditions that have heretofore sustained him, to a considered (and deeply personal) examination of Christian theology in an effort to re-explore the fundamental issues of being and faith, of ethics and social justice, of race, and of political practice in late twentieth-century America.

The book concludes with William Nash's "The Application of an Ideal: *Turning the Wheel* as Ontological Program," which considers Johnson's recent collection of essays on Buddhism and fiction writing. Nash argues that through the medium of non-fiction, Johnson achieves his most successful means to date of demonstrating how African Americans, especially African American artists, can pursue the practice of social and spiritual engagement in their work. Thus the present book, like the title of this most recent collection of Johnson's, brings the wheel around again: from his early engagement with philosophers and philosophizing in his short fiction, through his multiple philosophical studies in each of his novels and his non-fiction writing, and finally to his most recent reflections on Buddhism and the craft of fiction, Johnson offers an astonishingly rich body of work that both defines and provokes the category of philosophical black fiction and the philosophical novel as a whole.

NOTES

1. Although no one has undertaken a book-length biography of Johnson, several scholars have explored and commented on his personal history. For biographical information on Johnson, see Nash, *Charles Johnson's Fiction*, Chapter 1, esp. pp. 15–26; and Storhoff, *Understanding Charles Johnson*, Chapter 1, esp. pp 1–6. Both Nash and Storhoff provide basic outlines of Johnson's life and then emphasize details and developments that are most

pertinent to their individual arguments. One also gets a rich sense of Johnson's life from the interviews in James McWilliams's *Passing the Three Gates: Interviews with Charles Johnson*, as many of the interviewers pursue biographical issues, and Johnson's responses are quite revealing. For straight biography, see John Whalen-Bridge's essay in *Dictionary of Literary Biography, Volume 278*. This fine essay is the most current of a series of DLB entries on Johnson and supplants its predecessors. Johnson has also published several lengthy autobiographical essays: see especially "I Call Myself an Artist"; "*The Second Front*"; and a long essay in Gale's *Contemporary Authors Autobiography Series*, 18: 225–50. These essays are most compellingly read in chronological order, with the Gale essay coming first, because that approach provides a sense of the interplay between Johnson's fiction and his autobiography. Much of the information about his family provided in "*The Second Front*" figures into the history of a key character in *Dreamer*, which he was working on when he wrote the autobiographical essay—a point that Conner develops in his essay on *Dreamer* in this volume.

2. The phrase is bell hooks's; in her essay "An Aesthetic of Blackness: Strange and Oppositional," she uses it to counter the restrictiveness of black cultural nationalism with an aesthetic that simultaneously celebrates the empowerment of black people and rejects litmus tests that determine who might be "black enough" to warrant the attention or approbation of the black community. One can see how such a notion might appeal to Johnson in his quest to overcome restrictive notions of racial identity and racialized artistry.

3. Hence Johnson concludes "Whole Sight" by claiming that soon "black literature will be universally recognized as perhaps the truest form of Yankee fiction, the body of stories that, once broadened by *whole sight*, profiles the concerns of the Republic in the most vivid and memorable manner" (90).

4. Johnson typically names Du Bois, Toomer, and Ellison as predecessors in this tradition, occasionally including Wright as well. Rudolph Byrd argues for the inclusion of such figures as Toni Morrison, Gloria Naylor, James Baldwin, Cyrus Colter, Samuel Delany, and Ishmael Reed, at least in certain of their works (*Charles Johnson's Novels* 13). The crucial point is that this category is growing and it has many figures who play an important role in its formulation; however, no single author has so carefully defined the category in his or her writing as Johnson has, and no single author has given so many rich examples of "philosophical black fiction" in his or her fiction as Johnson has.

5. Byrd is the first scholar to articulate fully the parallels between Bakhtin's theories of language and Johnson's art. This is a substantial insight that will bear much fruit in Johnson scholarship.

6. See, for example, Timothy Parish's comment that "for Johnson, slavery is less a historical presence than a philosophical problem" ("Imagining Slavery" 82), or Molly Abel Travis's criticism of Johnson's "efforts to transcend race" and "[establish] a middle ground, a neutral space that denies the marginal and offers readers the familiar and unthreatening" ("Beloved and Middle Passage" 192–93). Such views reflect what William Gleason describes as Johnson's "professedly apolitical agenda" ("The Liberation of Perception," 706)—a view that Gleason's own writings on Johnson refute.

7. Nash makes the astute observation that Johnson's seminal essay on King—"The King We Left Behind"—signifies on the John Williams book, *The King God Didn't Save*, implying

that "Johnson shifts blame from the leader to those who mistakenly chose not to follow him" (Nash 185).

8. Johnson enumerates these same essential characteristics of King's teachings in his recent essay, "The King We Need: Teachings For a Nation in Search of Itself" (2005). The very title of this piece suggests a simultaneously political and philosophical view of King, that is, an emphasis on two fronts.

9. Indeed, it is important to note that the editors of this volume differ in the respective emphases they give to Johnson's political commitments. Whereas Nash sees Johnson's social activism as increasing with each of his novels (see Nash, pp.177 and 190, for example), Conner views Johnson's work as progressing into increasingly spiritual and religious avenues that resist specific political programs or solutions. Put differently, we each tend to emphasize different "fronts," while recognizing the essential point that *both* fronts are crucial to Johnson's overall thought and work. See Conner's review of Nash's book in *South Atlantic Review* 69:2 (2004: 124–28).

10. Johnson's present rejection of black cultural nationalism and the Black Arts Movement strongly defines his artistic credo, and he has suggested in recent years that the Black Arts Movement never appealed to him, after his youthful enthusiasm for it. The record of his published statements, however, indicates that this rejection is the end point of an evolution that began with him "adhering" to the principles of the Black Aesthetic. For a more extensive discussion of Johnson's attitudes about black cultural nationalism and artistry, see Nash, *Charles Johnson's Fiction*, especially pages 19–23; Little, "An Interview," especially pages 106–15; and Johnson's seminal essays on aesthetics and the black experience: "Philosophy and Black Fiction," "Whole Sight," and "A Phenomenology of the Black Body," as well as the first three chapters of *Being and Race*.

11. Consequently in *Dreamer* the central conflict is that of brothers: King and Chaym, Cain and Abel, the two sides of an ongoing opposition. As Chaym expresses this conflict to Matthew, "'You ever *thought* about what brothers are really like? Romulus and Remus, say. Or Jacob and Esau? How they can hate each other, especially if one is doing better?'" (55). But the novel's ongoing meditation on brotherhood and conflict reaches a new teaching in King's vision of the doctrine of "overlapping lives," which teaches that all barriers, including the "illusion" of "Race," can be overcome if our perception changes (83–84).

12. For a discussion of Johnson's debt to Nhat Hanh, see Storhoff, pages 9–10. See also Johnson's recent essay on Nhat Hanh and philosophies of peace: "And if peace is their goal . . ." (2004).

13. In a fine study of *Dreamer*, John Whalen-Bridge begins his analysis of the novel by describing the book as "a dialectical interplay between two worldviews, a typically Western one which we can call 'dualistic,' and one associated with Eastern philosophies which is commonly discussed as 'nondualistic.'" But as Whalen-Bridge's own careful qualifications suggest, this opposition between western dualism and eastern monism is far too simple for Johnson; and Whalen-Bridge goes on to complicate this approach by stating that *Dreamer* ultimately reveals "a cross-fertilization of Buddhist and Christian typological thinking" that reimagines "both Christian and Buddhist understanding, since its allusive and narrative strategies highlight the 'inescapable network of mutuality' in ways that question the gap between Christian *agape* and Buddhist *shunyata*" ("Waking Cain" 505, 517–18).

14. The notion of cross-fertilization also resonates with Johnson's creative practice of "genre-crossing," which he learned from John Gardner. The point of "genre-crossing" is to shake readers out of their preconceptions about fiction by mixing the conventions of particular literary forms usually seen as disparate, even incompatible. One might think, in this context, of *Oxherding Tale*, where Johnson fuses elements of an eighteenth-century British novel like Stern's *Tristram Shandy* with characteristic features of the nineteenth-century American slave narrative.

15. Byrd 4–5. This concept of the "palimpsest" is Byrd's "master metaphor" for understanding Johnson's "vision of cultural pluralism" (4). Johnson employs this term in *Dreamer* to describe the eclectic, layered genealogy of the Rev. Littlewood's church in the Illinois countryside (179).

16. Nash makes the point that Johnson's celebrated concept of "whole sight" in fiction is achieved first "by articulating a particular perspective in fiction, such as a 'black' point of view, and then expanding the 'expression and vision' of that viewpoint in an effort to access the universal" (*Charles Johnson's Fiction* 34). The concept is Joycean—through the microcosm one reaches the macrocosm—and is also the principle of a good storyteller—through the particular, one expresses the universal.

17. Johnson states in *Being and Race*, "It is this basic, genuinely exploratory element in creative writing that leads some phenomenologists such as Maurice Merleau-Ponty to conclude that philosophy and fiction—both disciplines of language—are about, at bottom, the same business" (32).

18. For a thorough description of Johnson's methods of teaching the craft of writing the short story and the novel—approaches that are, on the whole, resolutely Aristotelian in their emphasis on technique, structure, plot, and character—see his essay "A Boot Camp for Creative Writers." See also *Being and Race*, p.40, where he emphasizes the importance of these Aristotelian elements in good fiction. Conner's essay on *Middle Passage* in this volume treats the influence of Aristotle's *Poetics* on Johnson's work.

19. Professor Kevin Crotty of the Department of Classics, Washington & Lee University, assisted with these translations. Professor Crotty points out as well that the epigraph from Aquinas that opens *Middle Passage* is erroneous: it should read "Homo est quodam modo omnia."

20. See, for example, Jonathan Little's assertion that "Johnson draws from a richly eclectic mixture of traditions that fuse primarily Eastern religious and spiritual beliefs with traditional Western aesthetic ideals" (*Charles Johnson's Spiritual Imagination* 5). Storhoff's recent book on Johnson also emphasizes his "syncretistic sensibility" and how his work "cross-fertilizes Buddhism and Judeo-Christian traditions" (*Understanding* 14).

21. The most thorough discussion of Johnson's development of Husserlian concepts of phenomenology, particularly in *Being and Race*, is Nash's chapter, "The Aesthetic Articulated," in Nash, 2003, pp.30–50. See also Little, 1997, p.11. Conner's essay on *Dreamer* in this volume explores Johnson's immersion in both the secular and Christian existentialist traditions.

22. Johnson has stated that the refusal to abandon preconceptions is something that offends him in a deeply personal way: "What will enrage me is if somebody goes to my wife, or, particularly, to my son or my daughter, and fails to see them as radically individual and

unique and not like anybody who ever lived on this planet before or will ever live again. If they come at them with some umbrella term, some *bullshit* about who they think they are without asking them—that's ridiculous. I don't want them to do that to them. They've got to figure out who these kids are. That's the novelist's job as well. You don't deal in types or stereotypes. You've got to give up all presuppositions if you're going to have any success" (Bosche 90).

23. The quotation comes from Nash, "A Conversation with Charles Johnson," page 58. For Johnson's own view of how he situates Emerson among his influences, see his "Introduction" to the Signet Classic *Selected Writings of Ralph Waldo Emerson* (2003). For further discussion of Johnson and Emerson, see Nash, *Charles Johnson's Fiction*, 123–26 and 177.

24. William Gleason broke this ground with his outstanding essay, "The Liberation of Perception: Charles Johnson's *Oxherding Tale*." Subsequently, Jonathan Little, William Nash, Rudolph Byrd, and Gary Storhoff have treated Johnson's Buddhism in their book-length works. John Whalen-Bridge's 2003 interview, "Shoulder to the Wheel," offers a highly insightful discussion of Johnson's Buddhism, as does his essay on *Dreamer* contained in this volume.

25. With regard to Johnson's reading, he states in his 1995 "Introduction" to *Oxherding Tale*: "I studied over and over the 'Ten Oxherding Pictures' of twelfth-century Zen artist Kakuan Sien, the stunningly spiritual art of Nicholas Roerich . . . and devoured everything in print on zen by D. T. Suzuki, Eugen Herrigel, Christmas Humphreys, Alan Watts, and a library of esoteric books by authors from India, China, and Japan. I took college classes on Lao Tzu, Chuang Tzu, and the Vedas" (xi). This list, which he ties specifically to the process of researching and writing *Oxherding Tale*, forms the foundation of an encyclopedic knowledge of Eastern texts that Johnson has expanded in the two decades since the publication of his landmark second novel. After being awarded a MacArthur Foundation "genius grant" in 1998, for instance, Johnson took up the study of Sanskrit, so that he could read Theravadan Buddhist texts in the original. His engagement with Buddhism is deep, personal, and ongoing.

26. For a further discussion of Johnson's intellectual and personal motives in infusing his art with Buddhist principles, see Storhoff, 15–18.

27. Storhoff's *Understanding Charles Johnson* is especially skillful in assessing Johnson's particular debts to Thich Nhat Hanh. See pp.9–10, 21, 49, 166, and 183.

28. Johnson's 2003 address delivered to the Harvard Divinity School, titled "The Twenty-Sixth Paul Tillich Lecture," masterfully combines Johnson's interests in western phenomenology and eastern Buddhist thought. Like the address delivered before this same body by Emerson in 1838, Johnson's talk is a powerful investigation into the philosophical and poetic impulses that are at the heart of what William James terms "the varieties of religious experience." Conner discusses this address in his essay on *Dreamer* in this volume.

29. This is not to say that Johnson proselytizes for Buddhism—indeed, such an approach is antithetical to that tradition, as proselytizing relies on setting doctrines in opposition to one another and Buddhism seeks to overcome divisions.

CHARLES JOHNSON

THE GENESIS OF CHARLES JOHNSON'S PHILOSOPHICAL FICTION

LINDA SELZER

If historically the line between fiction and philosophy has often been blurred—as Plato's dialogues, Nietzsche's aphorisms, and the twentieth-century prolif-eration of existentialist literature in a number of genres all attest—this is especially true in the case of African American philosophy, which by necessity in America has had its roots in nonacademic forms of writing. As John P. Pittman points out in *African American Perspectives and Philosophical Traditions* (1997), to define philosophy only in terms of a specialist discourse is to leave out "an entire world of intellectual life, and for traditionally excluded groups, any 'representation' at all" (xii). Charles W. Mills makes a related point in *Blackness Visible: Essays on Philosophy and Race* (1998): he suggests that antholo-gies of African American philosophy are incomplete if they do not include as philosophically significant work such as Frederick Douglass's investigations of the meaning of freedom or Ralph Ellison's conceptual work on "invisibility" in *Invisible Man* (8ff., 167ff.). Others point out that the critique of racism lends itself to "narrative analysis," in part because narrative recuperates a subjective perspective that has been systematically rendered invisible by traditional philosophical discourses (Cuomo 7).

The factors that complicate the relationship of African-American thought and literature to Western philosophy—the historical reliance by black thinkers on nonacademic forms of writing, the need to recuperate perspectives that have been habitually repressed, the continuing efforts of black philosophers to infuse abstract arguments with narratological, phenomenological, and social immedi-acy—provide important critical contexts for understanding Charles Johnson's philosophical fiction, a discursive territory that Johnson has recently described as the place "where fiction and philosophy meet."[1] A careful analysis of one of his early short stories, "Alethia," specifies more precisely the particular prove-nance of his philosophical fiction. As a tale focused upon the experiences of a black philosopher in the white academy (and as one that takes a philosophical concept as its title), it is not surprising that "Alethia" centers upon the difficul-ties—both disciplinary and conceptual—encountered in the attempt to revise

I

Western philosophy in ways that make it more responsive to the lived experience of black Americans. More precisely, in "Alethia" Johnson uses the problematic relationship between a black professor and his student to critique the state of academic philosophy in the time period immediately before the story was published, to consider certain contradictions inherent in Western rationalism, and to enter into a philosophical disagreement between Kantian formalist and Schelerian nonformalist ethics—a disagreement that proves important to Johnson's own project of writing philosophically significant fiction.

Originally published in *Antaeus* in 1979 and included in Johnson's first collection of short stories, *The Sorcerer's Apprentice* (1986), "Alethia" centers on the apparent seduction of a fifty-year-old black philosophy professor by an undergraduate student from his Kant seminar, Wendy Barnes.[2] Raised on books about "Negro uplift"—stories about "men who tried, in their own small way, to create lives that could be, if disciplined, the basis of universal law"—the professor at the outset of the tale has pursued a higher education and earned a faculty position in a primarily white university (102). Isolated in his office or "the three small rooms" that he rents near Northwestern's campus, however, the professor also represents the alienation of the black intellectual who has failed to maintain what Cornel West, adapting Gramsci, has called an "organic" relationship to the black community (*Reader* 122). By threatening to accuse him of sexual harassment, Wendy blackmails the professor out of the academy and to a party on the south side of Chicago, where he experiences a drug-induced vision of unity with the black world he left behind. The ambiguous conclusion that follows ends in Wendy's bedroom, as she takes off her clothes and lies down next to him: has she saved the professor from a debilitating segregation in the white academy, or has she caused him to lose the last remnants of idealism and discipline that initially led him there?

The professor's association with Kant, the philosopher on whom he teaches his seminar, is important to Johnson's critique of academic philosophy in several respects. Kant is generally considered to be the first professional philosopher, one whose university appointment is frequently contrasted, for example, to the "philosophy of the marketplace" represented by a figure like Socrates.[3] Moreover, Kant's learned critiques have come to define the sort of technical work traditionally understood to merit the title of philosophical work in the West. As the philosopher most clearly associated with the European Enlightenment, Kant is also one whose work most clearly equates philosophical inquiry with the exercise of a rationality purified of personal inclination, emotion, and desire (one also thinks of Plato and Descartes). As Kant states in

Anthropology from a Pragmatic Point of View, "to be subject to emotions and passions is probably always an illness of mind because both emotion and passion exclude the sovereignty of reason" (*Anthropology* 155). Indeed, with his promulgation of practical reason as the synthesizer of universal truths in epistemology, his claims to disinterestedness in aesthetics, and his evocation of formalism in ethics, Kant made modern European philosophy practically synonymous with a purified rationality.[4] Kant is a signifier, then, for a specific path to philosophical enlightenment, one that is academic, highly technical, and decidedly rationalistic. This is precisely the path that the bookish professor, who describes himself as "living for knowledge," has chosen for himself at the outset of Johnson's tale (103). Before his encounter with Wendy Barnes, the professor's own "monkish and contemplative" life also recalls the bachelor Kant's ascetic and circumspect life, and the professor's medicine cabinet, stuffed with remedies for a variety of complaints, brings to mind Kant's own reputation as a notorious hypochondriac. In his work and in his life, then, the tale's black philosopher-narrator is clearly linked to Kant, an association that suggests that the modern professionalization of philosophy is partly responsible for the rarefied academic isolation that the professor finds himself in at the outset of Johnson's tale.

   Although the professor's association with Kant is strong, however, it is not complete. By describing himself as "stalking Kant," the professor suggests that the western philosopher in some sense still eludes him, and his inability to complete his own book suggests that his relationship to the discipline is problematic. More important, the ambivalence hinted at in the narrator's identification with Kant permeates the narrator's conception of his own position in the university, a position which is clearly complicated in ways that Kant's was not: by his blackness.[5] For the professor identifies not only with Kant, but also with "that towering sociologist W. E. B. Du Bois," whose classic statement on double consciousness he applies explicitly to his own position as a professor of philosophy. As he elucidates, "the Negro professor is, although reappointed and tenured, a kind of two-reel comedy" who no longer fits in the "bleak world of Chicago" he has left behind, nor in the academy, where, "like a thief come to the table, he hungrily grabs crumbs of thought from their genuine context, reading Hume for his reasoning on the self, blinking that author's racial slur" (99, 101–2).[6] Attracted to higher education but self-consciously aware of its traditions of racism, the professor is aware that his own position as a black philosopher deviates from the discipline's historical norms.

   The professor further complicates his position in the academy by contrasting his own reasons for entering the discipline as an idealistic "first-generation college student" with the philosophical motivation of his white teachers, who, "shaken by Wittgenstein," have "lost faith and were madly humping their teaching assistants" (102). Alluding to Wittgenstein's argument that a large number of philosophical questions should be dismissed as the simple result of confusion in the use of language, the professor's comment suggests that his white colleagues have become cynical about the practice of philosophy at the precise moment that he has entered the discipline. Based on his reading in books for Negro uplift, the professor has claimed an education in order to demonstrate that Blacks should be included in the formulation of universal Western norms, only to find, ironically, that the academy itself is abandoning those norms. Furthermore, by describing himself as a "thief" (and possibly as a stalker) the professor criminalizes his own presence in the academy and further betrays a sense of illegitimacy. It is clear that in spite of his tenure—and because of his blackness—the professor perceives his own position in the university as somehow precarious and potentially temporary, as his rental rooms near Northwestern suggest.

The professor's troubled idealism contrasts with the unabashed self-interest of his student Wendy, who attempts to blackmail the professor into giving her a "B" in the Kant seminar so she can remain in school. Wendy lays out her proposition in unmistakable terms: "If I don't ace this course," she tells the professor, "I'm gonna have to tell your chairman Dick Dunn and Dean David McCracken that you have been hounding me for trim" (105–6). In spite of their "philosophical differences," however, Wendy's determination not to be forced back into "factory" or "Day work" corresponds to the narrator's own desires to escape the "ugly, lovely black life" (104) he knew as a boy. The academically successful but culturally alienated professor and the academically marginal but culturally astute student represent two variations of first generation black college students, and the "rental library" books that Wendy carries signal—in addition to a lack of funds—that her own relationship to the academy is merely temporary (105). The professor's attempt to hold contemporary black Chicago at bay—he reads "Hebrew, Greek, or Sanskrit," but never "tabloids" or "lurid newspapers" (102–3)—is broken when Wendy enters his office, reminding him of the "well medicated blues singers, backing up James Brown down at the Regal" (105). Opposing a blues tradition to the professor's readings in various classical traditions, Wendy embodies the black world that the narrator perceives to make his position at the university problematic, and her threats of sexual scandal externalize his own inner doubts over his position in the academy, described earlier through tropes of criminality.

Reminiscent of one of Edgar Allan Poe's narrators, whose fascination with a female Other reveals the workings of his own conflicted psyche, the professor through his changing relationship with Wendy exposes the inner confusion beneath his own "outwar[d] calm" (100). Even as he complains of feeling trapped by Wendy's "endless tricks" (106), the professor recognizes that to some extent the "disaster was somehow all [his] own doing" (107). Arising anima-like from his own repressions, Wendy visits his office on the very day that he experiences a sudden, new vision of her during his Kant seminar, a re-evaluation that the professor attributes explicitly to his reading of Max Scheler (1874–1928). A prolific German phenomenologist, Scheler developed a non-formalist ethics specifically as a response to Kantian formalism. He grounded his own ethical system in love, which he understood to be an intentional relationship prior to intellectual abstractions: as he writes, "Man is, before he can think or will, *en amans*."[7] While Kant argues that moral behavior "wholly excludes the influence of inclinations" and secures his conception of duty in the universal laws synthesized by practical reason (*Foundations* 51), Scheler argues in contrast that one encounters value through acts of feeling. Scheler's ethics, then, privilege the very affectivity that Kant seeks to repress. Upon reading a passage attributed to Scheler—"contemplation of essence, the fundamental approach to Being peculiar to metaphysical knowledge, demands an attitude of loving devotion"—the professor is stunned to realize that his method for reaching truth, a purified Kantian rationalism, is suspect (100). For he has, as the professor tells himself, "misunderstood something that any schoolgirl knew instinctively—that living for knowledge, ignoring love, as I had, was wrong, because love—transcendental love—*was* knowledge" (103). As someone who has been "*devoted* to books" and who has spent his life "*embracing*" ideas, the pedantic professor's desire for truth has been misdirected (100, 102; italics mine). The implication is that Scheler has enabled the narrator to change his methods and to see Wendy anew, with the clarity of a phenomenological *epoche*—"the flash of clear vision . . . the gasp of recognition that slaps you, suddenly, when a tree drawing in a child's book . . . recomposes itself as a face" (84)—and that, by extension, the overly professionalized philosophical practice of the white academy could be reinvigorated through the adoption of phenomenological methods more responsive to black subjectivity.

Given Johnson's own interest in phenomenology, it is tempting to read the professor's sudden change of heart at face value. But although the narrative endorses the professor's reorientation, it also treats that new insight humorously, dramatizing what might be called "a seduction by phenomenological reduction." Johnson's short story is in fact structured around three separate moments of phenomenological insight: the first the professor's "fresh, new vision" of Wendy in the classroom (inspired by reading Scheler), the second a "new apprehension" that he experiences at the party (at least partly induced by drugs), and the third a moment of phenomenological surrender in Wendy's bedroom. By no means an uncomplicated tribute to phenomenology, however, the story in fact is designed to probe the irony, humor, danger, and possibility in the professor's evolving epistemic positions. Such ironies are made clear by the professor's reaction immediately after his new vision of Wendy, when he dismisses his class and retreats to his office, chastising himself for an interest in his student that is by no means purely transcendental: "O Shameful to have hot flashes for a student" (101). In light of his own equation of his vision to "hot flashes," the professor's appeal to Scheler must be read in part as a philo-sophical rationalization, or sublimation, of an erotic desire for Wendy that has been present from the outset, but repressed by the professor's Kantian disci-pline. Indeed, although he asserts earlier that he "seldom noticed" Wendy "while lecturing," the details the professor does notice—her "sandalwood perfume" and "black leather boots"—are sexually suggestive, and the fact that he describes her as "sashaying seductively" into class and "sitting with her knees pressed close together" reveals that he has been watching her rather more carefully than he admits (100–101). That Wendy Barnes comes to his office with her startling proposition the very day that the professor experiences his new "vision" of her in class suggests further that Wendy comes to his office in part because she is aware of his attraction to her and intends to use it to her own purposes. In any case, Wendy's scandalous proposal reduces the professor's prior idealistic mus-ings about "schoolgirls" who "know about love" to an elaborate joke at his own expense. Such narrative ambivalence is maintained throughout much of Johnson's tale: is the professor's idealism uplifting, naïve, or self-serving? Is Wendy's self-interest simply "vulgar" (as the professor initially finds her) and cynical (she suggests at one point that "civil rights are high comedy"), or is she a reliable guide for the professor out of the white academy to closer ties to the black community and a keener moral vision (105, 108)?

One thing is certain. Although the professor feels "trapped by Wendy"—he even describes her as having a face "like a trap door"—he is already trapped at the tale's outset both by his professional status as a black philosopher and by his intellectual commitment to a restrictively formal rationalism (106). From the outset the professor's attempt to "get over" through education is marked by mixed motives, propelled both by his idealistic boyhood dreams of living a life that could become, "with discipline," a universal law and by the more practical desire to escape a neighborhood fate that seemed to lead inevitably to "(a) drugs, (b) a Post Office job, (c) Marion Prison, (d) Sunset Cemetery (all black), or (e) the ooga-booga of Christianity" (101–2). In order to make his escape, the professor has "barricaded himself in by books" or buried himself in Padelford Hall, a building "as old . . . as a medieval fortress" (101, 103). But the release that Wendy—and Scheler—represent as an alternative to the rarefied world of the white academy is itself morally ambiguous. Wendy's threat to levy false claims of sexual harassment are clearly suspect, as is her inability to generalize norms of behavior more inclusive than those of her own personal self-interest, like those of civil rights. Scheler's phenomenology—proposed to answer Kant for ignoring the importance of affectivity in the apprehension of value—represents a liberating alternative to the restrictive life of discipline to which the professor has committed himself. But as a model of the professional philosopher, Scheler also represents a significant danger: his notoriously undisciplined private life could not be more opposed to the circumspection attributed to the unmarried Kant. As Herbert Spiegelberg points out, Scheler's "philosophical habitat was the café house" (231). Twice divorced, his love affairs led to the loss of more than one academic position.[8] The professor's growing sense that he is "Damned if I seduce her, damned if I don't" is therefore perceptive: he will be damned if he does seduce Wendy, because the principles upon which he has based his life will be compromised (and because his faculty position will be put at risk), and he will be damned if he doesn't seduce her, because he will remain trapped in an academic, epistemic, and personal discipline no broader than the narrow confines of Padelford Hall.

Set in opposition to the restrictive milieu of the white academy is the unruly environment of the area of black Chicago to which Wendy reintroduces the professor by taking him to a party in the "squalid Fifth Police District," an area referred to by the professor as a "sewer" (107). From the perspective of the professor's identification with a rationalist European philosophical tradition, black Chicago appears as an exoticized Other, which he consistently associates with matter, the body, and especially desire. Early in the tale the professor compares his attempt "to free himself from black Chicago" to the struggle of "Hegel's anxious Spirit . . . against matter" (101). His comparison alludes both to Hegel's description of the ascent of spirit and to the idealistic philosopher's judgment that Africans as a people had not achieved "the category of universality" because Africa is "the unhistorical, Undeveloped spirit, still involved in the conditions of mere nature" ("Introduction" 95). On the other hand, Wendy is the very embodiment of transgressive desire. For example, she drives the professor to the party "at over 70 miles per hour," breaking the speed limit and "Damned near blowing off both doors," while the tense professor sits next to her with his "black hat crushed against the roof, hands gripped between his knees" (107). But the suggestion that an unrestrained Wendy takes the reserved professor "for a ride" is complicated by his prior intimations of personal responsibility and his later admission at the party: "Even I was no longer sure what brought me here" (110). Like T. S. Eliot's J. Alfred Prufrock at another social gathering, he is clearly both attracted to and repelled by the pleasures the party affords, which provide the emotional release that, on one level, he so desperately seeks, while simultaneously threatening his carefully maintained self-control and the academic position that discipline has earned him. As the professor humorously—but perceptively—reflects, "Let me linger too long and I might never regain the university" (109). In his study of the categorical imperative, Roger J. Sullivan suggests that in developing his formalism, Kant assumes an internal conflict between reason and emotion (15). Feminist philosopher Robin May Schott argues further that by repressing emotion, Kantian epistemology practically guarantees the return of the repressed.[9] Through the professor's personal psychology and relationship with Wendy, Johnson effectively dramatizes the internal conflict between reason and desire in Kantian epistemology, the repression of affectivity, and the consequent return of the repressed.

The two primary locales of the short story, university and party, articulate a binary of mind/body, reason/desire, normativity/criminality. The party itself dramatizes both the collapse of the professor's personal discipline and the artificiality of the categories established by the professor's adherence to a rationalist epistemology that represses affectivity. At the first moment that he enters the apartment the professor becomes disoriented, overcome by "the raw ugly scent of marijuana hashish congolene and the damp smell of an old cellar that [he] could taste as well as smell these violent odors and take hold of them in [his] hands like tissue" (109). Grouping the hair-straightening product "congolene" with the "raw ugly scents" of the old cellar and with those of hashish, the professor's response to the party once again associates the black community with impurity, materiality, and criminality. But his synesthesia—captured by odors that he can "taste" and hold in his hands "like tissue"—also signals a blurring of his normal categories of discernment (an alteration that is reinforced at the sentence level by the lack of commas between sentence elements). As the professor's confusion increases when he "unconsciously" swallows a pellet that someone presses into his hand, the party makes clear that his categories of interpretation are not *apriori* or universal, but artificial and changeable.

The release of the affectivity he has previously repressed enables the professor to experience at the party a second vision of Wendy that is part LSD hallucination and part phenomenological insight. As he watches Wendy dance, "now fast, now slow," then lowers his eyelids to contemplate her after-image, the professor achieves a new sense of unity with Wendy, the other partygoers, and, indeed, with the entire unruly population of Chicago:

> I suddenly saw Wendy—not as the girl who shotgunned me with blackmail back at Padelford Hall, who made me jump like a trained seal; who stood outside me as another subject in a context of wills—but, yes, as pure light, brilliance, fluid like the music, blending in a perfectly balanced world with the players Muslims petty thieves blacks Jews lumpenproles Daley machine politicians West Indians loungers Africans the drug peddlers who, when it came to the crunch, were, it was plain, pure light, too, the Whole in drag, and in the evanescent, drugged instant, I did indeed desperately love her. (111)

Interpreting the professor's second vision as "an individual transcendence that connects [the professor] to a larger appreciation of the whole," Jonathan Little finds in his insight an expression of Johnson's "own version of the Black Aesthetic," because, rather than "fleeing blackness . . . the narrator learns to see within it the particular and distinctive beauty it affords" (*Charles Johnson's Spiritual Imagination* 123).

On the other hand, elements of the professor's vision indicate that his intellectual emancipation from European rationalism at this point in the narrative is incomplete. Indeed, the imagery of the second vision suggests, ironically, that the professor's identification with the black community is predicated upon the erasure of its particularity. For the second vision of Wendy—realized after the professor turns inward and reflects upon her after-image—replicates the generalizing tendencies of Kantian rationalism. At the moment of his insight, Wendy loses her particularity—both the specificity of her prior actions (she is no longer "the girl who shotgunned me") and of her name, as she becomes simply, "the girl" (111). This process of abstraction continues during the professor's revelation, as "the girl" is transfigured into "pure light, brilliance, blending in a perfectly balanced world" (111). The professor's qualification that he does "most desperately" love her *"at this moment"* (italics mine) suggests that he does not love Wendy as a particular woman, but only insofar as her particularity can be transcended.

Earlier in the narrative the professor, drawing on Scheler, defines Mind as an "opening that, if directed toward another, allowed him (or her) to appear . . . as both moral and beautiful" (103). The conclusion that he draws from this statement is that "Nature needed man to clarify its meaning" (104). While the professor's conclusion expresses a new appreciation for an intimate relationship between mind and world, it also reveals a will to control, or at least, a will to define. At the party, Wendy occupies the position of Nature, while the professor, observing her, is in the position of mind, whose purpose it becomes to clarify her meaning. He fulfills that purpose by transcending Wendy's concrete qualities in order to realize an idealized vision of "pure light." The fact that the professor strips Wendy of her distinctiveness—including her color—at the very moment that he "most desperately love[s] her" calls into question, at this point in the tale, both the precise nature of the professor's reintegration into the black community and the degree to which his insight frees him from an abstracting Kantian formalism.

If the professor's second vision is captured in the secular imagery often associated with the quest for purity characteristic of European rationality, the party also figures the professor's change in perception through a trope of homosexuality that is more inclusive of particularity and more responsive to the needs of affectivity. Of all his experiences at the party, the professor is most confused by "the flashy men in white mink jackets who favored women, the women who looked, in their pale, fulgurating light, like men" (109). Because he has organized his life in the academy around inflexible dualisms, it is precisely homosexuality's blurring of binary categories that most disturbs the professor's thinking. But the trope of homosexuality suggests that meaning (and subjectivity) may be better expressed through "masquerade" than through categorical purity. The professor through his identification with the other men at the party is thus led to recognize those aspects of himself and the black community that he had earlier attempted to repress: "that man, the one in the Abo Po, lightly treading the measure, was me. And this one dressed like Walt (or Joe) Frazier was me. If I existed at all, it was in this Kaleidoscope party, this pinwheel of color, the I just a function, a flickerflash creation of this black chaos, the chaos no more, or less than, the I" (110–11). A needed corrective to his earlier position of normative rigidity and epistemic superiority, the professor's identification with the men at the party suggests a path away from the false universalism of European rationalism, built on dualistic (and exclusionary) categories into a more inclusive position that does not subsume the other—as does perhaps his vision of Wendy—in categorical purity. As Johnson suggests in "Philosophy and Black Fiction," "the Black world *appears* in countless guises" (82).

Whether interpreted as a moment of transcendental insight, an attempt to transcend the particularities of black life, or a liberating expression of repressed need (or as some combination of all three), the second vision of Wendy does not conclude Johnson's narrative. Awakening in her bedroom the next morning, the professor discovers that a "stylized purity of line" has returned to his perception, and he reflects upon the meaning of the previous night's events. Did he "dream the connectedness of Being the night before," or does he "dream distinctions" now (111–12)? His intellectual quandary marks the return of the professor's dualistic patterns of thought and of his tendency to over-intellectualize. Admonishing him for "still thinking like a fat boy" (112), Wendy takes off her clothes and joins the professor in bed. As he raises his arm in order that "she can move closer" and "at last lets [his] mind sleep," Johnson's short story ends. Earlier in the tale the professor criticizes other faculty for losing their idealism and "madly humping" their students: has he joined his disillusioned peers?

Given the specific character of Schelerian phenomenology (which differs from Husserl's in important respects), the narrative's extended trope of books, and Wendy's evolving role in the short story, it is likely that the professor's affair does not comprise a "fall" from transcendental heights, but a further step away from Kantian formalism toward Scheler's nonformalist ethics.[10] In describing effective philosophic practice, Kant, Husserl, and Scheler each advocate different paths. In "What is Enlightenment?" Kant summarizes the period's intellectual motto as "Dare to trust your own reason," and he locates enlightenment in the individual's exercise of his or her own reason.[11] His formalist ethics require that reason be purified of personal inclination and desire in the service of universal truth. The proper philosophical path is, then, to follow the dictates of a reason so disciplined. Husserl, on the other hand, urged philosophers to turn "back to the things themselves" in an attempt to ensure that inquiry did not limit itself to either the abstract conceptions of received theories or the "sedimented" accumulations of common-sense knowledge.[12] Scheler, however, found Husserl's attempts to turn phenomenology into a rigorous science itself overly analytical and rationalistic, and he stressed that the merely rational could not account for the richly existential, which is characterized by a phenomenological abundance that overflows the analytical or conceptual. The professor's relationship with Wendy Barnes implies the same.

Moreover, the tale's ambivalence in regard to the practice of phenomenology suggests that Johnson is aware that the method can carry its own dangers. Before the professor's change of heart, for example, he is described as practicing some "perceptual tricks" he has learned from "Husserl's *Ideen*" (103). By describing Husserl's exercises as mere tricks, Johnson suggests that phenomenology—or at least Husserlian phenomenology—can run the risk of degenerating into mere mental operations or perceptual games. This is precisely the practice that Scheler hoped to avoid: to Scheler, as philosopher John Staude summarizes, "phenomenology was not so much a method—in the sense of mental operations—as a special attitude," an orientation whereby "one could enter into a . . . relationship with things" (Staude 21). Against the Kantian philosophical subject who trusts the "sovereignty of his own reason," and unlike a Husserlian transcendent ego that analyzes its own acts of consciousness as they construct meaning, Scheler proposed, as philosopher Michael Barber suggests, that the "authentic phenomenologist turns toward being like a lover or a friend" (143). This evolving philosophical disagreement in fact mirrors the movement of Johnson's narrative: if Kant believed that value was ascertained by acts of reason that required a mastery of affectivity (the professor's position at the outset of the tale), and if Husserl suggested that meaning was constructed through acts of intention that implied a certain mastery of an object for the sake of knowledge (the professor's second position), Scheler argued that value was discovered through a loving surrender to the object or the Other. At the very moment that the professor lets his own "mind rest" and allows Wendy to reveal herself to him, he comes closest, then, to realizing Scheler's nonformalist ethics.[13] From this perspective, the professor's earlier vision of Wendy at the party can be read as a momentary "irrealization" that frees him from his preconceptions about her nature and prepares him, at the conclusion of the tale, to accept Wendy on her own terms.[14]

Johnson's critique of Kantian formalism is intensified throughout the narrative by his skillful development of an extended trope of books, manuscripts, and papers. Certainly the tale abounds with allusions to books, from revered works of philosophy to children's coloring books, and from great works of literature to the professor's grade book. For the professor, books initially hold the promise—like Kant's formalist ethics—that abstract norms will provide effective models for life. Comparing the books he reads about "Negro uplift" to Plutarch's *Lives of the Noble Grecians* (102), the professor from his boyhood reading through his classical training to his philosophical study of Kant characteristically turns to books to discover patterns for thought and action (102).

But, in a way that recalls Ralph Waldo Emerson's contention that books, poorly used, can be the most dangerous of things, Johnson criticizes the professor's reliance on books by compounding images of the limitations that their forms can impose: from the "paint-by-numbers curriculum" the professor encounters in college, to the books that "barricad[e]" him in Padelford Hall, to the mental "tricks" the professor learns from Husserl's *Ideen*, to Wendy's judgment that the professor's life amounts to nothing but "the Book—that dry ream of windy bullshit—you can't finish" (108). In other words, from the time he is "a lonely little fat boy" the professor limits his "sources" about life, narrowing his search for meaning to pre-existing paradigms. Significantly, the professor's practice as a philosopher reveals the same second-hand methodology. When he lectures, he approaches Kant "by way of a playful verse attributed to Bishop Berkeley" (100), thereby interpreting the work of one philosopher through that of another. The practice of philosophy as ever more analysis of received tradition is precisely the model that phenomenology hoped to disrupt by turning the discipline to the "everyday" world of lived experience, a reorientation, Johnson's short story suggests, that would also better account for the lived experience of black Americans.

Significantly, Johnson's trope of the book also resonates with Scheler's belief that—because of the propensity of concepts either to obscure or to displace the *qualities* of the object—a certain "de-symbolization of the world" is required if one is to perceive afresh.[15] This process of de-symbolization is dramatized at the party, where the book—representing rationality, abstract norms, and the white academy—is trumped by music, the agent of experience, desire, and the black community. As the professor recounts, "It played hob with my blood pressure. It was wild, sensual, clanging and languid by turns, loud and liquid, an intangible force, or—what shall I say?—spirit angling through the air, freed by cackling instruments that lifted me, a fat boy and student still, like a scrap of paper, then dropped me, head over heels" (110). In a reversal of the professor's earlier identification of spirit with the white academy and materiality with the black community, at the party music proves the more potent spiritual force, triumphing over the reified word, a mere "scrap of paper." The final paragraph of the short story reinforces that potency as Wendy—who had earlier been reduced to an "F" student in the professor's grade book—sits with "one bare foot on [the professor's] briefcase," an image suggestive of the triumph of unembellished life over abstract thought.

Representing the aspects of phenomenological experience that do not fit into the professor's formalist preconceptions, Wendy Barnes plays several important roles in the narrative. Certainly Johnson is interested in more than simply a realistic presentation in the development of her character, as can be detected when Wendy—her hair "crack[ling] with electricity"—assumes a prophetic voice, making pronouncements on the condition of philosophy, the professor, and contemporary society in language that far outstrips her usual vocabulary (as the professor remarks afterwards, "if I'd known she was this smart, I'd have given her an A the first week of the term," [109]). As indicated earlier, Wendy signifies in part the return of the repressed, both as an agent of the black world the professor has abandoned for the white academy and as the embodiment of the personal desire that he has repressed as part of the discipline of Kantian rationality. Wendy's unbridled commitment to her own personal interests is precisely what Kantian ethics attempts to suppress in order to achieve its formalism. But Wendy also makes claims to represent a certain kind of knowledge. As she tells the professor, "I know how this place works" (105). Over the course of the short story, the roles of teacher and student in fact become reversed. When Wendy first enters his office the professor tells her, paternalistically, "There now, tell me about it" (105); but by the end of the tale, it is Wendy who corrects the professor, chiding him as, "You poor fool" (112). The professor's original commitment to received norms created a need to control—both his own inclinations and the "criminality" he associates with the black community. His second vision at the party, while providing a needed corrective to his preconceptions about the black community, nevertheless demonstrated that his commitment to abstraction failed to account for the phenomenological richness of the other. But as Wendy disrobes and reveals herself to him in all her embodied particularity at the end of the tale, the professor gives up rational control and allows himself to be taught by the other. The final role that Wendy plays in the short story, then, is as the embodiment of *alethia* itself, understood in specifically Schelerian terms as "a guide away from symbolizing thought" to the "self-given phenomenon."[16] In performing the role of guide for the professor's journey out of Kantian rationalism, Wendy signifies upon the role of Diotima in the *Symposium*. In Plato's famous dialogue, Diotima instructs Socrates and the other men at Agathon's drinking party on the proper philosophical path to truth, which she describes as an ascent from the sensuous love of the beloved's body to the rarefied love of ideal forms. By leading the professor out of his study, back to the black community, and ultimately to her own bed, Wendy comically reverses the philosophical journey that Diotima describes, as she educates the professor in the phenomenological abundance that overflows rationalist forms.

The alienated professor's re-introduction to the black world in "Alethia" invites comparison to James Baldwin's renowned story, "Sonny's Blues," in which an educated older brother who has also distanced himself from the black community comes to a new understanding of his younger brother's motivations, his family's history, and his community's resilience. Like the estranged professor of Johnson's tale who initially disdains the "braying" and "crackling" music that he hears at Wendy's party, later to experience its power, Sonny's older brother initially dismisses jazz and the blues as "good time" music, which he associates with the forces (like drugs) that threaten the black community. Through the power of his younger brother's playing, however, he is led to a new appreciation for the blues, his brother, and the black community. But although both of these stories chart the return of an educated but alienated black man to his community, important differences between them in theme and narrative technique help to define the particular orientation of Johnson's philosophical fiction. For example, as a powerful piece of realistic fiction, Baldwin's narrative is characterized by unified character development and a carefully maintained tone appropriate to its serious elaboration of the historical, familiar, and communal ties that bind the black community. On the other hand, the professor and student in Johnson's tale are not so realistically or even very individualistically drawn, and the tale's tone is markedly mixed, as is its genre, which draws on elements of the seduction tale, horror story, and romance.

As is often the case in his fiction, Johnson's characters resemble the emblematic characters one finds in a fable or allegory, and like allegory, the tale is designed to be read on several levels: as an amusing satire of the professor's problematic sexual encounter with a student that raises certain ethical questions (such as whether the professor is the seduced or seducer), as a critique of the practice of academic philosophy (especially insofar as the practice of philosophy fails to accommodate the lived experience of black people), and as an exploration of certain contradictions within reason itself as historically realized in European philosophy at least since the time of Kant. Interestingly, the tale also demonstrates a certain critical distance on Johnson's part toward his own attraction to Western philosophy, reinforced by the inclusion of autobiographical details (such as the fact that the professor lives near Northwestern, near the area where Johnson himself grew up, or that he has an office in Padelford Hall, still Johnson's address at the University of Washington).[17] Both Baldwin's and Johnson's approaches to the short story, as illustrated by these two tales, offer certain opportunities and limitations. Baldwin's realism, for example, buys him immense emotional power, while the satiric distance often required by Johnson's critique can have the effect of distancing readers from his characters, even as it creates opportunities for multiple readings, humor, and philosophical complexity.

To write effective philosophical fiction, Johnson must work to maintain a difficult balance between phenomenological immediacy and philosophical complexity in the place "where fiction and philosophy meet." In "Philosophy and Black Fiction," an article published only a year after "Alethia" first appeared and one that reflects Johnson's thinking about the relationship of philosophy to black fiction at the same time the short story was composed, Johnson speaks explicitly about the "area where fiction and philosophy overlap" (80). His analysis of this discursive territory demonstrates that he does not recognize the bifurcation of reason and desire that rationalism presupposes: for there is, Johnson asserts, an "analytic dimension native to literary art" (79) and, further, "feelings" themselves are "shamelessly analytic" (83). Since he understands conception to be informed by the emotions that accompany intentionality, Johnson's phenomenological orientation leads him to reject the possibility of a reason purified of emotion. As he explains, "We aim perceptually at something and, through the emotions of anger or love, cause it to *appear* before us as it could not otherwise" (83). Indeed, the belief that thought and inclination are *never* separate provides Johnson with an epistemological rationale for practicing philosophically engaged fiction. By working with philosophy in a literary mode, Johnson is able to achieve a phenomenological intensity that more abstract forms of philosophical writing often lack (or, as is suggested by his short story "Alethia," that they systematically repress). But in creating fiction with a serious philosophical orientation (often dense with philosophical allusion), Johnson must be careful not to sacrifice the phenomenological immediacy that philosophizing in fiction wins him in the first place. By his own admission, not all of Johnson's work manages this difficult balancing act successfully. But at its best—as in this tale about a seduction by phenomenological reduction that is at once satiric, serious, and philosophically significant—Johnson balances those demands superbly.

At one point in "Alethia" Wendy is described as having a face "like a trap door," but by the end of the tale she comes to embody the sort of "unpredictable possibility" that Johnson attributes to the artistic use of language. A trap door, after all, does not simply signify the presence of a trap, but also a way *out* of that trap. If conventional language has the power to calcify perception, language also has the power, Johnson asserts, to break down established habits of interpretation: "it's like a trap door, [it] drops you down to this whole other level of seeing" (O'Connell 29). As Johnson elaborates in a recent interview: "Ideas do not begin in some abstract realm floating high above human experience. Rather, they originate in the historical muck and mud of our daily experience, cloaked in the immediate particulars of this world, and only later do we abstract them for the purpose of study and reflection. What a philosophical novelist does—what I do—is simply return those ideas to the palpable world of experience from which they first sprang. That way, I hope, readers experience the ideas viscerally, with flesh put back on their abstract bones" (Ghosh 374). Despite his critique of inherited conceptual forms and of the manner in which conventional language can conceal the world's complexity, Johnson throughout his career vigorously maintains that the defamiliarizing power of art has serious *intellectual* as well as aesthetic effects.

In "Where Philosophy and Fiction Meet," Johnson explains that when he was faced with criticism from his family and friends for switching his major from journalism to philosophy as an undergraduate student at Southern Illinois University, he found support for what he calls his "need" for philosophy in "the finest works of African American literature" (92). To the friends and family who criticized his decision, he spoke about the philosophical background of other black writers, and he pointed to the example of W. E. B. Du Bois's "great hopes to develop a philosophical method for the interpretation of race relations" (92). Moreover, Johnson discovered in African American literature itself a philosophical tradition, a "tradition of broaching fundamental questions of being and race, culture and consciousness" (92). The explosion of interest over the past two decades in marking out a black philosophical tradition that incorporates a number of works of African American literature suggests that today others agree with Johnson's estimation. In any case, it is clear that African American letters provided Johnson with both a cultural genealogy for his passion for philosophy and a creative venue through which that passion could be expressed. Speculating in "Where Philosophy and Fiction Meet" that the "vitality of philosophical discourse has passed in the latter half of this century from the small province of academic seminars to the pages of our finest stories," Johnson echoes the critique of academic philosophy and the dissatisfaction with traditional philosophical discourse found in "Alethia." He concludes that the novelist might "reach a broader audience than his counterpart does in stuffy journals" (92). By unabashedly claiming the literary as a powerful discursive site for black philosophical agency, Charles Johnson locates the genesis of his fiction precisely in the attempt to open wide the halls of academic philosophy to a new world of artistic and intellectual possibility.

NOTES

1. Johnson has made several comments to this effect over the years. This particular quotation comes from Mudede's interview, "The Human Dimension" (236–45).

2. My analysis of "Alethia" builds on the work of Jonathan Little (*Charles Johnson's Spiritual* Imagination 122–24), William Nash (*Charles Johnson's Fiction* 92–94), and Gary Storhoff (130–35), who offer the fullest treatments of the short story to this point.

3. See, for example, Pittman's claim that "up until Kant none of the canonical philosophical writers were 'professionals'" (xi).

4. Philosophers who examine Kant's attitudes toward the emotions, inclinations, and desire include Roger J. Sullivan and Robin May Schott.

5. See Nash, *Charles Johnson's Fiction* (93).

6. See Hume's comments on race in his infamous footnote in "Of National Characters," 228.

7. Scheler is here translated and quoted by Frings, 41.

8. Scheler lost his academic appointment in the German university system due to scandals after his first divorce. Although he found work afterwards as a Catholic educator, he lost that position after his second divorce, when Catholic students and clergy were forbidden to attend his classes. For an analysis of Scheler's personal difficulties, see Staude.

9. See Schott's discussion of the consequences of such a repression in *Cognition and Eros: A Critique of the Kantian Paradigm*, especially Chapter Eight, "Kant's Treatment of Sensibility" (101–14). In "The Gender of Enlightenment," Schott points out that Kant's attempt to exclude the erotic from rationality depends upon an "assumption that his rational posture is itself wholly nonemotional" (327). Schott argues that Kant's claiming of a position of objectivity is "already an emotional posture" (329), a position with which Johnson's phenomenological orientation would lead him to agree.

10. Although he reaches this conclusion for different reasons, Nash also understands the implied sexual relationship as a positive development (93).

11. This is one translation of Kant's famous dictum. See "What is Enlightenment," 54.

12. As Speigelberg points out, Husserl's essay on "Philosophy as a Rigorous Science" illustrates Husserl's hopes for scientific rigor in the discipline and ends with his motto, "Back to the Things" (120–21).

13. Although it is not the focus of this particular reading of the short story, it should also be mentioned the professor's abandonment of rationalism also resonates with Zen Buddhism's call to put aside one's attachment to one's thoughts and "let be" what appears before consciousness without judging it, which in turn can be related, perhaps, to the early state of "irrealization" in the Husserlian epoche, described in more detail in note 14.

14. Although at times Johnson can sound as though he rejects black particulars in favor of a deracialized universal—as when he suggests in "Philosophy and Black Fiction" that "aspects of the Black world become, after the *epoche*, only the occasion for universal reflection"—it is important to note that this bracketing (or ir-realization) is only a single step in a process, one designed to aid thought in overcoming not particulars but *presuppositions about those particulars*. Although the relationship in Johnson's work between universals and particulars may seem contradictory, this often results from a failure to understand their

relation in terms of a phenomenological method that unfolds over time. In other words, I would argue that Johnson understands the bracketing of particulars—in this tale Wendy's specificity, and by extension, that of the black community—as an *initial* step in a process. The goal is not to abandon the particulars, but to prepare oneself to see them afresh, and by doing so to arrive at new universals (concepts). Or as Johnson explains in "Philosophy and Black Fiction": "From the fibrous particulars of Black life a perception anchored in racial experience is bodied forth, and we come to understand somewhat how new seeing—revitalized vision—occurs in black fiction" (81). Thus the narrative line in "Alethia" dramatizes almost precisely the process of phenomenological practice that Johnson describes in "Philosophy and Black Fiction."

15. For a discussion of the importance of "de-symbolization" in Scheler's work, see Stuade (21ff) and Spiegelberg (241ff).

16. See Spielgelberg, 241.

17. There are other biographical references in the tale. Wendy threatens to report the professor for sexual harassment to his "chairman Dick Dunn and Dean David McCracken" (106). At the time that Johnson wrote the short story, Dick Dunn was in fact his chairman at the University of Washington, and David McCracken, who worked in the Dean's office, had an office directly across from Johnson's in Padelford Hall.

"IN-ITSELF-FOR-ME"

Decomposition and Art in Charles Johnson's Oxherding Tale

GENA CHANDLER

An Artist must be free to choose what he does, certainly, but he must also never be afraid to do what he might choose.
—LANGSTON HUGHES, "The Negro Artist and the Racial Mountain"

That the presence of the world is precisely the presence of its flesh to my flesh, that I "am of the world" and that I am not it, this is what is no sooner said than forgotten.
—MAURICE MERLEAU-PONTY, *The Visible and the Invisible*

In October 1999, New York's Brooklyn Museum became the staging ground for an important exhibition of Britain's new and emerging young artists. The museum's director, Arnold Lehman, marked the exhibition as "the most creative energy [in art] that's come out of Great Britain in a very long time" ("The Art of Controversy"). That exhibition, "Sensation: Young British Artists from the Saatchi Collection," represented an official American "coming-out" party for a collection of contemporary British artists who were challenging the boundaries of taste and aesthetics in the contemporary art world while simultaneously challenging the historical biases against the value of British art. The exhibit included 90 works from the private collection of Charles Saatchi, art patron and progenitor of contemporary Brit Art. Two of the more controversial artists of the exhibit, Chris Ofili and Damien Hirst, perhaps caused the greatest furor as their works pushed the boundaries of the art world's (and then-mayor of New York Rudy Giuliani's) oft-protected culture of taste and decorum. "Yes . . . but is it art?" became a rallying cry of officials and patrons alike as the artwork pushed the moral boundaries of the contemporary art world.[1] Ofili's "The Holy Virgin Mary" juxtaposed sexually explicit photos of human genitalia with a portrait of a black Madonna adorned with elephant dung, and Hirst's "A Thousand Years" presented a glass enclosure containing a decomposing cow head with bluebottle flies and maggots happily eating on the fleshy composition. In an ironic twist, Hirst's decomposition was nourished from within the enclosure with sugar and water but also included an insectocuter facilitating a continuing and macabre cycle of life and death. So concerned with the threat these works posed to the general public and to public aesthetic sensibility, the exhibit came with a mock health warning. The warning advised parents of young children and the faint of heart and taste to abstain from viewing the exhibit: "There will be works of art on display in the Sensation exhibition which some people may find distasteful. Parents should exercise their judgment in bringing their children to the exhibition. One gallery will not be open to those under the age of 18." The "Sensation" exhibit became a conceptual and philosophical staging ground for larger cultural query on the nature, function, and value of art.

Beyond the visceral textures of their art, both works interrogated the process and condition of organic decay through blending structural and conceptual means. The decomposition present in Ofili's and Hirst's work were not only larger embodiments of their artistic expressions and ideas, but also embodied the spaces of their viewers' lived experiences. While Hirst's "A Thousand Years" traverses the boundaries of constituent organic parts of an everyday cow, he makes a larger conceptual statement about the solvency of its constituent parts in understanding the fluency of moral and aesthetic boundaries. Similarly, Ofili's "The Holy Virgin Mary" repositions racialized and culturally constructed notions of virginity, womanhood, and spirituality in his rendering of the Virgin Mary in *black-face and form*. The image not only changes popular expressions of her sexuality but also challenges her moral function and use. In examining his own art, Hirst notes his fascination with blending the culturally unacceptable with the culturally pleasing: "What I like is that contradiction: a really gorgeous photograph of something horrific." Hirst's fascination, however, is not without meaning: "I want to make people think, not to totally shock the shit out of them for the sake of it" (Chaundry). The negative responses to these works of art comes not just from his viewers' ability to make a value judgment on the art, but from their ability to relate to the work from the space of their own experiences. In this exhibit, interrogating the interpretive space where seeing occurred means residing in the scenes of decomposition and decay. The larger questions of aesthetics, taste, and moral value inherent in the debate over these and other works in the "Sensation" exhibit (eventually leading the city to threaten to revoke the museum's lease and funding) also raises important questions about the artist and the artist's interpretive space. The city and the museum were not alone in trying to control that space through placing a value on the works being shown; the artists also tried to control the viewers' very space of seeing. The city was attempting to dictate to viewers what was an appropriate experience to be seen, while the artists were trying to challenge the experience of what could be (i.e. what was *possible* to *be*) seen.

These issues of seeing the site and space of decomposition are at the very heart of Charles Johnson's *Oxherding Tale*. Johnson's self-described " 'platform' book" ("Introduction" xvii) engages readers as cultural agents of taste and aesthetics through various scenes of sensory and structural decomposition; these scenes specifically seek to direct the gaze to *seeing* different spaces of artistic production, value, and moral consciousness in the ever-changing spaces of black creative discourse. The voyeuristic tenor of Johnson's literary art in these decomposing spaces in the novel makes readers look upon and makes them privy to the inner-life, inner-workings, and the *inter-texts* of the novel's central character, Andrew Hawkins. Furthermore, Johnson's model drives readers to look in ways that challenge presuppositions from the limited range of their experiences. Johnson's self-reflexive play on the classic slave narrative tradition bends our interpretive sight to query Andrew's unlikely conception and engage with various instances of decomposition and decay in the traditional *bodies* (tragic mulatto, slave narrative, race man) of African American literary structures we know and expect. In a striking scene early in the novel, Andrew participates in the act of skinning a deer. This and other moments of sensory and structural decomposition are not merely intended to shock the reader and maintain our interest in the bodies on display, but are an attempt to challenge and expand our interpretive faculties, making us look upon the scene and consider new directives in our artistic understanding while we, as viewers of Johnson's art, understand the wealth of his experiences in the world and the multiple reflections on those experiences affective in his lived existence. The furor over the "Sensation" exhibit mimics the furor that Johnson works to construct here in his literary art and the transcendence he hopes to effect by challenging the interpretive spaces of black writing and creative production: "Why else do we fling books into the fire if not because, in the case of great fiction, and deep within our depths, the writer is leading us in a direction we know is inevitable but toward which we sometimes *do not wish to go*, especially if it will shatter our smugness, or displace us from our fondest prejudices" (*Being and Race* 39). Decomposition allows Johnson to access that space "deep within our depths" that "trespasses" on the spaces where black fiction has not wanted to go but inevitably contains. Andrew and the slave narrative become the perfect interpretive model to question these spaces because of their physical engagement with the common spaces where (as in the "Sensation" exhibit) everything sacred and fouled resides.

Decomposition works two ways in *Oxherding Tale* to challenge the interpretive space of art and the artist's mode of seeing. On a basic level, decomposition refers to an organic breakdown of constituent parts.[2] Thus, there are literal and figurative sites of decomposition or breakdowns in the novel. These sites reveal scenes of putrescence and decay either of physical bodies or of specific bodies of discourse. In *Oxherding Tale* those bodies of discourse revolve around black creative production and art. Under this structure, decomposition also refers to a reversal or a removal of meanings. These meanings reside in central forms or compositions traditionally found in black creative discourse or, more specifically, in the tradition of African American literature. Thus, an opposite rendering (a literal organic breakdown) of what readers traditionally expect or a *de-composition* takes place. Additionally, the term *decomposition* can also refer to a fusion of meaning on a pre-existing structure. The *Oxford English Dictionary* notes that decomposition is a "further composition" or "a compounding of things already composite (made up of various parts or elements)." In a similar way, in these literal scenes of putrid decay and rotting, Johnson adds new levels of interpretive meaning and possibility for black creative production. He plays on what the reader already knows and assumes to be true about various *composite structures* in the novel and then, like an artist, adds new layers and textures of meaning. These textures of meaning expand the ways in which we see and understand these spaces as they literally decompose or break apart and *open* before the reader.

Johnson's own questioning of the nature and function of art in *Being and Race: Black Writing Since 1970* makes a strikingly similar conclusion about the nature of seeing, noting that "art is not doing its job, if you only see what you think you should see" (Lyke 43). Just as phenomenology denies an empirical system with established meanings, Johnson impugns the traditional structures of African American literature and its canonical stories. In these scenes of structural decomposition then, Johnson challenges the ways in which we see these spaces of inquiry (the tragic mulatto, slavery and freedom, the slave narrative tradition, and the artist) and effectively challenges the means by which we interpret them by expanding our aesthetic and interpretive palate. Many possible forms emerge out of the various *de-compositions* that appear in the novel. Using the slave narrative and the inter-text of black philosophical fiction as referents, Johnson decomposes the skin (read tradition) around black creative discourse by positioning the archetypal figure of a mulatto character as an emerging artist challenging fiction and form. Decomposition allows readers to see the interpretive spaces that open up when the strictures of skin are peeled away, rot away, or are eaten away—all literal scenes of decomposition in this novel. More importantly, he provides us a view inside the development not just of a man moving toward enlightenment, but of an *artist* shaping and drawing his own space out of an interpretive engagement with the wealth of experiences he has with and through the use and function of his body.

To appreciate Johnson's aesthetic vision of art here and the positioning of Andrew as artist, I suggest that we frame our discussion with the perspective provided by phenomenology, specifically the phenomenological principle of the "in-itself-for-me."[3] The trajectories of this and other phenomenological structures provide valuable insight into reading Andrew as a developing artist with an emerging aesthetic presence.[4] From a theoretical level, Johnson's discussion in *Being and Race* about the challenges facing the black writer to produce art helped to develop the rich critical commentary surrounding his re-visioning of the African American slave narrative tradition and its traditionally tragic story of the mulatto slave.[5] "Our faith in fiction," Johnson notes, "Comes from an ancient belief that language and literary art—all speaking and showing—clarify our experience" (*Being and Race* 3). *Oxherding Tale* works to challenge that faith by making us believe in the possibility of other experiences than an essential and monolithic black aesthetic. It also moves to challenge the position of the black body as "stained" and imbued with the skin or stricture of tragedy.[6]

Andrew, our mulatto character, is neither tragic nor sentimental. His conception is wholly comic, his existence as a slave moves symbolically from house to field, his education is not based on basic literacy, but rather on an engagement with philosophical inquiry and interpretation, and his path to enlightenment becomes an immersion within the complicated range of the senses. Andrew functions as an apprentice artist under the guise of Johnson's own artistic and philosophical muse about the nature of black fiction because he suspends all presuppositions, all theories attached to the experiences and meaning of black literary art (*Being and Race* 29). Andrew reflects his body's worldly experiences. As a mulatto, his body reminds us not to privilege one racial identity over another, and it also reminds us to consider the range of his experiences. The connection between his consciousness and his body's function in the world links Andrew with Merleau-Ponty's basic premise in *The Phenomenology of Perception*: "The world is not an object such that I have in my possession the law of its making; it is the natural setting of, and field for, all my thoughts and all my explicit perceptions. Truth does not 'inhabit' only the 'inner man,' or, more accurately, there is no inner man, man is in the world, and only in the world does he know himself" (xi). Man (the universal human) is not governed merely by a set of empirical laws imposed upon his person, but man is a reflection of the world governed by his experiences. The laws of the South, the laws of his community (black or white), do not stand before or against the laws of his body and the way it experiences the world. Thus, understanding Andrew and the experiences that he recounts in the novel about decomposing spaces works not merely from the recognizable context of black fiction, but from the locus of his experiences. His black body, "stained" with the tragedy of blackness, is the first place readers are prone to look for meaning, but that body has to be read within the context of Andrew's experiences. Using Merleau-Ponty's perspective then, we can understand that Andrew's physical body "is to be compared not to a physical object" (here merely the physical distinction of its color or composition), but rather to a work of art because it is a "focal point of living meanings, not the function of a certain number of mutually variable terms" (*Phenomenology* 150–51). If readers attempt to read, or interpret his body, his art, through an empirical lens of what they *know*, they end in "the experience error" (5).

Andrew Hawkins's slave narrative begins with a study of his physical composition in the novel and in the narrative of slavery. His story—black and slave—begins by an unlikely conception and ends with a reckoning with an unlikely composition he makes for himself—William Harris, white Revolutionary War descendant. During a night of drinking (48 ounces of Madeira) between Jonathan Polkinghorne (master of the plantation) and George Hawkins (butler and slave), Polkinghorne devises an idea to avoid the sure censure awaiting either man who dared return home to his wife drunk. Polkinghorne surmises that "there's no harm in switching places for one night, is there, with me sleeping in the quarters and you upstairs" (5). The resulting switch leaves George Hawkins in bed with the mistress of the plantation, Anna Polkinghorne, and Andrew Hawkins as the product of their union. This scene becomes an important staging ground in challenging what readers see in the slave narrative tradition from the locus of what they have come to know. It brings the art of this piece and Johnson's philosophy of art into our field of vision and into the interpretive space. Here Johnson challenges "our faith in fiction" and what "we think we should see" by engaging with our experiences. Miscegenation is not a new element in the history of slavery, nor is the mulatto character, but the paradox Johnson creates in Andrew's conception and his physical place in the world provides the space that allows him to deconstruct and decompose the solvency of fiction and form and expand his art.

This paradoxical decomposition becomes an important staging ground for interpretive inquiry because it grounds readers in the experience of "imperfect knowledge" and rejects the epistemological "mistake [of circumscribing] being within the parameters of human cognition" (Dillon 2–3). It refers to the central paradox of experience that grounds Merleau-Ponty's phenomenology and its challenge to the classic discussion of knowledge and experience in Plato's *Meno*, when Meno asks, "And how will you inquire, Socrates, into that which you do not know? What will you put forth as the subject of inquiry? And if you find what you want, how will you ever know that this is the thing you did not know?" (206). As a mulatto, Andrew's physical body animates this paradox. He lies betwixt and between epistemological faith in specific structures of the slave narrative tradition and his own expansive ontological space that transcends any epistemological certainty. Inquiry is the basis of Andrew's life because his body is a continual space of uncertainty and query and Johnson, as several critics have noted, animates this concern in his use of the Buddhist quest motif.[7] Andrew is continually searching for meaning outside of the space of his basic cognition. Thus, Andrew's body becomes the perfect space to initiate the aesthetics of decomposition: "When I look back on my life, it seems that I belonged by error or accident—call it what you will—to both house and field, but I was popular in neither, because the war between these two families focused, as it were, on me, and I found myself caught from my fifth year forward in their crossfire" (8). The decomposition between house and field establishes Andrew's own understanding of himself between two different worlds, not belonging fully to either. His experience, early in life, teaches him that his body is a reminder of "the experience error," and his decision later in life to pass as a white man, represents his own "experience error" learned early in childhood about his meaning in both the white and black worlds. Andrew feels that this final creation is permanent until he is forced to *see*, in Reb and the Soulcatcher, the spaces outside of this field of vision. So while arguably Andrew does not initially create anything or see himself as a creator because of his limited mobility and expressive awareness as a slave, his apprenticeship to these different types of experiences in the range of his physical encounters helps him to develop his own unique aesthetic and his own unique work of art.

From the initial story of Andrew's conception and the shift of his position as tragic, the novel's earliest literal space of decomposition, the skinning of the deer, serves to read the other sites of decomposition in the novel. Andrew begins to connect the composition of his body with his ability to decompose the spaces of enslavement in his physical world and to expand the interpretive possibilities around his lived experience:

> Despite the cold, I was gulping air, my heart fluttering and unstable in my chest when I cut along the soft belly, pulling the blade from pelvic bone to chest, through tissue tough as rubber. My fist inside then, holding down the hot coils of intestines, I slid my sleeve in deep as I could, cutting loose the diaphragm, the windpipe—it felt like an old hose with wires on it—and then, against my will, I began crying softly into one hand as the other pulled free a handful of smoking heart, lungs, and intestines onto the snow-covered ground. (27)

The decomposition of the deer marks a central presentation of Andrew as artist and the emergence of his body as art. Andrew recognizes the living being behind the deer's skin and begins to understand its skin merely as a covering of the deer's existence. What lies beneath the skin becomes important to understanding that existence and is an important phenomenological model about the nature and function of art. Johnson states that art exists as "enriching experience by organizing the pieces such that some sense that was embodied there, buried, but not clearly seen, is bodied forth" (McCullough 11). Art here becomes what Andrew can body forth out of the pieces of decay.

Additionally, what lies beneath is only understood in relationship to the lived experience in the world. Andrew's body, like the deer's, is not an empty vessel but a constellation of meanings. The heart, lungs, intestines represent the critical "chiasm" of the deer or the "intertwining" of its flesh and thus its experiences in the outer and inner world which Andrew now holds in his hands.[8] Andrew understands that his experience in seeing the deer killed, in skinning the deer, and in the consumption of the deer will shape meaning and his life forever. Here is where his art takes on value. That value is not an empirical value system driven by preconceptions about his art, but a value driven by his own personal and lived experiences, a value driven by what life and meaning he sees in the space of decomposition. This moment empowers Andrew to query his own industry, even his own hands, as art-*forms* out of the work of his own body:

> It was hot work, I can tell you. The effort left me panting. Then it was as if someone ran a finger across my mind. What if all Ezekiel's talk abut how poleaxing preceded porkchops was saying that violence of the shotgun blast, the instant before the final explosion of dust, stayed sealed inside like a particle, trapped in the dying tissues, and wound up on the dinner table—as if

everything mysteriously blended into everything else, and somehow all the violence wars slavery crime and suffering in the world had, as Ezekiel suggested, its beginning in what went into our bellies? (27)

Art and the artist combine in a space where creative production, moral imperative, and freedom are most challenged. For Andrew, and for the many battling with the dynamics of race in the novel, those worlds and experiences are driven under the moral wrangling of human slavery and oppression. The interpretive line is not in focusing on the loss of form, in the visceral decay of the deer, now a gruesome mass of entrails, blood, and loose skin. The interpretive line focuses instead on the connection of his body literally inside and outside of the deer and its relationship to his understanding of the world. The decomposition of the deer becomes one of the central turning points in Andrew's development and movement towards personal autonomy and freedom.

The dividing line between his and others' experiences blurs and he begins to see connections between "everything else" and his body as he questions the idea of consuming the flesh of the deer. For Freidrich Schiller, any philosophy of art attempting to arrive at purposeful meaning must assume a moral center (Eldridge 12). The artist, however, while always in conversation with and informed by other artists, eventually bodies forth his own art out of the range of those experiences. Andrew begins to read his own freedom and social character in connection with his activity of skinning the deer and he begins to understand the challenges of blending the autonomy of art with the freedom and, by extension, significance of his own life. The connection between one art and this art created by the violence of Andrew's hands connects them on the level of moral and aesthetic value. Thus, the question of whether it *is* art (its aesthetic value) gets obscured by the more important question of how he plans to use his ability and power to create art both in himself and in that which he touches. His decision is informed by the wealth of his experiences but will be manifested through his personal choices. A combination of theories emerges in his final query about the deer (his father's needs, Ezekiel's commentary on vegetarianism), but what he is left with is his own response to the act as his body (his arms, his hands) touches and transforms the deer. The choice, however, while informed, must not be driven by the aesthetics, the presuppositions of others, or his own latent fears: that is what becomes tragic and that is the larger moral question connected to his work as artist.

The skinning of the deer and the lessons learned there will come full circle by novel's end with the other aesthetic lesson that Andrew learns about the importance of seeing and having "Whole Sight" in his interpretive space.[9] The inability to express autonomy as a slave in the peculiar institution of slavery mimics the peculiar institution of and ideological investment in blackness that Johnson writes against. That investment *sees* blackness and its forms through a particular light—a particular vision of the black artist. Andrew's initial vision is ideological and proscriptive. That vision is driven by an ideology of beauty and an attempt to place value on something that has different meaning for all of us. So, Andrew's quest in the novel commences in the most ideological of spaces—romantic love. He desires to marry and to free Minty, the slave girl, whom he has known since childhood, but whom he does not *really* see until "he *really* saw her for the first time" as "purified features in a Whole" (15). Master Polkinghorne, however, has another *vision* and it does not involve losing his most valuable piece of *property* to the whims of love. He instead decides to send Andrew into the arms of the insatiable Flo Hatfield, the "genius of love," and to a most certain death. Ironically, Andrew's path further into bondage, and his bondage to an aesthetic ideal of love, will eventually help to free him and body forth his art. The vision of Minty, however, has to decompose before that can happen: "I advanced into the guestroom with one foot always forward, not wanting to face this, afraid, aye, of what I thought I would see: so many profiles of Minty spun before me, like flashcards— a frightened girl condemned to stay forever in the shopwindow, on the Block; a servant girl whose laughter affected me like straight gin . . . and another Minty I did not recognize, reduced to rotting flesh. . . . She was disintegrating. Sugar in water. Form into formlessness" (166). So the last sight of decomposition in the novel, Minty's literal rotting away as a victim of pellagra, functions as the second frame in which Andrew, the artist, develops in the novel. Minty represents an aesthetic of beauty that drives Andrew to upset his comfortable vision of life for the unknown and, as another formative space of decomposition, she will serve as a directional path in shaping his art.

From the framing spaces of structural and conceptual decomposition in the novel, we can now critically circle back to the first and perhaps most important space of de-composition (not a literal decay of the body's constituent parts but a breakdown of its meaning in relationship to Andrew's lived-experience)— Andrew's physical body:

Beneath the sausage-tight skin of slavery I could be, depending on the roll of the dice, the swerve of the indifferent atom, forever poised between two worlds, or—with a little luck—a wealthy man who had made his way in the world and married the woman he loved. All right—be realistic, I thought.

Consider the facts: Like a man who had failed or been rudely flung into the world, I owned nothing. My knowledge, my clothes, my language even, were shamefully second-hand, made by, and perhaps for, other men. I was living a lie, that was the heart of it. My argument was: Whatever my origin, I would be wholly responsible for the shape I gave myself in the future, for shirting myself handsomely with a new life that called me like a siren to possibilities that were real but forever out of reach. (17)

He becomes an expression of personal autonomy, and his body, his skin, is the art which he chooses because it is the one space during and after his slave existence where he exercises his freedom and exerts control. Andrew's awareness of his ability to enact, in this instance, freedom for himself by using his skin (that renders him light enough to pass) to his advantage also enables him to create himself anew and determine his own artistic vision of himself as well as his artistic vision of the larger world. Andrew's understanding of his "responsibility" for "the shape I gave myself" in both future and present tense establishes an ethic of artistic creativity that enables Andrew to create his own existence—his own way of understanding his world. His *conscious* awareness of that ability to enact freedom in his own life connects indistinguishably with the literal shape and form of his bodily composition. Andrew also assumes a position placing him squarely in charge of his own value—rather than have his existence determined by the "sausage-tight skin" of slavery he chooses to shed that skin, and shift into a shape which befits his whims, his location, his time. He has the chance to expand the interpretive space around him and literally move outside of the framework of merely mulatto and slave. He becomes one of the many shape-shifters in Johnson's novels—those who are able to change their fate by creating a new skin (read being) for themselves.

For instance, in *Faith and the Good Thing*, our unlikely heroine finds that she has more in common with the elusive and structurally abstruse Swamp Woman than originally assumed and, by novel's end, the burnt, useless skin that she suffered through the roles of "innocent, whore, and housewife" (*Faith* 195) is shed for the discarded skin of the bog woman. They literally exchange skins and experience: "The Swamp Woman removed a fresh suit of skin from the box. She slipped it on, tugging at its loose seams, then zipped up the back. Faith held her breath: the hair on the suit was formed around its head in a full mushrooming natural; the skin was creamy and the color of caramel, the eyes in the head were slightly asymmetrical and the breasts—small" (194). The Swamp Woman assumes the skin and thus the experiences of what she reminds us she has never been—"a foolish, young girl"—and devilishly exclaims that she "ain't never tasted the Good Thing in quite that way" (194). Faith's decision to assume the skin of the Swamp Woman makes her privy to a larger truth, not only her ability to create but her ability to fashion her own art out of experience. Her body becomes an extension of her experiences and, in her encounters, she is able to shape herself and her art: "Faith almost knew what she [the Swamp Woman] would encounter, could predict it, because she'd been there herself. That awareness made her feel like an oracle. It convinced her that prescience was not so much a gift of magic as it was the product of experience" (194). Faith also recognizes phenomenology's presuppositionless tenor in her rejection of scientific relativism and her acknowledgement of a prescience (forethought) driven not by scientific theory but by the extent of her body's experiences. Her own encounters in the skin of "a foolish, young girl" enable Faith to understand what will happen to the Swamp Woman now that she has assumed that same skin. Yet Faith also knows that the Swamp Woman will have to experience for herself what it means to be that "foolish, young girl" and craft her own meaning out of that space. Similarly, Andrew's conception of the politics of skin and racial mixing enables Johnson to extend his discussion of the skin as a limited covering that merely reflects one vision of Andrew's relationship to the world, his experiences, and his vision as an artist.

The unlikely spaces of decomposition in the novel (the decomposition of the slave narrative, decomposition of the deer, and the decomposition of skin) prepare us as readers for the unlikely purveyors of this artistic sense in Andrew's creative development. While arguably there are many in the novel who provide instruction and influence which Andrew will use to develop his own interpretive vision and body of art, two figure prominently in fostering Johnson's critical model and in positioning Andrew as an artist: Reb, the Coffinmaker, and Bannon, the Soulcatcher. One sculpts art (shapes) in wood from the seeming space of nothingness; the other assumes the body of those he wishes to possess and *embodies* them from the inside out. Bannon catches slaves by catching souls and he catches those souls by embodying their experiences. Reb is a man without experiences to embody because he assumes an ascetic lifestyle and denies himself the pleasure of the senses in order to work in the service of his art. Both work from opposite ends of the artistic spectrum but both are serious about their art. Bannon is the hunter who eventually seeks to hunt and capture escaped slaves Reb and Andrew, and Reb is the elusive prey that cannot be caught. Bannon tells Andrew that his artistic technique fails on Reb because Reb defies imitation: "For me to capture a Negro the *right* way, as Ah told you, Ah have to feel what he feels, want what he wants, 'fore Ah knows him good enough to hep him finish hisself" (173). Reb, however, is ascetic and thus as Bannon surmises wants "Nothin'!" and exclaims, "How the hell you gonna catch a Negro like that? He can't be caught, he's *already* free" (173). Neither man functions in the space of mimesis, but as Johnson has noted in the development of his own art, art does not begin *ex nihilo*, it begins somewhere. It does not begin in an essentialist system of ideas or, in the case of Reb, in a particular technique, but in experience and that experience and the way we engage with experiences will differ for each of us.

One is a sculptor, a woodcarver, a coffinmaker who provides dead souls a vessel to the netherworld; the other is the one who ferries these souls to the netherworld. Both men, however, create their art through a fluid engagement with the body of experience. The fluidity of form that both of these men exact with their hands is a fluidity of consciousness as well. Consciousness is a personal space that the individual controls: one is consciously in the world and one is consciously out of it. The ability to shape out of nothingness or without the strictures of mimicking form and function allows each man to excel at his craft. Reb is void of technique, and Bannon's technique goes only so far as to let his prey catch itself. He gets inside the skin of his victim and assumes its shape only long enough to lead his prey to the slaughter, and then assumes his own body again and allows his victim to foster his own death, just as Andrew's race-obsessed father (Johnson's model of a race man) does when the Soulcatcher comes for him: " 'Ah did indeed snuff George Hawkins after the Cripplegate uprisin', but he was carryin' fifty-'leven pockets of death in him anyways, li'l pools of corruption that kept him so miserable he *begged* me . . .'" (174). Is it any coincidence that both of these men deal specifically in the spaces of decomposition? Both men experience the breakdown of constituent parts, every time they engage with their art. Reb buries the dead; Bannon facilitates death. Johnson uses this space of decomposition to remind us of his own artistic vision as a writer and the vision that this novel supports: "I don't believe that art imitates. There is a mimetic element, but I really think that what a writer does is create an experience on the pages of the book for the reader. You're creating experience. You're not transcribing experience. If you talk about the African-American past in your work, you're obviously interpreting an experience. It's all filtered through consciousness, and the consciousness obviously of the author" (Little, "An Interview" 109). Experience, not mimesis, grounds what these men do as well and Andrew's ability to recall his personal experiences with both of these men will eventually lead him to develop his own unique aesthetic, and thus develop his own unique artistic vision. First, he has to achieve the ability, Johnson notes, to "get out of his own way" (Rowell 545).

Reb and Bannon move against technique and thus against a mechanical or formal presentation of skill. Art *is* in phenomenology, and technique for each of these men is not engagement in a formal system but an engagement away from self. Reb's role as an ascetic allows him to "get out of his own way" and simply create rather than mimic art:

> "Technique?" Reb laughed. "You wanna know what I do? I don't do nothin', Freshmeat, leastways, nothing you'd understand. . . . I try to forget every casket I've made. After a day I can't remember none of 'em. After two days, I forget whatever instructions the family of the dead person give me, and whether they gonna like it or not. After five days, I forget the fact that I makes coffins. Seven days go by and I forget all about myself, and that's when I start looking round for a tree that wants to be a coffin." (47)

Asceticism denies Reb all physical and sensory pleasures, so his art simply comes into being/is without being influenced by an empirical and rational system of knowledge. Instead, he grounds his art in his consciousness and thus in his experience. He is disciplined but not limited by his directional path; it simply guides the meaning of his life and his art. He instructs Andrew in an important difference between being *ascetic* and being *aesthetic* and ascribing to a particular vision of beauty rather than a wide range of artistic fields. Reb's perceptive range allows him to escape the South and the Soulcatcher. In *Understanding Charles Johnson*, Gary Storhoff asserts, "Reb's understanding of the self as always evolving—a consistent theme in Johnson's work—literally saves his life and Andrew's" (87); it also helps him to fashion his finest work of art, a coffin for Abraham Lincoln—the father of freedom. I would extend this reading and suggest that it is also another important space that focuses on decomposition in the novel. In all of the spaces where decay takes place, form emerges out of formlessness. Reb is able to enact for himself and for Andrew the very real spaces of freedom and art where the individual and his experiences are allowed to create and fashion space freely without the strictures or the institutions of *slavery*.

Bannon is the conceptual opposite of Reb, but he still serves an important vision of the artist that will eventually help to liberate Andrew at the end of this enlightened quest and help him emerge into the space of an artist. When Andrew first encounters the Soulcatcher, he learns an important lesson about the need for depth and width in an artist's vision:

> The Soulcatcher's voice, I swear, was black. The kind of deep-fried Mississippi Delta twang that magically turned *floor* into *flow*. *Door* into *doe*. Yet this was

the same man, now framed by lofts of hay and straw in Flo's barn, cribs and bins for grain, that I'd seen months earlier in her yard—a manhunter, a great, slack-shouldered monster with a gray Cathedral beard, a racial mongrel, like most Americans, but the genetic mix in the Soulcatcher was graphic: a collage of features that forced me . . . to stare. (67)

Bannon's body is a visual query on the art of seeing. Andrew's compulsion to *stare*, signifying his eyes wide open, plays on the importance of seeing in this novel. What Andrew thinks he sees in Bannon's body comes from the space of his experience: the "deep-fried Mississippi twang, the deltoid nose of the Wazimba, the coarsely textured hair like his fathers." Andrew's mistake or "experience error" is in his rational and empirical approach to reading those images solely as black, despite the evidence his own eyes and experience provide to the contrary: "And, more startling, his clothes were a cross between house—Rob Roy jeans, a redingote, cartridge belts, and Ivanhoe cap—and fields. I could not shake the feeling that Bannon was in masquerade" (68). While Bannon's appearance is *graphic*, visually descriptive and vividly *drawn* for Andrew to interpret, Andrew fails to see the range of interpretive possibilities Bannon's body provides for him. Instead he sees Bannon's masquerade as an expression of pretense and a disguise that needs uncovering.

Bannon, however, is not in disguise at all. He simply defies naming. Andrew has forgotten the lessons of skin and decomposition he learned earlier. That lesson comes to a head when the aesthetic paths of Bannon and Reb come together. Bannon, interestingly enough, becomes the catalyst for Andrew's movement into physical and artistic freedom. He brings the interpretive palate of Andrew full circle and reflects the changing tenor of the artist's gaze: "my gaze dropping from his face to his chest and forearms, where the intricately woven brown tattooes presented, in the brilliance of a silver-gray sky at dawn, an impossible flesh tapestry of a thousand individualities no longer static, mere drawings, but if you looked at them long enough, bodies moving like Lilliputians over the surface of his skin. Not tattooes at all" (175). In this site of decomposition, Bannon's body is not disintegrating or rotting away, but it is moving simultaneously into spaces of form and formlessness. For phenomenology, the "brilliance of the silver-sky at dawn" that Andrew describes represents the "point- or object-horizon" structure or "perspective" (Merleau-Ponty, *Phenomenology* 68). As Merleau-Ponty explains, "to look at an object is to inhabit it, and from this habitation to grasp all thing in terms of the aspect which they present it" (68). Bannon's body is no longer a series of "static drawings" but a moving, living, ever-changing "tapestry of a thousand individualities." What is visible to Andrew as a reader of Bannon's text has no boundaries and in a similar way Johnson now makes sure that our understanding of black creative discourse has no boundaries as well. The horizon becomes a presentation of "objective space" and Andrew is met with a vision of artistic freedom—a vision of an artist whose work develops "in-itself" and "from himself" that he can now use to construct his own life. All the people that Bannon has killed, or touched, or who come in contact with his body, are now a part of the tapestry that colors his skin. The once static images—the color injected beneath the skin's surface—have changed and continue to change as Bannon embodies the experiences of his world. Andrew develops his own spaces of seeing art and thus his own space as an artist because he now sees the symbolic in Bannon's body. Moreover, despite the decomposition and destruction which created this artwork, Andrew's interpretive faculties are now wide enough for him to see his art as one artist's artistic interpretation of freedom.

Andrew Hawkins comes into Being or sense for us as readers by Johnson's unlikeliest of artistic compositions and bodies forth new interpretive spaces for his literary art. Thus, Johnson's portrait of the artist in Andrew connects to his own unique artistic development in the literature, or more accurately, his own spaces of de-composition where the creation of his own literary art begins by breaking down the constituent parts of forms to reflect meaning in the world within the body of his work. Reflecting on the symbolic states of decomposition in his own work, Johnson explains: "as a young novelist, I found the problem of what is or is not the 'black' experience staring at me more steadily than I could stare at it, particularly after I'd written six bad, apprentice novels, three that aped the style of James Baldwin, Richard Wright, and John A. Williams" (*Being and Race* 5). Johnson's attempt to "ape" or mimic these artists elucidates his quest to become part of the composition of the African American literary tradition. Of course, his development as an artist can only evolve through the decomposition of the tradition within that tradition. More importantly, we learn from Johnson early in his treatise that art does not begin "ex nihilo" but in conversation with other models (artists) whom he has been influenced by and whose work he has experienced. He contextualizes this statement by noting that writing or the *art* of writing "doesn't so much record an experience—or even imitate or represent it—as it *creates* that experience" (*Being and Race* 6). The model adheres to Johnson's phenomenological tenor and phenomenology's concept of *epoché* or "bracketing" where all presuppositions are brought together to *create* a "fresh, original vision" (5). While the black writer, for Johnson, unlike his white counterpart, may have trouble in determining where to begin, the beginning fruits of his artistic impulse are easily located: "We [as artists] *encounter* in some form [art], blunder into it—or have it placed before us by teachers or parents—as being different from others in the world" (3–4).

Similarly, Reb's first "encounter" with Andrew structures or *brackets* him within this phenomena of art. Reb demands of Andrew, " 'You *folks*, I say, or white people?' " Andrew responds, " 'Oh folks,' I assured him, 'Definitely folks.' " But Reb is not convinced: " 'You ain't folks or white,' he snorted. His eyes studied me. 'You fresh meat, boy' " (36). Andrew is the one space in the novel where a literal, physical "decomposition" does not occur, but a symbolic one does. Reb's naming of Andrew here marks the solvency of his physical form and its meaning in both the sensory and the corporeal worlds. While others around him physically and literally decay, Andrew remains intact. In other words, he never gets away from his body. It always remains in connection with his consciousness and always remains a part of the conscious way he understands the world. The skin that sheaths his body changes depending on the viewer and the way he is *perceived*, but the physical composition of the body and the meaning that it has for him in the world, or his flesh, remain the same. James B. Steeves's explanation of Merleau-Ponty's vision of the flesh provides an important space from which to read this rendering of Andrew in Johnson's novel: "The flesh is the structure of transfer and reversibility between sensing and being sensed, between consciousness and world. It involves an engagement with the world and a distance from it as well, allowing us to be involved with beings while remaining separate from them" (138–39). Thus, Andrew's fleshy composition remains consistent in its opposition to perceived ideas and norms. Nonetheless, he always remains in contact with the world of experience through his body. He continuously *becomes* a larger *embodiment* of forms. Andrew's task consists in recognizing his form in the midst of his *feelings* of formlessness.

Just as Andrew moves from an apprenticeship into his own artistic vision, Johnson's apprenticeship to the corpus of black creative production embodies an alternative vision of black art and brings *Oxherding Tale* and this interrogation on decomposition full circle. Instead of an organic breakdown or breaking apart of constituent forms as a means to expand interpretive spaces in the novel, Johnson's body of work becomes a composite space of meaning. Moreover, his apprenticeship to the "prescience" of his literary influences (Richard Wright, James Baldwin, and John A. Williams) enables Johnson to solve his own artistic and literary paradox. The "flesh" of this text embodies a pre-existing form (an experience) that brings Johnson's artistic vision into wide focus—even perhaps without Johnson having fully experienced this vision or having known of it consciously *before* it embodies the heart of this novel.

Perhaps more than any other influence on *Oxherding Tale*, Wright's literary body in *Native Son* provides the most important contextual model to consider the inner workings of the artist, as writer, designer, and interpreter of art. According to Johnson, *Native Son* constructs the most "consistent, coherent, and complete racial universe" of American writing and is imbued with layer after layer of meaning (*Being and Race* 14). Wright's phenomenological universe bodies forth through Bigger Thomas—a symbolic and literal space of decomposition. Bigger compounds the intimate, artistic expressions of Wright's private, prescientific consciousness and his public realm of creative production and intent.[10] Bigger is a model where we as readers become agents in the action and actively participate in the creation of new interpretive space.[11] Just as a painting or work of art forces us to gaze and see meaning for ourselves in the space of the artist's vision, Bigger is Wright's literary canvas on which he writes the imaginative novel and expands his readers' imaginative capabilities.

Andrew's emergence as an artist, not an artistic model, at the end of this oxherding tale, therefore, is no coincidence, because he manifests Johnson's own emergence as an artist who *creates* form rather than "apes" it. Johnson's encounters with interpreting Wright's art (Bigger in *Native Son)* progenerates his own "fresh, original vision." The final decomposition in the novel is a composite artistic rendering of Charles Johnson and his symbolic Reb, his fictive Allmuseri, and his literary sifu—Richard Wright. In a concomitant blending of his encounters with Wright's *Native Son* and Wright as craftsman, Johnson, as artist, comes to know what his literary and personal consciousness in his earlier artistic development attempted to "ape." While he can never imitate what his teachers have taught him, he can create experience and thus art in the composite spaces of this and other creative works. Johnson is able to body forth new meaning if he releases himself from the deterministic rhetoric around blackness and black being. Thus, in Andrew, Johnson "brackets" the experiences and failures learned from Wright's naturalistic project and canvas in *Native Son* (Bigger) and he embodies his own phenomenology of seeing in the experiential "black" text (Andrew). While Bigger is an *artform* in which Wright attempts to express "the emotional and mental climate of [the] time" that was "damned up, buried, and implied" (Wright 452) within an alternating historical and ahistorical racial universe, Andrew is a literal and literary *form-maker* who challenges the very heart of Johnson's art and the very possibilities of black creative discourse. What naturalism and its scientific determinism will not allow Bigger to do—thereby limiting Wright's art—phenomenology and its pre-suppositionless tenor will allow for Andrew, and by extension, for Johnson. As Andrew's narrative quest begins, so too does Johnson's, and the remaining imaginative field decomposes into infinite, artistic spaces of literary transcendence.

NOTES

1. The phrase, "Yes . . . but is it Art?," refers to a 1993 *Sixty Minutes* Interview by correspondent Morley Safer (see "Yes . . . but is it Art?"). In this series, Safer examined the commercial and aesthetic value of contemporary art.

2. The *Oxford English Dictionary* defines decomposition as "the action or process of decomposing; separation or resolution (of anything) into its constituent elements."

3. The phenomenological concept of "in-itself-for-me" comes from Merleau-Ponty's *The Phenomenology of Perception* and his discussions about the body. In this concept, experience is always discussed in relationship to the way the body *experiences* the world. As such, this theory allows us to interpret experience based on what we know and what we do not directly know but *experience* through the body's contact with various worldly phenomena. Thus, meaning in the world is relevant both in relation to itself—"in-itself"—and in relation to the ways in which we experience the world for ourselves—"for me"—through our bodies.

4. Several scholars have probed the depths of Johnson's work through the lens of phenomenology. See in particular Rushdy's seminal essay on phenomenology and Charles Johnson's fiction, "Phenomenology of the Allmuseri: Charles Johnson and the Subject of the Narrative of Slavery."

5. For a larger discussion of Johnson's recasting of the slave narrative form, see Coleman, "Charles Johnson's Quest for Black Freedom in *Oxherding Tale*," and Ouimet, "Freedom through Contamination: Collapsed Boundaries in Charles Johnson's *Oxherding Tale and Middle Passage*." For an important discussion of Johnson's revision of slave narrative form through a postmodern reading, see Rushdy, "Serving the Form, Conserving the Order: Charles Johnson's *Oxherding Tale*."

6. Johnson deconstructs this idea in his essay "A Phenomenology of the Black Body" (Byrd 109–22), which originally appeared in *Juju: Research Papers in Afro-American Studies*, Winter 1976.

7. There have been several important studies on the quest motif in *Oxherding Tale*. See especially Byrd, "*Oxherding Tale* and *Siddhartha*: Philosophy, Fiction, and the Emergence of a Hidden Tradition," and Gleason, "The Liberation of Perception: Charles Johnson's *Oxherding Tale*."

8. The term *chiasm* is Merleau-Ponty's rejection of Husserl's distinction between the inner and outer world—*Lifeworld* (Dermot 429). Merleau-Ponty develops this idea in his posthumous work, *The Visible and the Invisible*. In his notes to *The Visible and the Invisible*, Merleau-Ponty defines *chiasm* as "the application of the inside and the outside to one another" (264). *Lifeworld* or *Lebenswelt* refers to the phenomenology of Edmund Husserl.

The *Lifeworld* for Husserl was the foundational basis for all of human perception and his way of naming that reality. Merleau-Ponty challenges the boundaries of reality. See Edmund Husserl, *The Crisis of European Sciences and Transcendental Philosophy*, Trans. D. Carr. Evanston: Northwestern University Press, 1970.

9. *Whole sight* is Johnson's concept of understanding an expansive, multi-layered view of black creative discourse. He discusses this idea in his seminal 1984 essay "Whole Sight: Notes on New Black Fiction." Additionally, Nash deconstructs the idea of whole sight in relation to Johnson's complete fictional discourse (see *Charles Johnson's Fiction*, 34–36).

10. Wright's discussion in "How Bigger was Born" on the intent and function of the imaginative novel is important to the discussion provided here. I am particularly interested in Wright's expression of the nature and texture of the imaginative novel as a work of art: "In a fundamental sense, an imaginative novel represents the merging of two extremes; it is an intensely intimate expression on the part of a consciousness couched in terms of the most objective and commonly known events. It is at once something private and public by its very nature and texture" (433).

11. Johnson provides an interesting reading of Wright's *Native Son* that reflects this phenomenon in *Being and Race*. In examining his own experience reading Wright, Johnson comments: "Wright reminds us through his method—eidetic description, or presenting things in their lived essence (meaning) for a historical subject—that the world we live in is, first and foremost, one shaped by the mind. . . . No where does he cheat by resorting to narrative summary, or 'telling.' . . Indeed, the relentless pace of *Native Son* is fueled precisely because most of the book is unmediated scene, as in play. We see everything. We are forced to be witnesses to every thought and emotion of a national tragedy two centuries in the making. More: it is *we* whom Wright turns into murderers" (14).

BONDAGE AND DISCIPLINE
The Pedagogy of Discomfort in The Sorcerer's Apprentice

HERMAN BEAVERS

Have little thought and as few desires as possible.
—LAO TSU

I

Reading *The Sorcerer's Apprentice* prompted me to revisit Paolo Friere's *Pedagogy of the Oppressed*, in part because the question of failed pedagogy frames the opening and closing stories in the collection. But I also decided a turn to Friere was appropriate because reading Johnson's stories and discovering in them the investment in Eastern philosophical tenets characteristic of his other works of fiction, I determined that if pedagogy was at issue in these stories, it is best described as a *pedagogy of discomfort*. In light of the ways that we find aspiration and desire working in each of these stories, I'm proposing that at issue is the ability of Johnson's characters to loose themselves from the bondage that arises out of wanting [to be] more. Johnson's stories employ a variety of formats—the fairy tale, the parable, the allegory, and science fiction—to confront the problem of African American identity. But because Johnson's characters have to endure the misery that accompanies the failure to achieve their ambitions, it would seem that Jonathan Little is correct in his characterization of the stories in *The Sorcerer's Apprentice* as "surprisingly pessimistic" (109).[1] However, I would point to two aspects of the stories that suggest the possibilities for a different conclusion. The first is to be found in the subtitle of the collection, "Tales and Conjurations," which to my mind makes the intention of these fictions of a much more speculative sort. As evidenced by his selection of story formats, Johnson eschews Wrightian social realism, which uses instances of African American discomfort to indict racial inequity and injustice, to explore the ways that discomfort can signify possibility. Second, I would suggest that in putting forward characters who enact a variety of failed pedagogies,

Johnson indicates his sense that hegemony assumes forms so intertwined with the "everyday" that its disruption can only be accomplished via calamitous circumstance.

Hence, in "The Education of Mingo" and the title story, we find their respective plots turning on the interaction between pedagogue and student. The stories are further linked by the suggestion that failed acts of pedagogy are liberating, offering the possibility for escape. Though this would seem to suggest nothing more than an exercise in the counterintuitive, I would suggest that there is much more afoot. For in each instance, escape is not without its costs. For those unfamiliar with his work, Paolo Friere, the great Brazilian educator and activist, opens his classic volume, *Pedagogy of the Oppressed*, by describing humanization both as humankind's "central problem" and "an inescapable concern." Turning his attention to those he deems "the oppressed," Friere asserts their problem is that rather than recovering their humanity, they hope to supplant the oppressor by becoming oppressors in their own right. In his view, the teacher-student relationship is "fundamentally narrative" in character, a condition which is underscored by the fact that the "relationship involves a narrating Subject (the teacher) and patient, listening objects (the students)." Friere continues, "The teacher talks about reality as if it were motionless, static, compartmentalized, and predictable. . . . His task is to fill the students with the contents of his narration—contents which are detached from reality, disconnected from the totality that engendered them and could give them significance. Words are emptied of their concreteness and become a hollow, alienated, and alienating verbosity" (57). The result is that narration turns the student into " 'containers,' into 'receptacles to be "filled" by the teacher' " (59), which ultimately determines the teacher's worth. Friere refers to this approach to educating as "banking education," a modality whose main problem is that "it will never propose to students that they critically consider reality" (59). Further, it makes the teacher an agent of the status quo, embracing the notion that they are founts of knowledge, which means that they, too, are alienated from themselves.[2]

In "The Sorcerer's Apprentice," Allan Jackson envisions the life of a sorcerer as a combination of white magic and tangibility; in this instance, the ability to overwhelm the physical world with a mastery of technique. At the story's outset, Rubin Bailey, a sorcerer not long out of slavery, living in South Carolina, thinking that his days are growing short, chooses Allan Jackson to become his apprentice. Both Allan and his father, Richard, are delighted that such an honor has been bestowed upon their family; Allan loves the sorcerer, who "remember[s] the white magic of the Ekpe cults and Camaroons," especially because the old man's craft "comforted the sick, held back evil, and blighted the enemies of the newly freed slaves with locusts and bad health" (*Sorcerer's Apprentice*, 149). In his quest for higher knowledge, he wants nothing better than to work miracles and to do good. Though Rubin warns him to the contrary, Allan falls asleep thinking, "To do good is a very great thing, the *only* thing, but a magician must be able to conjure at a moment's notice. Surely it is all a question of know-how" (150).

Living in the days just after the end of slavery, Allan's quest for mastery as a sorcerer refers, if only allegorically, to Du Bois's *Souls of Black Folk*, where he argues that the end of African American striving lies in achievement as "a co-worker in the kingdom of culture, [by escaping] both death and isolation, to husband and use his best powers and his latent genius." Looking at Johnson's body of work, we find such thinking echoed in his second novel, *Oxherding Tale*, where his protagonist, Andrew Hawkins, observes: "For the men of my period the dream of contributing to the Race, of Great Sacrifice and glory, drew us back from desire. We wanted to do something difficult—see?—like tame the West, spearhead a Revolution, or pin down the universe like a butterfly on the pages of a book. We wanted trials. Tests of faith. We could not live, the men of my age, without a cause, a principle. Something greater than living day to day, and to which we could devote ourselves entirely" (43). One might be hard-pressed to grasp why Rubin does not endorse such thinking. When finally he consents to teach Allan the trade of sorcery, his pedagogy is curious in that it dislodges technique and intention. He resists Allan's desire to circumvent the veil and tells him, almost antithetically, "You are the best of students. And you wish to do good, but you can't be too faithful, or too eager, or the good becomes evil" (150). As pedagogue, Rubin embodies Chaung Tsu's insistence that the Way avoids conscious striving, for such a path "is fundamentally a way to self-aggrandizement and it is consequently bound to come into conflict with Tao" (Merton 24). This conflict becomes manifest in "The Sorcerer's Apprentice" when Rubin tells Allan: " 'What I know has worked I will teach. There is no certainty these things can work for you, or even for me, a second time. White magic comes and goes. I'm teaching you a trade, Allan. You will never starve. This is because after fifty years, I still can't foresee if an incantation will be magic or foolishness' " (151). By problematizing technique, Rubin also nullifies the connection between talent and virtue. Moreover, he controverts Allan's propensity to bifurcate experience into "right" or "wrong" displays of technical skill. Though Allan is praised by Rubin for his "native talent, which did not come from knowledge," the student believes it to be "wholly unreliable."

Viewed in DuBoisian terms, Allan's distrust of "native talent" would seem the correct sentiment. Johnson's use of Taoist philosophy in "The Sorcerer's Apprentice" intimates that there is an alternative path to be sought. The relationship between Rubin and Allan demonstrates the pedagogical model to be found in Chaung Tsu's admonition:

If you wish to improve your wisdom
And shame the ignorant,
To cultivate your character,
And outshine others;
A light will shine around you
As if you had swallowed the sun and the moon:
You will not avoid calamity. (Merton 115, my emphasis)

Though this would seem to suggest a negative outcome, Johnson uses Chaung Tsu's admonition as the ground upon which he will establish the "break" from the commonsensical nature of hegemony. But in "The Sorcerer's Apprentice," this will take the form of Allan's quest for excellence, seen in Western terms as man's "natural" state of being. In his hands, this quest becomes destructive, a source of failure. For example, when Allan cannot cure a sick infant, in spite of the fact that his memory is a place "where techniques lay stacked like crates in a storage bin," he loses all faith in his training. Though he has mimicked Rubin Bailey's techniques to the letter, the child's death leads him to conclude that his talent is for "pa(o)stiche" (164), imitation, rather than innovation and success.

Here, it would be useful to juxtapose Allan's circumstance against the one depicted in "The Education of Mingo." Once again, we need to consider the failed pedagogue, here in the form of Moses Green, who buys a bondsman named Mingo and decides to educate him to the ways of Western culture. Though the auctioneer has informed Moses that Mingo is the "youngest son of the reigning king of the Allmuseri, a tribe of wizards," Moses dismisses this information. In his mind, "nearly everybody in the New World from Anabaptists to Whigs" is an "outrageous liar." Hence, Moses' worldview is framed by skepticism, if not outright disregard, for all the systems of belief, political, religious, and otherwise, that surround him. While this need not be an issue in and of itself, when we consider the fact that Moses is a slaveowner, his distrust of ideological systems means that he eschews the rhetorical tools undergirding the act of enslavement. Orlando Patterson clarifies the importance of this when he argues that the relationship between master and slave requires "the tacit support of those not directly involved with it," and he concludes "the master's power was nothing in isolation from fellow members of his community" (10). Lacking this reinforcement, Moses remains free to define the nature of his relationship with Mingo because it turns on a cultural, rather than a materialist, axis.

However, Moses' location outside the purview of the dominant ideological systems of his day in no way suggests that he fails to embrace racial hierarchy. Mingo's blackness is all that is required to substantiate his assumption that the African is cultureless. Nonetheless, Moses is confident that he can guide the bondsman into the parameters of western culture. Realizing that Mingo speaks no English, Moses informs him, " 'S all right. I'm going to school you myself. Teach you everything I know, son, which ain't so joe-fired much—just common sense—but it's better'n not knowing nothing ain't it?" (4). Moses' confidence in "common sense" as a curricular foundation needs to be understood against his decision to institute an "education" that is based not only on racial inferiority, but intended to sustain it. That he offers to teach Mingo "all [he] knows" leads me to conclude that we are not to take Moses' role of "master" seriously, for he views Mingo, not as property, but as his tutee.

Here, one might also consider Heidegger's definition of "common sense," where he observes:

> Common sense concerns itself, whether "theoretically" or "practically," only with entities which can be surveyed at a glance circumspectively. What is distinctive in common sense is that it has in view only the experiencing of "factual" entities, in order that it may be able to rid itself of an understanding of Being. It fails to recognize that entities can be experienced "factually" only when Being is already understood, even if it has not been conceptualized. Common sense misunderstands understanding. And therefore, common sense must necessarily pass off as "violent" anything that lies beyond the reach of its understanding, or any attempt to go out so far. (*Being and Time* 363)

Heidegger's assessment of common sense as "violent" is underscored by Mingo's turn to violence, where he murders one of Moses' neighbors and his sweetheart, Harriet Bridgewater. Little describes Harriet as a "romantic conjurer" (110), meant as a juxtaposition against Moses' aesthetic misguidedness. But this assessment ignores Harriet's rootedness in an assessment of blackness that reflects the racial imaginary produced during the Enlightenment. When

Moses declares Mingo's ability to feel what he feels, Harriet, paraphrasing Aristotle, reminds him that slaves are "tools with life in them and tools are lifeless slaves" (10). She goes on to warn him about getting too close to "that Wild African," and underscores her warning by quoting Hume and relating the philosopher's refusal to believe in a bondsman's ability to play the piano by ear. In short, she gives voice to the *common sense* of Western thought. Thus, when Mingo, as Moses' doppelganger, murders Harriet, we see why Johnson includes the detail of Harriet reading Mary Shelley's *Frankenstein*: this suggests that such thinking is ultimately the undoing of Western culture, for in rejecting Moses' connection to Mingo as dangerous, Harriet also serves as a touchstone for what will drive slavery and colonialism—the notion that the African is *Other*. Though Moses is deeply hurt by Harriet's death, we must contend with the issue of what it means for Mingo to have intuited her murder as something Moses desired. And the implication of Mingo's act is perhaps a bit more speculative than we might conclude on a first reading of the story.[3]

At this point, we might pose the question: if Johnson's story is not a rumination on slavery in the nineteenth century, what ends is it trying to achieve? One suggestion is that Johnson's story can be understood as a revision of Daniel Defoe's *Robinson Crusoe*. What is essential here is the manner in which Friday, like Moses, substantiates Crusoe's world. Since it is a world largely of his own creation, Friday's presence, his initiation into Crusoe's ways of doing and thinking, works to verify, in the Hegelian sense, the physical, the concrete.

Further, it is against the backdrop of the *Other* that both Crusoe and Moses construct themselves. For example, when Crusoe elects to instruct Friday "in the knowledge of the true God," he does so only to discover the benefits of his role as pedagogue: "I had God knows, more sincerity than knowledge in all the methods I took for this poor creature's instruction and must acknowledge what I believe all that act upon the same principle will find, that in laying things open to him, I really informed and instructed myself in many things, that either I did not know or had not fully considered before, but which occurred naturally to my mind upon my searching into them for the information of this poor Savage" (Defoe, 159). Like Crusoe, Moses views Mingo's education as a serious project. Where he differs is that his decision to expose Mingo to all he knows, from alpha to omega, deemphasizes his power. For Moses' distance from institutional power requires him to limit Mingo's access to knowledge, not only because it consolidates his power, but because it reinforces Mingo's subordinate status as well. Though there is a strong parallel to be drawn between Friday and Mingo, especially in light of their ability to please their masters, let me suggest that the similarities are superficial at best. For I would suggest that it is not power Johnson wants to examine here, so much as it is the relation between phenomenological issues and epistemological ones.

As such, Johnson's story depicts the manner in which Moses' contact with Mingo's otherness ultimately changes him—if it does not liberate him outright—in ways that reveal the instability of the Western tradition to which Harriet Bridgewater has been so intimately bound. Hence, Moses recognizes that "Education, as he dimly understood it, was as serious as a heart attack. You had to have a model, a good Christian gentleman like Moses himself, to wash a Moor white in a single generation. As he taught Mingo farming and table etiquette, ciphering with knotted string, and how to cook ashcakes, *Moses constantly revised himself*" (5, emphasis added). For Moses' act of self-revision alters his relationship to his surroundings. He moves from skepticism (which results after all from the unreliability of institutional knowledge) to positionality, where he must designate good from evil. He takes to "policing all his gestures, standing the boy behind his eyes." He comes to feel, looking at Mingo, at once "like a father, now like an artist fingering something fine and noble from a rude clump of foreign clay. It was like aiming a shotgun at the whole world through the African, blasting away all that Moses, according to his lights, tagged evil and cultivating the good; like standing, you might say, on the sixth day, feet planted wide, trousers hitched, remaking the world so it looked more familiar" (5–6). Certainly, Moses possesses god-like power in bringing Mingo to a state of Western awareness. But the passage above also points at the manner in which Mingo serves a talismanic function, for it is Moses' propensity to reposition Mingo "behind his eyes" that serves to render the unknown familiar. Those things he finds objectionable in the personal sense achieve ideological status when he passes them onto Mingo as negative experience, as evil. His location within the sphere of "common sense" likewise means that he can associate what once was experientially based insight with nature, where whim and fancy become synonymous with reality itself.

But further, Mingo serves as a site for Moses to negotiate the distance between mimesis and alterity. In needing to "make sense of things for Mingo's sake," Moses worries that his actions may somehow deform what he knows as common sense. This uncertainty, Michael Taussig argues, is indicative of the politics of identity as they are affected by the mimetic faculty:

Pulling you this way and that, mimesis plays this trick of dancing between the very same and the very different. An impossible but necessary, indeed an everyday affair, mimesis registers both sameness and difference, of being like, and of being Other. Creating stability from this instability is no small task, yet all identity formation is engaged in this habitually bracing activity in which the issue is not so much staying the same, but maintaining sameness through alterity. (Taussig 129)

Following on Taussig's observation allows me to insist Moses' decision to "educate" Mingo is grounded in the mimetic act, the need to create a world within a world, by overwhelming the foreign with the familiar. This is demonstrated when Moses wavers between telling Mingo that lightning is electricity or the Devil beating his wife. Though his initial impulse is to equate lightning with folklore, he chooses to assign it meaning via scientific discourse. Feeling that he can't "waffle on a thing like that," Moses works out what Taussig (via Adorno and Horkheimer) describes as a Western historical development whereby "mimesis becomes . . . a repressed presence not so much erased by Enlightenment science as distorted and used as hidden force." The last sentence of the paragraph relays the significance of Moses' shift in consciousness: "He made it a point to despoil meanings with care, choosing the ones that made the most common sense" (*Sorcerer* 6). I want to emphasize the use of the word "despoil" here because it intimates a fundamental aspect of Moses' project. The OED definition of "despoil" is "to strip of possession by violence or plunder, to deprive violently." Just as Crusoe attempts to move Friday from "cannibal" to Christian without understanding the cosmological and epistemological suppositions that call for the warrior to eat his enemy, thereby committing an act of conceptual violence, Moses' instruction likewise needs to be understood as destructive, but not in the ways that slavery might lead us to believe.

As Mingo gets "the hang of farm life" Moses grows in his awareness of how the slave is not merely a source of labor, but a site of labor as well. The rudiments of farm life—"patience, grit, hard work, and prayerful silence"—which Mingo comes to grasp with such difficulty, become the site where mimesis and alterity form a conceptual grid where Moses can conclude, "everything about him and the African was as different as night and day. . . . Mingo's education, to put it plainly, involved the evaporation of one coherent, consistent, complete universe, and the embracing of another one alien, contradictory, strange" (6). Here, Johnson initiates a parody of the ideology that foregrounds what will become the European colonial project. As it turns out, Moses discovers that Mingo has killed a white man on a neighboring farm and, later, his lover, Harriet Bridgewater (who has dismissed slaves as "tools with life in them"). When Moses inquires about Mingo's motives for murdering his friends, Mingo replies: " 'What Mingo know, Massa Green know. Bees like *what* Mingo sees or don't see what Massa Green taught him to see or don't see. Like Mingo lives through Massa Green right?' " (15), and he concludes, " 'Massa Green, he owns Mingo, right? . . . So when Mingo works, it bees Massa Green workin', right? Bees Massa Green workin', thinkin', doin *through* Mingo—ain't that so?' " (15). Mingo's actions have proceeded from the fact that as subjects "wired together," the African has absorbed all of Moses' inclinations and desires, both conscious and unconscious. Not only does this suggest an interesting play on Orlando Patterson's assertion that slavery is an example of human parasitism, but as if to underscore the point, Moses arrives at Harriet's house after Isaiah's murder to find her reading Mary Shelley's *Frankenstein*—which is described as a "recent tale of monstrosity and existential horror" (17).

The horror, as it were, is the manner in which the western subject's strug-gle to "be" is coming undone. But, as Johnson's protagonists remind us, this quest is always already enmeshed in a world of materiality and masculine energy. And we must remember that the motivation for Victor Frankenstein's tale is his encounter with Robert Walton, whose ill-fated attempt to sail to the North Pole is only partially motivated by his desire to achieve notoriety. The other part of that motivation issues from his desire to restore his family's com-promised patriarchal status. Johnson's use of Eastern religious tropes can be understood as critiques of reified constructions of race and gender, if only because Taoism denigrates that which we have traditionally associated with masculine power: aspiration, agency, and mastery.

As I noted above, Johnson brings together issues of creativity, revision, and reproduction in order to address the subject of transformation. Too often, these stories suggest, we confuse transformation and transcendence, which marks the manner in which what we believe to be important narrative forms in African-American cultural practice—the slave narrative, the conversion narrative, the recovery narrative, the rags-to-riches narrative—are ultimately bound up in melodrama that leans far too heavily on a circumscribed notion of racial inferiority. In the case of "The Education of Mingo," the story's nine-teenth-century setting would appear to suggest that the story is an historical fiction; however there are numerous cues that intimate that Johnson, as in *Oxherding Tale* and *Middle Passage*, wants to insinuate bondage of a broader sort.[4] Moses Green's largest requirement is "for a field hand and helpmate—a friend" (3). But this means that Moses is not situated within the conventional ideology of the slaveholder; that is, Mingo's value to him does not issue from his status as property, but as a companion.

While it is true that Mingo's education involves erasure and reinscription, what Johnson suggests, in a manner so nuanced to be almost imperceptible, is that Moses is freed from the constraints of the "common sense" of hegemony. Hence, when he and Mingo leave for Missouri ("somewheres in the west"), it is an ironic move because Moses has been disconnected from the kind of thinking embodied by Harriet Bridgewater. The ending is ambivalent to be sure, but it also in its way suggests that in matters of imprisonment, liberation is more likely to be found when bodies are in motion than at rest.

However, if pedagogy of the sort Moses directs towards Mingo is inherently corrupt, Johnson's "Alethia" is a story that, like "The Education of Mingo," underscores the ways that pedagogues, as purveyors of the status quo, are as much in need of liberation as their students. Hence, Johnson's depiction of an elderly professor's burgeoning love affair with Wendy Barnes, a female student who has threatened to accuse him of sexual harassment should he give her a failing grade, is about what happens when we *give in* to our desires. Though I would agree with Jonathan Little's assessment that the story ends on an ambivalent note, what interests me here is that the professor, like Ezekiel Sykes-Withers in *Oxherding Tale*, follows through on his desire to direct (as Marx has directed Sykes-Withers to do) his ruminations on the nature of existence *towards* someone. Though the scenario ends with the professor awakening in a tenement on Chicago's South Side, one look at him and Wendy Barnes says, "You're still thinking like a fat boy." However, upon saying this, she crawls back into bed with the old man, as if, once again, to suggest that liberation is a product of counterintuitive thinking, which we cannot conceptualize as much as we can stumble upon it.[5]

II

Though I have spent the bulk of this essay on the first and last stories of *The Sorcerer's Apprentice*, I want to insist that this is in no way meant as a dismissal of the remaining stories. Rather, I would speculate that a more productive juxtaposition is to be found in a linkage of either story to the second story in the volume, "Exchange Value"—in the case of the opening story because we move from Johnson's rumination on the ways that the slave liberates the master to an instance where property comes to enslave its owner. Told through the eyes of Cooter, "Exchange Value" has to do with what transpires after he and his brother Loftis steal nearly $900,000 in money and merchandise from their neighbor, Miss Bailey. As they are acquiring their newfound prosperity, Cooter ruminates on how such accumulation could exist in the face of Miss Bailey's destitution. Looking at the dead woman's face as the authorities carry her away, Cooter concludes "I seen something in her face, like maybe she'd been poor as Job's turkey for thirty years, suffering from that special Negro fear of using up what little we get in this life—Loftis, he call that entropy—believing in her belly, and for all her faith, jim, that there just ain't no more coming tomorrow from grace or the Lord, or from her own labor, like she can't kill nothing, and won't nothing die . . . " (37). Though he lacks the ability to characterize his analysis as such, Cooter's assessment of Miss Bailey's plight is steeped in the realm of chaos theory. Thus, he concludes: ". . . so when Conners will her his wealth, it put her through changes, she be spellbound, possessed by the promise of life, panicky about depletion, and locked now in the past 'cause *every* purchase, you know, has to be a poor buy: a loss of life" (38). As clearly as he sees Miss Bailey's plight, however, Cooter and Loftis soon fall into a similar pattern. Cooter returns home from a night on the town, having gorged himself on soul food and bought an expensive leather coat, to find that Loftis has changed the locks on their apartment and barricaded himself in with a weird assortment of cardboard and razor blades. Though Cooter finds Loftis's behavior strange, even more so when the latter decides to go to work as usual, he is no less affected by their take. He has concluded that he and Loftis are "like wizards," who can "transform [Miss Bailey's] stuff into anything else at will. All we had to do . . . was decide exactly what to exchange it for" (35).

It is here that "Exchange Value" can be seen to inhabit the same thematic territory as "The Sorcerer's Apprentice," for Cooter and Loftis are both young men who believe themselves to be well-steeped in the ideological realm of capitalism. But in an ironic turn, their acquisition becomes synonymous with imprisonment because, for all the ways that they are raised to the level of "wizards," they are, like Allan Jackson, caught in a veritable maelstrom of potential, unable to free themselves. The difficulty, as Johnson would have it, is that the complex demands placed on blacks by notions of "racial authenticity" or theories of racial uplift, ultimately create a vortex from which they cannot escape. In Cooter's and Loftis's case—and Miss Bailey's as well—it becomes a matter of figuring out which items have sufficient exchange value to transform potential into surplus.

But Johnson proposes that racism makes such thinking a trap. The fear of depletion, which leaps like a virus from Miss Bailey to Cooter and Loftis, is reminiscent of the vortex, whose energy draws everything to the center. In this instance, when Loftis tells Cooter, "As soon as you buy something, you lose the power to buy something" (36), he is describing entropy, a fall into randomness. Because neither of them can guarantee that spending money will create a surplus, Loftis goes off to work as usual, saying "It's Wednesday, ain't it?" and thereby suggesting that the ways that he and Cooter come to embody the hegemonic forces of commodification is by embracing the everyday even more deeply than before. Unlike Moses Green and Allan Jackson, who run toward calamity, Loftis and Cooter, in trying to avoid it, become ensnared in a vortex of sameness and stasis. And thus, it could be that Johnson is trying to suggest the ways that racism arises out of capitalist enterprise, for neither Loftis nor Cooter reach the alternative conclusion that they can *extend* their holdings through expenditure. In this sense, we can also read "Exchange Value" as a story that ruminates on the nature of art, for creativity rests, Johnson intimates, on action, not stasis. Having acquired the resources to alter their circumstances, Loftis and Cooter eschew creativity (expenditure) in favor of critique (conservation).

This brings us to "Menagerie, A Child's Fable," with its replication of the fable's propensity to utilize archetype to make its case—which, incidentally, has political implications as well as philosophical ones. To accomplish this, Johnson sets in motion a story that chronicles the movement from order to chaos, tyranny to anarchy. Tilford's Pet Shoppe, owned by the evil and cruel Mr. Tilford, is occupied by every manner of pet: mammal, fish, or fowl. This "menagerie" is watched over by Berkeley, whom Johnson describes as "a pious German shepherd," and who among "watchdogs in Seattle . . . [is] generally known as one of the best" (43). Berkeley's is an existence rendered meaningful by the seriousness with which he approaches his work. Unlike Tilford, "whose ways [are] mysterious to Berkeley," the watchdog is distinguished by the fact that he knows "exactly where he was at every moment, what he was doing and why he was doing it" (44). He is, in other words, the embodiment of the fully-realized Western subject.

But when Tilford leaves the Shoppe and does not return, having left all the food bowls empty, the animals' cages uncleaned, Berkeley realizes that something has gone awry. It is Monkey, the one animal for whom Berkeley harbors a dislike, who points out the dilemma and its only solution in view of the fact that the pets are faced with the prospect of starvation: Berkeley must open all the cages and let the animals run free. Monkey's analysis is poignantly put forth: " 'We've got a crisis situation here.' Monkey sighed like one of the elderly, tired lizards, as if his solution bothered even him. 'It calls for courage, radical decisions. You're in charge until Tilford gets back. That means you gotta feed us, but you can't do that, can you? Only one here with hands is *me*. See, we all have different talents, unique gifts. If you let us out, we can pool our resources. I can *open* the feed bags'" (48). What Monkey suggests is that in addition to the issue of sustenance, there is an equally difficult problem of representation. Or, put more precisely, Johnson reveals once again the tension between representation and materiality. For what is at issue is whether Berkeley, as emblem of the status quo, can meet the needs of those bound by its hierarchical arrangements. As Tilford's surrogate, Berkeley must provide leadership. It falls upon him to create a structure in which the animals can survive. But lacking the physical attributes—e.g. Monkey's digital dexterity—he can only remove the impediments to survival, he cannot maintain them. And so he ponders "the possibility of chaos" that accompanies releasing the animals because he knows that "the chances for mischief [are] incalculable" (48).

But this gets at the story's underlying dilemma: is Berkeley liberated because Tilford's absence marks his passage from an ancillary status to a superordinate one? Or is it the case that, like the animals released from their cages, his life as "pet" is nullified and his life as an individual has begun? If it is a matter of the former, Berkeley's situation is bound by the responsibility to maintain order because that is what Tilford represents: hierarchy, control, and routine. However, as a subject schooled in the dictates of liberal individualism, Berkeley's position is one characterized by a mix of "procedure and fair play," which undergirds his ability "to see all sides" (52). Ironically, however, this attitude leads to the Pet Shoppe's demise, for Berkeley realizes that his desire for order could only be achieved by subordinating the other animals's needs and desires and, more problematically, assuming that all the animals have the same position vis-à-vis power as he. Though his size and the fact that he has teeth (not to mention the abilities that come with being mammal) allow him to enforce the law, what is clear is that Berkeley's life is perched between hypotaxis and parataxis.

For his part, Monkey is the perfect foil to Berkeley's devotion to order and duty. When Berkeley resists the idea of opening the cages, Monkey accuses him of fascism. When Berkeley blanches at the thought of releasing the tarantula from his cage, Monkey accuses him of bigotry. In what stands as an excellent study in the ways liberalism functions in the public space, Johnson's fable could be read as an endorsement of authoritarianism. But here, Tortoise provides the reader with the clue that Johnson is up to something thematically unconventional. When Monkey tries to free Tortoise from his cage, the latter resists, snapping at Monkey's fingers rather than allowing himself access to freedom.

"No one questioned it. Tortoise had escaped the year before, remaining at large for a week, and then he returned mysteriously on his own, his eyes strangely unfocused, as if he'd seen the end of the world, or a vision of the world to come. He hadn't spoken in a year. Hunched inside his shell, hardly eating at all, Tortoise lived in the Shoppe, but you could hardly say he was part of it" (49). Tortoise, having experienced "freedom," understands that aspiration and desire are what give it its contours and ultimately render it unachievable. But I submit the story is not a dismissal of the value of multiculturalism, even though the Pet Shoppe is consumed by fire, Berkeley is killed when Monkey shoots him with Tilford's gun, and a deadly essentialism has led the animals to look to their own narrow interests. Rather, like Jonathan Little, I believe the story is meant to insist that liberation of the sort the Pet Shoppe fails to achieve is produced by a leap of imagination capable of transcending racial, national, and sexual difference (Little 116). Ironically, however, as the character of Tortoise is meant to suggest, this comes, not through a utopian vision of the future, but rather through what Megan Boler and Michalinos Zembylas refer to as a "pedagogy of discomfort," which they argue "recognizes and problematizes the deeply embedded emotional dimensions that frame and shape daily habits, routines, and unconscious complicity with hegemony" (111).

III

Allan Jackson's failed sorcery induces a level of misery and discomfort such that his only recourse is to commit suicide. For, in his view, he is an imitator of the art, not a true practitioner. Having discovered that "Talent . . . was a curse" (165), Allan sets about calling forth the demon kings, whose task it will be to destroy him. In a move that proposes the dialectical nature of pedagogy, when Allan tells the demons that he is a student, "one who studies beauty, who wishes to give it back, but who cannot serve what he loves," the demons agree that he is wretched, having denigrated Rubin's white magic into black magic. However, it would be wrong to read this as Johnson's capitulation to an integrationist aesthetic that resituates blackness in the null space created for it by the Enlightenment. Rather, we find ourselves in a moment when Allan Jackson's life as a "race man" is so uncertain, he can only imagine a life characterized by discomfort and disillusionment: "If he returned home, his days would be a dreary marking time for magic, which might never come again, living to one side of what he had loved, and loved still, for fear of creating evil—this was surely the worse curse of all, waiting for grace, but in suicide he would drag his father's last treasure, dirtied as it was, into hell behind him" (168). But it is his father's unconditional love for Allan that leads him to erase the chalk circle in which he has initiated the spell to call forth the demons. As they await his decision, Allan steps toward his father and at that moment he feels "within his chest the first spring of resignation, a giving way of both the hunger to heal and the anxiety to avoid evil. Was this surrender the one thing the Sorcerer could not teach? His pupil did not know. Nor did he truly know, now that he was no longer a Sorcerer's apprentice with a bright future, how to comfort his father" (168). The demons turn away, "seeking better game," the signal that Allan has, in ways reminiscent of Andrew Hawkins, achieved a level of release that has come on the heels of his recognition of his emotional bond with his father, as well as the need to empty himself of all aspiration, embracing instead a life of failure and underachievement.

I want to bring this discussion to a close by turning back to where I began: failed acts of pedagogy. Although I have devoted a great deal of attention in this essay to failed students and failed teachers, I want to turn to *The Way of Chaung Tsu*, where we find this parable, which I quote here at length:

> In the age when life on earth was full, no one paid any special attention to worthy men, nor did they single out the man of ability. Rulers were simply the highest branches on the tree and the people were like deer in the woods. They were honest and righteous without realizing that they were "doing their duty." They loved each other and did not know that this was "love of neighbor." They deceived no one yet they did not know that they were "men to be trusted." They were reliable and did not know that this was "good faith." They lived freely together giving and taking, and did not know that they were generous. For this reason their deeds have not been narrated. *They made no history.* (Merton 76, emphasis added)

I choose to read Chaung Tsu's parable as an act which serves as a blueprint for a world that does not denigrate difference so much as deemphasize it altogether, an instance where the buzzwords of multiculturalism—diversity, pluralism, democracy, inclusiveness—characterize a society infused with a singular goal.

But what conclusions can we draw about ourselves if Johnson is asking us to become a people who "ma[ke] no history?" Does it mean that we should devalue the past, engage in a discourse of forgetfulness (cultural amnesia as in the United States notwithstanding)? I think not, largely because the assertion of memory is so important to the emergence of new literatures, so heavily associated with acts of breaking silence and bearing witness. Johnson's fiction, because it resists the impulse to reproduce racial identity as a coherent, essential event, can be an important tool in this project. For in *The Sorcerer's Apprentice*, he provides us with numerous instances of failed pedagogy, as if to suggest that sensation, spirituality, and calamity—all of which can be dismissed in the rational world of logic as arbitrary, if not altogether ineffectual—are much surer paths to liberation than aspiration and desire. To be sure his characters are often, like Rudolph in "China" or the narrator of "Popper's Disease," symbols of discomfort or disenchantment, but this, Johnson suggests, is the price of being liberated from the illusions borne of desire. In this sense, the stories are consistent with what we have read in Johnson's novels: the problem of desire, as Horace Bannon puts it in *Oxherding Tale*, is that "what destroys a man, what finally unstrings him, is his appetites" (173).

If, as Henry Giroux observes, the value of multiculturalism lies in recognizing that critical forms of pedagogy are "fundamentally involved in the production of narratives of that which is 'not yet,' " then an emphasis on "process" and not "arrivals" can go a long way toward helping our students, who at times embody the desire to "know" so deeply that they set themselves on a path to not knowing, to becoming more comfortable with a postmodern view of history "that is decentered, discontinuous, fragmented, and plural" (Giroux 122). Certainly this project, though not without its interruptions and false starts, rests on our ability to persuade students that "there is no there there." Johnson's stories ask us to consider what happens when the pedagogies of emptiness and discomfort are conjoined. They therefore force us to think seriously about his call in *Being and Race* for African American writers to eschew the kind of cultural nationalism that leads them to be engaged in "image control"—the effort to define black life against that put forward by the mainstream—and embrace, as he refers to it, "the complexity of Being" (17, 20). What this means is that Johnson dramatizes the sense that fictional characters do indeed embody change, but what is perhaps of greater interest is their ability to embody *interchange*, that is, their ability to embody both affective and effective states of being. Hence, the fictions in *The Sorcerer's Apprentice* call us to embrace our own forms of incompleteness, inviting us to recognize that who we are results from the ways that instruction and misguidedness constitute the Way.

NOTES

1. See, for example, Jonathan Little's assessment of Johnson's stories in *The Sorcerer's Apprentice.* Assessing the stories against Johnson's novels, Little concludes that Johnson's stories are a departure from the transcendent arcs to be found in the longer works, insisting that "the stories generally focus on the pain and suffering of African American existence, unalleviated by the possibility of spiritual transcendence" (*Charles Johnson's Spiritual Imagination,* 109).

2. Here, I think it important for me to articulate my great admiration for Friere's work. Indeed, I consider reading *Pedagogy of the Oppressed* as one of the most transformative experiences in my graduate education. I find his arguments so persuasive that they have influenced how I approach my work in a classroom and continue to reveal new insights with each encounter.

3. Even if it is true that Johnson wants us to understand the dangers of certain forms of aesthetic license, as Little (110) suggests, we must also contend with the possibility that Johnson wants us to ponder the notion that the Western subject embodies the unconscious desire to undo its assumptions.

4. Though Moses Green has purchased the African as he would any slave during antebellum slavery—at an auction (where he pays in Mexican coin)—the story is set in southern Illinois, a free state, which means that Mingo cannot be considered "property" in the conventional sense. In the literal sense, location affects how we must read this fiction. Johnson's decision to set the story outside of the antebellum South means the reader cannot interpret this fiction as solely a commentary on the evils of slavery, which means that Johnson has a different emphasis.

5. Unlike Sykes-Withers, who believes he is achieving Alethia, only to end up with Althea (*Oxherding Tale* 87–94), the professor achieves it, but not through conscious thought, and as Little suggests, we need to pay close attention to the fact that he achieves in a drug-addled state (Little 124).

TO UTTER THE HOLY
The Metaphysical Romance of Middle Passage

MARC C. CONNER

Perhaps the mystery of American cultural identity contained in such motley mixtures arises out of our persistent attempts to reduce our cultural diversity to an easily recognizable unity.
—RALPH ELLISON

In the age of the world's night, the abyss of the world must be experienced and endured. But for this it is necessary that there be those who reach into the abyss. . . . To be a poet in a destitute time means: to attend, singing, to the trace of the fugitive gods. This is why the poet in the time of the world's night utters the holy.
—MARTIN HEIDEGGER[1]

"The highest and, indeed, the truly serious task of art," states Nietzsche, is "to save the eye from gazing into the horrors of night and to deliver the subject by the healing balm of illusion from the spasms of the agitations of the will" (*Birth* 118). For Nietzsche, this constitutes the supreme achievement of Attic tragedy, in which the frenzied and annihilating power of Dionysus is contained by and expressed through Apollo's "healing balm of blissful illusion" (127). Consequently Nietzsche defines "the tragic myth" as the "symbolization of Dionysian wisdom through Apollinian artifices" (131). It would seem that the more horrific and devastating the vision depicted, the greater the demands are for the Apollinian artifice. In the African-American context, there can be no more horrific subject matter to treat than the Middle Passage. This is the great, unspeakable horror in the American and African-American past, an area so daunting that it has received conspicuously little treatment in art.[2]

When Toni Morrison took on this subject in a highly allusive, indirect fashion in her magisterial *Beloved*, she dedicated the novel to "*sixty million and more*," in an attempt to pay homage to the vast unnumbered victims of this holocaust. Exact counts of the victims of the trans-Atlantic slave trade vary widely;[3]

nevertheless the point of Morrison's figure is surely not historical argument, but rather the intimation of the unnumbered and forever unnamed victims of this horror. Indeed, the figure may best be understood in a Biblical sense: "sixty million and more" surely connotes an unnumbered host of dead, just as the 144,000 in Revelation is not a literal figure, but rather conveys "a great multitude, which no man could number, of all nations" (Rev. 7:9). The effect of this figure is more akin to Kant's mathematical sublime, in which the concept of "a progressively increasing numerical series" brings the imagination to the "point of excess . . . like an abyss in which it fears to lose itself" (*Critique* 102, 107). And as with Kant's sublime, the key point is that this terror resists all representation.

This context of near-silence in the face of the unrepresentable helps us to appreciate, then, the sheer audacity of Charles Johnson's third novel, which devotes itself to a detailed and historically informed fictional account of its title matter, the Middle Passage. Johnson sets himself the task of putting into print, of giving cogent expression to, what John Hope Franklin terms the "veritable nightmare [of] the voyage to the Americas" (44). As Orlando Bagwell asks in his preface to *Africans in America*: "Why should we revisit a past wrought with pain, anguish, guilt, and embarrassment? Why should we study a history filled with such tragedy?" (ix). Johnson seeks to imaginatively reconstruct a period in history that many would prefer not to see—that is, he consciously chooses as his subject matter the defining tragedy in African-American history.

Yet Johnson's audacity goes even further. For his treatment of the Middle Passage does not have the solemnity, the grave and somber tone, and the hallowed language, that marks Morrison's *Beloved* or Hayden's "Middle Passage." Rather, much of Johnson's novel follows the form and language of the adventure tale, the sea voyage, even of the Roman Comedy whereby the tricky servant schemes and connives his way to freedom. The novel is filled with rather startling humor, from its beginning—"Of all the things that drive men to sea, the most common disaster, I've come to learn, is women" (1)—to its ending— "We groped awkwardly for a while, but something was wrong. Things were not progressing as smoothly as they were supposed to. ('Your elbow's in my eyeball,' said I; 'Sorry,' said she; 'Hold on, I think I've got a charley horse.')" (208). This is a strange, even apparently irreverent, register for a novel about a slave ship making the dreadful passage from America to Africa and back again.

Johnson has entered such territory before, beginning with the satiric cartoons contained in his 1970 book, *Black Humor*. In one illustration, Johnson depicts the huddled slaves in the hold of a ship bound on the middle passage, and one African raises a hand and suggests, "Say, why don't we have a sing-along?" In another, the white overseer says to an enthusiastic group of male slaves awaiting auction, "Well, you can't *all* go to stud farms" (*Black Humor* 22, 23).[4] Such challenging representations have generated criticism for Johnson's fictional account of the Middle Passage, often in the form of an unfavorable comparison to Morrison's straightforwardly tragic depiction in *Beloved*. Molly Abel Travis argues that "the middle passage Charles Johnson offers to his read-ers is much more accommodating than Morrison's," and that Johnson's "humor and intellectual musing," unlike Morrison's narrative complexity, "offers readers the familiar and the unthreatening" (186, 193). Similarly, Vincent A. O'Keefe asserts that the novel's "narrative techniques do not allow readers the oppor-tunity to experience the perceptual disorder (or middle passage) necessary to decalcify perception," unlike "most of the narrative strategies of *Beloved*" (641)—meaning, I take it, that Johnson's humorous narrative does not make the reader sufficiently uncomfortable about slavery. Several initial reviews of the novel expressed a similar concern. Richard Sincere wrote in *The Washington Times* that "remarkably, despite the overarching presence of the slave trade and the vivid depictions of the mistreatment of Africans by their captors, Mr. Johnson has little that is explicitly negative to say about race relations in the antebellum American republic" (F1). Another reviewer complains that Rutherford "fails to react to his predicament with sufficient horror," and that he "takes nothing seriously enough" (Dixon X6). And another concludes that "the question of how Rutherford can live with himself, having sailed on a slaver . . . seems resolved in the end by an artificial jollity" (Keneally 8).

This is complicated terrain in Johnson scholarship, and it brings us into a stark confrontation with Johnson's refusal to emulate the protest tradition in African-American fiction, his conscious decisions to challenge expected repre-sentations, and his steadfast denial of all racial and identity stereotypes, whether affirming or negating of African-American cultural pride. While this is surely a rich and fascinating context for discussing *Middle Passage* and one that has received superb critical commentary,[5] my concern here is somewhat differ-ent. I am interested in how Johnson embarks upon a story of supreme tragedy, and how closely he approaches the tragic in this novel both as a narrative form and as a philosophy. At the same time, Johnson weaves throughout the novel a contrary impulse: the forms and worldviews—meaning, for Johnson, the phi-losophy—of comedy. In other words, the forms—or, more accurately, the modes—Johnson employs in telling this story are the tools he uses for working through the philosophical implications—the *worldviews*—that determine and are determined by those modes.[6] Thus the conflict of modes is also the means by which the novel's other conflicts—of race, of history, of politics, of ideas, of genders—are themselves conducted and, ultimately, resolved. For in the end Johnson's novel seeks to transcend both tragedy and comedy—the annihilating powers of Dionysus, the healing balm of Apollo, and the *comos* of the comic festival—in an effort to connect philosophy with a new (or very old) literary form that enables humanity to survive and ultimately transcend a world of profound suffering.

I

"DUALISM IS A BLOODY STRUCTURE OF THE MIND": THE TRAGIC ARGUMENT OF *MIDDLE PASSAGE*

"All men by nature desire to know," asserts Aristotle in the famous opening sentence of his *Metaphysics* (114). The third chapter of Genesis expresses this same view: "And the woman saw that the tree [of knowledge of good and evil] was good for eating and that it was lust to the eyes" (3:6, Alter 12). The problem of knowledge is more explicit in Genesis, where it specifically inaugurates what Robert Alter terms the "moral ambiguities of human origins" (7). But in Aristotle too, we can trace a connection between humanity's lust for knowledge and humanity's fallenness, or the tragic state. Aristotle attributes the workings of tragedy to "an error of some kind"—the famous *hamartia*—but an error that he insists "is not due to any moral defect or depravity" (*Poetics* 21). The Greek term is akin to the sense of missing the mark, or taking a wrong turn in the road. Thus, as Malcolm Heath argues, the Aristotelian view of tragedy "excludes the interpretation of *hamartia* as a moral flaw"—but this is not the same as asserting "that *hamartia* has no moral content at all." There can certainly be moral implications or consequences to the error—the example of Oedipus's mistakes comes readily to mind—but these implications do not reveal a wickedness in the character himself. Rather, *hamartia* "includes errors made in ignorance or through misjudgment," as well as "moral errors of a kind which do not imply wickedness" (Heath xxxii–xxxiii). As another scholar confirms, tragedy consists in "an action with its surface painted in ethical and intellectual colours" (Jones 48). Thus, we cannot condemn the tragic hero for his mistakes, even though the consequences are horrible for many. Wither, then, the cause?

Northrop Frye argues that the cause is not to be found in the error itself; it resides, instead, in the world that led to the error—the world of human fallenness, the broken and fragmented world that *follows upon* the initial attempt to satisfy the lust for a knowledge beyond the human:

> As soon as Adam falls, he enters his own created life, which is also the order of nature as we know it. The tragedy of Adam, therefore, resolves, like all other tragedies, in the manifestation of natural law. *He enters a world in which existence is itself tragic*, not existence modified by an act, deliberate or unconscious. Merely to exist is to disturb the balance of nature. . . . This fact, in itself ironic and now called *Angst*, becomes tragic when a sense of a lost and originally higher destiny is added to it. *Aristotle's hamartia, then, is a condition of being, not a cause of becoming.* (*Anatomy* 213, my emphasis)

Put differently, tragedy—for both Aristotle and the author of Genesis—ensues because the human world is so structured that such an outcome is inevitable.

In *Middle Passage*, Johnson takes this tragic view of existence and assigns it to one of his most eloquent characters, the Mephistophelean Captain Falcon. Imperialist, slave-trader, and ruthless exploiter of others, Falcon is also the spokesman for the philosophy of the dualistic self, the self split into warring factions. "'*Man* is the problem,'" Falcon tells Rutherford, for "'conflict . . . *is* what it means to be conscious. Dualism is a bloody structure of the mind. Subject and object, perceiver and perceived, self and other—these ancient twins are built into mind like the stem-piece of a merchantman. We cannot *think* without them, sir'" (97–98). The inevitable result of this dualism is warfare among others as well as within oneself: "'there will be slaughter and slavery and the subordination of one to another 'cause two notions of things never exist side by side as equals'" (97). As many scholars have pointed out, Falcon's philosophical position is part of Johnson's critique of one strand of western thought, the Cartesian dualism that argues for a split between mind and body, self and world, which has led to many bloody horrors from the Enlightenment to today.[7] I would add that Falcon is also Johnson's spokesman for the tragic worldview. His restless search for knowledge and for dominion ultimately resolves into "his belief that one must conquer death through some great deed or original discovery" (143)—precisely the doomed quest that impels the eating of the fruit in Genesis 3, to "become as gods knowing good and evil," and to "reach out and take as well from the tree of life and live forever" (3:6, 22, Alter 12, 15). As Rutherford notes, Falcon "had the air of a man who desperately wanted to die" (52), for his desire for knowledge is nothing more nor less than his desire for his own death.

This death-drive in Falcon follows from his philosophy, which ultimately is a desperate insistence upon solipsism, upon the primacy of his individual self. He says of other people that " 'I suppose they've never been real to me. Only I'm real to me' " (95). This disregard of any surrounding social world, a refusal to attach oneself to any sense of community, is the very embodiment of *thanatos*, the death-drive. Freud gives eloquent definition to the heart of this drive in *Civilization and Its Discontents*, when he notes that

> besides the instinct to preserve living substance and to join it into ever larger units, there must exist another, contrary instinct seeking to dissolve those units and to bring them back to their primaeval, inorganic state. That is to say, as well as Eros there was an instinct of death. . . . Civilization is a process in the service of Eros, whose purpose is to combine single human individuals, and after that families, then races, peoples and nations, into one great unity, the unity of mankind. . . . But man's natural aggressive instinct, the hostility of each against all and of all against each, opposes this programme of civilization. This aggressive instinct is the derivative and the main representative of the death instinct. (77, 81–82)

Falcon embodies this death instinct, the aggressive stance of each against all, and thus he is the opponent of life, of the drive to form communities and to attach human to human . . . of love itself. Thus in his final interview with the Captain, Rutherford realizes that Falcon "was adrift from the laws and logic of the heart" (143).[8]

Falcon is Captain of the ship called *The Republic*, and hence he stands for the death-drive of America itself, which has shown itself nowhere more conspicuously than in the shameful history of slavery and racial injustice—what Ellison describes as "the ambiguities and hypocrisies of human history as they have played themselves out in the United States" (*Collected Essays* 193). From the moment Rutherford boards *The Republic*, he is aware that it is a vessel of death: "I had an odd sensation, difficult to explain, that I'd boarded not a ship but a kind of fantastic, floating Black Maria, a wooden sepulcher" (21). The ship's opposition to the social world is asserted by Falcon in his first interview with Rutherford: " 'there's not a civilized law holds water,' " he states, " 'once you've put to sea' " (32). And by the time the disastrous storm begins to rage, the ship has become "a shrinking casket . . . plunging into a trench, as if into Hell" (81).

Falcon's attitude toward the sea matches the death-drive of his quest. He tells Rutherford of an earlier voyage in which Falcon was driven to cannibalism to stay alive. He states: "'The sea does things to your head, Calhoun, terrible unravelings of belief that aren't in a cultured man's metaphysic'" (33). The eating of another human may well be the logical culmination—what Beckett might term the "Endgame"—of *thanatos*. This sense of nihilism driving *The Republic* informs the first mate Cringle's view of the sea as well: "'Three quarters of the world's surface,' said Cringle, 'is covered by that formless Naught, and I dislike it, Calhoun, being hemmed in by Nothing, this bottomless chaos breeding all manner of monstrosities and creatures that defy civilized law'" (42). Consequently, it follows almost of necessity that the ship compels all aboard towards apocalypse, the end of things. When the ship departs from Africa with its terrible cargo of enslaved humans, the guns of the ship and of the fort all fire "so thunderously the air shook. Abruptly, all was confusion" (60). Portending doom and destruction, this apocalyptic thunder matches the mission of death that Falcon, and his world-view, insists upon.

Falcon's quest—and perhaps the quest of western dualism itself—ultimately arrives at a confrontation with the unrepresentable, with that which can neither be comprehended nor withstood. The drive towards death, towards self-immolation, must, if it be honest, ultimately come to the face of death itself—and Hamlet's undiscovered country remains as inscrutable for us as it was for him. It is no accident that Nietzsche, in *The Birth of Tragedy*, arrives at Hamlet as his example of the man who has most thoroughly explored the abyss of existence: "the Dionysian man resembles Hamlet: both have once looked truly into the essence of things, they have *gained knowledge* . . . true knowledge, an insight into the horrible truth" (60). For Nietzsche, such a confrontation with the unrepresentable—which Nietzsche, like Aristotle and the author of Genesis, crucially understands as the pushing of knowledge to its uttermost limits—is precisely the point, the *raison d'etre*, of tragedy itself. For at this moment, when "existence is negated along with its glittering reflection in the gods or in an immortal beyond . . . art approaches as a saving sorceress, expert at healing. She alone knows how to turn these nauseous thoughts about the horror or absurdity of existence into notions with which one can live" (60). Such for Nietzsche is the impulse of tragedy: "The Greek knew and felt the terror and horror of existence. That he might endure this terror at all, he had to interpose between himself and life the radiant dreambirth of the Olympians" (42). Art, by which Nietzsche understands Greek tragedy, originated in the desperate attempt to enable humanity to look into the abyss and yet live.

In *Middle Passage*, Johnson expresses this same impulse in his intimation of the Allmuseri God. This god has been variously interpreted as the return of Rutherford's repressed memories of his father (Storhoff 178–79), as the figure who offers Rutherford "a new understanding of black being" (Nash, *Charles Johnson's Fiction* 144), as the source of "a traumatic self-transcendence and an immediate and profound apprehension of a fundamental spiritual unity that revises individual identity and conventional categories of perception" (Little, *Charles Johnson's Spiritual Imagination* 143)—in short, in various metaphorical manners. All of these interpretations are legitimate and accurate, as far as they go—but ultimately Johnson may not intend the god as a conventional metaphor at all. Perhaps Nietzsche gives us a more direct way of understanding this figure: "For a genuine poet, metaphor is not a rhetorical figure *but a vicarious image that he actually beholds in place of a concept*" (63, emphasis mine). A concept that one beholds as an image—such is the way Johnson presents the god, as the artifice through which the unrepresentable can be intimated. In short, when he confronts the Allmuseri god, Rutherford comes to the point of Dionysian self-annihilation, thinly veiled in the life-preserving form of Apollinian illusion. We arrive, at this point in the novel, at the very heart of the tragic. And it is precisely at this point that the novel begins to turn away from its tragic impetus.

II

"EVERYTHING IS READY FOR A WEDDING": THE COMIC ARGUMENT OF *MIDDLE PASSAGE*

In Johnson's 1998 novel, *Dreamer*, we are told that on Martin Luther King, Jr.'s, nightstand table there are two books: "*The Writings of Saint Paul*" alongside "Nietzsche's *The Anti-Christ*" (24). These two textual markers can be taken as the twin poles of Johnson's vision in *Middle Passage*, with the first half of the novel dominated by the Nietzschean mode of tragedy, but the second half moving toward what we might rightly term a Pauline vision of regeneration and renewal. By invoking Paul in his depiction of King, Johnson calls our attention to the key elements of Pauline theology that appear throughout his fiction, particularly the emphasis on "faith," defined by Rudolf Bultmann as the opportunity "to open ourselves freely to the future": "Such faith is simultaneously obedience, because it is our turning away from ourselves, our surrendering all security, our renouncing any attempt to be acceptable, to gain our life, to trust in ourselves, and our resolving to trust solely in God" (18). The comparisons here to Johnson's eastern thought, with its emphasis on selflessness and releasing oneself from the things of this world, are rich.[9] And Paul—like Johnson— is fundamentally a comic writer: in his letters we find the repeated emphasis of "a fundamental change in perception," a "pattern of transformation," and the insistence that "God has created a new world on the model of self-giving love" (Brown 147). These principles form the very foundation of a comic vision.

After his confrontation with the god, Rutherford falls into a faint, or a sleep, or some other sort of "long interval passed in the most unimaginable quietude" (171). This disappearance, we are told, lasts " 'three days full,' " after which he awakes and Squibb, the cook-turned-healer, tells him, " 'Yuh need to bleed . . . and pray' " (172). Following his sublime encounter, Rutherford enacts his own passion, sacrificing his body at the climax of his epiphany, allowing its disappearance, then submitting to its ritualized renewal through blood and prayer. When he regains his awareness, he learns that Cringle has sacrificed himself, asking Squibb to end his life in another formalized ritual:

> "Cringle closed me fingers round the handle. He instructed me that if I preferred not to kill him face to face, he'd turn his back to me. Don't you know he told me to cover his mouth, plunge the knife between his shoulder blades, then pull it free and cut his throat from behind. . . . In a kind of daze I done what he wanted, standin' back from meself, then unstringin' him, and it was in a daze that I lay back, short-winded and watchin' the Africans cut away Cringle's head, hands, feet and bowels, and throw 'em overboard." (173–74)

This is a ceremony of combined sacrifice and suicide, and it recalls the Samurai practice of *junshi* or *seppuku* (also termed *hara-kiri*), in which the warrior disembowels himself then has his *kaishaku* or assistant cut his throat or behead him "to minimize the period of suffering." In the Samurai tradition, such an act was understood as "a type of self-sacrifice," meant to show one's fidelity to one's lord (Kakubayashi 218, 219, 223).[10] Johnson characteristically combines this eastern rite with the Christian tradition of Eucharistic sacrifice, with the result that Cringle's act balances Falcon's earlier grim delight in the eating of a fellow human; whereas for Falcon this represents the tragic impulse of consuming the other, for Cringle the impulse is comic in the most ancient sense: for comedy depends upon successful sacrifice, and the more Divine the

Comedy, the greater the need for this willing sacrifice. Rutherford is in awe of Cringle's gesture: "Cringle's death silenced me. By any measure, he had been the best mate among us, the most magnanimous and gentle during our ordeal, the most generous in the face of hopelessness—in fact, a sailor who gave hope, steadied the ladder for others, and solved more problems than he created" (174). Through what Storhoff describes as "Cringle's self-sacrificing transformation" (176), at the end he is able to put into action the Christian virtue that he has grasped at, but that has eluded him: "Greater love hath no man than this, that a man lay down his life for his friends" (John 15:13).

Rutherford then explains the changes in Squibb, who has transformed from his initial state—a constant drunkard who will even steal food meant for starving children—to a remarkable figure of selfless service. "As our mates perished," Rutherford reports, "Squibb was pressed into service. . . . I think I know how these demands and duties, all in the face of probable death, tested him. . . . Whatever was needful he did." Rutherford explains this as "a Way," in the oriental sense, and one that specifically counters the novel's tragic impulse, for it is an attempt "to solder that deep schism Falcon believed bifurcated Mind" (175–76). Squibb has undergone one of the key elements in comedy, the *basanoi* or "ordeals" that serve as "tests or touchstones of the hero's character" (Frye, *Anatomy* 166). In this regard Squibb offers a miniature version of Rutherford's own progression; for just as Squibb can be understood as the parasite or social outcast who is redeemed and welcomed into society by the conclusion, so too Rutherford begins the novel as the thief, even as the tricky servant or *dolosus servus* so common to Roman comedy.[11]

Indeed, *Middle Passage* from the very beginning bears a strong resemblance to the structures of comedy. It opens with the major element of all comedy: the block or obstacle to young love. Traditionally this block takes the form of an older man who tries to bar the impulses of *eros*; yet Johnson magnifies the comic effect by making the block actually Rutherford himself, the young man. He comments, "I'd always felt people fell in love as they might fall into a hole; it was something I thought a smart man avoided" (7). When Isadora presses him on the marriage question, he responds, " 'No, Isadora . . . I don't believe I'll ever get married. There's too much to do. And see. Life is too short for me to shackle myself to a mortgage and marriage' " (10). Ironically, Rutherford views marriage and "life"—that is, the principle of *eros*, of generative community— as opposites. He here associates marriage with the commitment to the home, literally the house ("mortgage"), which he also fears. This indicates that Rutherford's avoidance of marriage rests upon a fundamental confusion, a mistaken association of the life principle with its opposite, imprisonment and paralysis and the loss of freedom, which is actually the result of the tragic world-view. As Frye argues, "tragedy seems to lead up to an epiphany of law, of that which is and must be," whereas "the action of comedy, like the action of the Christian Bible, moves from law to liberty." Rutherford believes he is flee-ing law and all of its restrictions by fleeing Isadora, but in truth he moves inex-orably towards an ever-constricting web of limitation and confinement the more he moves into Falcon's solipsistic and death-obsessed world. In short, he suffers from a confusion of world-view, mistaking comedy for tragedy and vice versa. For "just as comedy often sets up an arbitrary law and then organizes the action to break or evade it, so tragedy presents the reverse theme of narrowing a comparatively free life into a process of causation" (*Anatomy* 208, 181, 212). Consequently, Rutherford actually flees marriage not through fear, but through misunderstanding, and particularly a misunderstanding of himself. What Rutherford requires is to undergo his own *basanoi*, the trials in the wilderness (here depicted as the sea) that will transform and redeem him.

The novel's opening impulse then may be understood as the flight from society into the "green world" typical of Shakespearean comedy—with the sea standing in for the forest. As Falcon tells Rutherford in their first interview, "'there's not a civilized law holds water . . . once you've put to sea'" (32). Indeed, Johnson realizes that the sea is a perfect locale for the function of the green world, in which transformation and liberation are precisely the desired end of the flight. For change is the defining principle on board the *Republic*: "the *Republic* was physically unstable. She was perpetually flying apart and re-forming during the voyage. . . . Captain Falcon's crew spent most of their time literally rebuilding the *Republic* as we crawled along the waves. In a word, she was, from stem to stern, a process. She would not be, Cringle warned me, the same vessel that left New Orleans, it not being in the nature of any ship to remain the same on that thrashing Void called the Atlantic" (35–36). Johnson alludes here to the ancient philosophical puzzle known as "Theseus' Ship," which is at least as old as the pre-Socratic philosophers. Plutarch describes this problem as follows: "The ship wherein Theseus and the youth of Athens returned had thirty oars, and was preserved by the Athenians down even to the time of Demetrius Phalereus, for they took away the old planks as they decayed, putting in new and stronger timber in their place, insomuch that this ship became a standing example among the philosophers, for the logical ques-tion of things that grow; one side holding that the ship remained the same, and the other contending that it was not the same" (Plutarch 14). Put differently, the problem asks, if the Athenians were to replace each and every part of the ship as it sailed, such that not a single sail or plank remained after its voyage, can it still be said to be the identical ship as that which first set sail? The problem is one of identity over time, or the persistence of identity even through change. To Johnson, this is the very heart of his own philosophical investigations in this novel:

> I suggest on this ship that these characters interpenetrate and change and transform each other. On the ship the people who survive—this is probably true of everything I write—are the ones who are capable of change. It's Squibb who is transformed by his exposure to the Allmuseri, to the extent that, even when he's working with Rutherford to save his life, his touch is almost like the Allmuseri. And it's Rutherford who learns their language and part of their vision, which he brings back to his encounter with Isadora. Those two survive and the little girl and some of the African kids. The characters who don't survive largely are those who cannot change. The nouns die in my books and the verbs go on. I think life is a process, more process than product. (Blue 137)

The first significant transformation of self is that of Tommy, the cabin boy, after he goes into the hold and beholds the Allmuseri god. He re-emerges on deck "with only half his mind—or could it be it was twice the mind he had had before . . . *as if he had been baptized in the Deep*" (68, emphasis added)—which could stand as the epigraph to Rutherford's entire journey in the novel. Rutherford describes this as "a sea change," a term he uses again when referring to Squibb's transformation (69, 176). This alludes to Shakespeare's *The Tempest*, a work that, like *Middle Passage*, begins in tragedy but moves towards comedy—or even beyond comedy, a point I will return to in the final section of this chapter. When Rutherford is pulled from the wreck of the *Republic*, a passenger asks, " 'What kind of fish are they?' " (185), which also points us towards *The Tempest*, when Trinculo encounters Caliban and exclaims, "What have we here, a man or a fish? Dead or alive? A fish . . . a strange fish!" (II.ii.24–27). Thus the "sea change" applies to Rutherford as well, who emerges by the novel's final chapter as a profoundly different man, so transformed that, as he comments, "our own mothers would not have known us" (185).

This transformation is of course the defining principle of comedy. Through the flight from society, law, and the block to love, and the entrance into the world of transformation, the comic hero is himself transformed and as a result is able to transform his social world as well. Thus, "the movement of comedy is usually a movement from one kind of society to another. . . . At the end of the play the device in the plot that brings hero and heroine together causes a new society to crystallize around the hero, and the moment when this crystallization occurs is the point of resolution in the action, the comic discovery, *anagnorisis* or *cognition*" (Frye, *Anatomy* 163). It is striking that Frye uses the same term for the central moment of "recognition" (*anagnorisis*) in comedy that Aristotle uses for the parallel moment in tragedy (*Poetics* 18–19). This suggests how closely comedy and tragedy can be allied—indeed, the closer a comedy approaches tragedy, the more successful it ultimately is (as is most clearly evident in the example of the Divine or Christian Comedy, in which the extreme of tragedy— the very death of God—becomes the extreme of comedy—the resurrection and regeneration of all life). Frye notes—in a phrase that describes the final stage of *Middle Passage* quite well—that in many comedies "the fear of death, sometimes a hideous death, hangs over the central character to the end, and is dispelled so quickly that one has almost the sense of awakening from nightmare" (179).

This is surely Rutherford's condition in the final *denoument* of Johnson's novel. After his three days' ordeal, Rutherford undergoes a simultaneous purgation and rebirth. He lies in "pools of my own milky perspiration," "sprawled in a purging fever," feeling "that I was on fire." Then, he vomits or voids himself of what remains of his former self, the self that the confrontation with the god has brought to the surface: "I brought up black clumps I can only liken to an afterbirth or a living thing aborted from the body—something foul and shaped like the African god, as if its homunculus had been growing inside me—and voiding this was so violent a thing I was too weakened to rise again, and lay jackknifed for a long time with my face flat against the splintery rind of the hull, listening to the swash and purl of waters below me" (177–78).[12] Rutherford at this point is in a state quite similar to that of Ellison's Invisible Man when he awakens in the Factory Hospital, hardly knowing even his own name or identity. As he lies in anguish in the hull of the ship, Rutherford realizes that "Try as I might, I could not remember my full name," and in a sense of loss that explicitly echoes Ellison's hero, he laments, "I had not known before that everything, within and without, could break down so thoroughly" (179–80).[13] Fittingly, therefore, the "swash and purl of waters" is reminiscent of the opening of Genesis 1, where "the spirit of the lord moved across the face of the waters," suggesting the recreation that will occur here.

The Ellisonian parallel is particularly strong in light of what follows. For in the depths of his anguish, Rutherford "desperately dreamed of home," a home that he acknowledges is a place of suffering, slavery, injustice, outrage—"hardly the sort of place a Negro would pine for, but pine for them I did." He describes his condition in the United States as "the strangeness and mystery of black life," a formulation that echoes what John Callahan calls the "epigraph" of *Invisible Man*, the definition of American existence as "the beautiful absurdity of their American identity and mine" (*Invisible Man* 559; Callahan 84). Johnson then gives what may well be his most Ellisonian evocation of America as a place of conflict and chaos, yet filled with possibility: "If this weird, upside-down caricature of a country called America, if this land of refugees and former indentured servants, religious heretics and half-breeds, whoresons and fugitives—this cauldron of mongrels from all points on the compass—was all I could rightly call *home*, then aye: I was of it. There, as I lay weakened from bleeding, was where I wanted to be. Do I sound like a patriot? Brother, I put it to you: What Negro, in his heart (if he's not a hypocrite), is not?" (179).

The parallels to Ellison's integrative view of America are powerful, and have been oft-noted.[14] I would go further and suggest that this, too, is a sentiment shared ultimately even by Morrison, though her writings seem so much more ambivalent about the possibility of America as home or haven to African-Americans. Near the end of *Beloved*, Paul D returns to Sethe in the hopes that she will survive her own harrowing ordeal, and that he will be able "to put his story next to hers." " 'Sethe,' he says, 'me and you, we got more yesterday than anybody. We need some kind of tomorrow' " (273). Such a desire is not far removed from Johnson's hopes for an America that will allow for survival and continuity. And Paul D then recalls his wanderings across the countryside during his flight from slavery, offering a vision of America that is quite similar to Rutherford's descriptions of the nation: "in all those escapes he could not help being astonished by the beauty of this land that was not his. He hid in its breast, fingered its earth for food, clung to its banks to lap water and tried not to love it" (269). It seems that for Morrison, as for Ellison and Johnson, the truest American might well be the African-American, a conviction that echoes Du Bois's pronouncement at the dawn of the twentieth century: "Actively we have woven ourselves with the very warp and woof of this nation. . . . Would America have been America without her Negro people?" (*Souls* 189).

The moment when Rutherford, along with Squibb and three of the Allmuseri children, is fished from the sea marks the novel's decisive shift from its tragic to its comic paradigm. Rutherford moves from the utter despair of the lost to the profound gratitude of the found. Just before the ship goes down, he laments, "my friends could help me no more than a man who falls overboard during a gale, the sea taking him instantly. I gave myself up for lost" (181).

Here Johnson alludes to the poem that stands behind this entire novel, and one that offers powerful expression of the forlorn state of the man who is utterly lost—Cowper's "The Castaway":

> Obscurest night involved the sky,
> The Atlantic billows roared,
> When such a destined wretch as I,
> Washed headlong from on board,
> Of friends, of hope, of all bereft,
> His floating home forever left.
> . . . .
> No voice divine the storm allayed,
> No light propitious shone,
> When, snatched from all effectual aid,
> We perished, each alone;
> But I beneath a rougher sea,
> And whelmed in deeper gulfs than he. (Cowper 214–15)

Recalling both the terrifying plight of the castaway of its title, who, like Melville's Pip, is faced with the "awful lonesomeness . . . of such a heartless immensity" (*Moby-Dick* 347), as well as the status of the one who hears or relates such a tale and must thereby face her own existential isolation, this poem approaches the heart of the tragic condition with a power almost unmatched in western poetry.[15] Were Johnson to allow the tragic paradigm to claim his novel, *Middle Passage* would end here, "whelmed in deeper gulfs."

But of course the novel continues, and in a rather startlingly rapid manner, Rutherford is propelled into a paradigmatic comic conclusion. He and the other survivors are taken aboard the *Juno*, and so the ship of state shifts from one representing an enslaving republic to one whose reigning deity is the protector of marriage. Indeed, Rutherford quickly learns that the ship's very purpose on those waters is marriage: " 'everything *is* ready for a wedding,' " Isadora tells him, though Rutherford must overcome Papa and replace him as the appropriate groom for Isadora. This is easily accomplished, because Rutherford's transformation has simultaneously given him the physical skills to overcome Papa's brute force (his assumption of the Allmuseri martial arts enables him to evade and throw Papa's muscle, Santos), and also the emotional and philosophical education that enables him to see beyond himself and to ascend into the life-giving and charitable roles of husband and father. He feels now towards

Baleka, the orphaned Allmuseri child, as a father feels towards his daughter, and indeed Rutherford's very being is now inseparable from that of Baleka: " 'Whenever Baleka is out of my sight I am worried. If she bruises herself, *I* feel bruised. Night and day I pray all will go well for her, even after I am gone. . . . I cannot *eat*, if you must know, until I am sure she has eaten first, nor sleep if she is restless and, to make matters worse, if she is quiet for too long, I worry about that as well . . .' " (195).

Isadora remarks on the transformation in Rutherford from the man who fled from home and love at the novel's start, exclaiming, " 'you *have* changed, Rutherford,' " and the contrast is extraordinary when compared to the Rutherford on board the *Republic*, about whom McGaffin notes that Rutherford has no family, no beloved, that in fact " 'it don't matter wot happens to *you*, does it?' " (86). The Rutherford at novel's end is deeply implicated in others: Baleka, Isadora, Squibb all depend upon him; he is determined to return to Illinois and reunite with his brother; he has begun to right the scales of American injustice by exposing Papa's exploitation of his own people . . . in short, Rutherford *matters*, in profound ways, to the larger community around him, a situation that reaches towards the very heart of the difference between tragedy and comedy:

> In comedy the erotic and social affinities of the hero are combined and unified in the final scene; tragedy usually makes love and the social structure irreconcilable and contending forces, a conflict which reduces love to passion and social activity to a forbidding and imperative duty. Comedy is much concerned with integrating the family and adjusting the family to society as a whole; tragedy is much concerned with breaking up the family and opposing it to the rest of society. (Frye, *Anatomy* 218)

The overall movement in *Middle Passage* from the tragic to the comic seems evident, and, as many scholars have noted, does account well for much of the novel's major ideas, themes, and arguments. Storhoff in particular declares the book's fundamental embrace of the comic at the end, asserting that "Johnson ends his philosophical novel in a satiric romp with the conventions of romantic comedy—certainly a needed comic relief after the grimmest aspects of the *Republic*'s destruction" (180–81). However, although Storhoff goes on to emphasize that "Johnson stresses the serious transformation that has occurred," nevertheless this concluding view of the novel as "satiric," as mere "comic relief," is too drastic a reduction of Johnson's ambitious aims in *Middle*

Passage. For the novel's conclusion signals its ongoing movement away from the comic as well, as it evades the Scylla of tragedy and the Charybdis of comedy in search of an alternative aesthetic—a middle passage, one might say— that can give ultimate expression to Johnson's radical philosophical and social argument that rises to the surface through the novel's conclusion.

III

"AND COUNTLESS SEAS OF SUFFERING": *MIDDLE PASSAGE* AS METAPHYSICAL ROMANCE

The description Falcon gives of the Allmuseri God shows a divinity that transcends both the human and the natural domains. The God " 'sustains everythin' in the universe,' " working " 'to ensure that galaxies push outward and particles smaller than the eye dance their endless, pointless reel.' " Its ongoing task is " 'its labor of creating and destroying the cosmos, then creating it again, cycle after cycle' " (100). Rather than being limited by natural time, by the Alpha and the Omega, this God *contains* both creation and apocalypse, absorbing the end of things and then transforming it into renewal, again and again. Consequently, unlike tragedy, which is defined by the limits of human life, and unlike comedy, which is defined by the cycles of natural life, there is in *Middle Passage*—and indeed, in all of Johnson's fiction—an intimation of existence that transcends such categories. At the novel's end, Johnson invokes this transcendent category, in an effort to bring into relief the novel's ongoing effort to detach from this world and release oneself into a larger domain of being.[16]

Rutherford's experience with the Allmuseri God is the essential moment in the novel, the decisive break with Rutherford's past after which all is changed utterly for him. Prior to this moment, Rutherford is well defined as what Mircea Eliade calls "non-religious man," one for whom "habitation has lost its cosmological values . . . the cosmos has become opaque, inert, mute; it transmits no message, it holds no cipher" (178). McGaffin expresses this view of Rutherford when he says, " 'Calhoun'll go his own way, like he's always done, believin' in nothin', belongin' to nobody' " (88). Rutherford's initial fear of marriage and of home is precisely an acknowledgement that he does not see value outside of himself—he confesses, "if you must know, I didn't feel worthy of [Isadora]. Her goodness shamed me" (17–18) . . . one of many ways in which he mirrors Falcon, the self-reliant solipsist.[17] But the confrontation with the God reverses all of this, offering the sort of experience that Eliade describes as "a founding of the world":

> It is the break effected in space that allows the world to be constituted, because it reveals the fixed point, the central axis for all future orientation. When the sacred manifests itself in any hierophany, there is not only a break in the homogeneity of space; there is also revelation of an absolute reality, opposed to the nonreality of the vast surrounding expanse. The manifestation of the sacred ontologically founds the world. In the homogeneous and infinite expanse, in which no point of reference is possible and hence no *orientation* can be established, the hierophany reveals an absolute fixed point, a center. (21)

This is the essence of Rutherford's transforming experience before the Allmuseri God. This hierophany, or revelation of the sacred, establishes a sense of the holy for him, much in the way that Rudolf Otto has famously defined "the Holy": as the "absolute overpoweringness" of the "*mysterium tremendum*," bringing about both "the annihilation of self, and then, as its complement . . . the transcendent as the sole and entire reality" (19, 21, 25). The universe takes shape around this fundamental event in both space and time, which "makes it possible to obtain a fixed point and hence to acquire orientation in the chaos of homogeneity, to 'found the world' and to live in a real sense" (Eliade 23). Consequently, from this moment onward, Rutherford's movement towards a life lived in orientation towards the sacred is established.

Now, this is not exactly the domain of the comic. The movement of comedy is fundamentally a movement towards society. Although it may depend upon a metaphysics that is more expansive than that of tragedy—indeed, I would argue that comedy certainly does present a much more comprehensive and complex metaphysical view than tragedy—nevertheless its immediate impulse is human, concerned with the marriage and sexual union of the lovers. Curiously, *Middle Passage*, while moving in this direction all the way to the final page, turns aside at the very end. Here, Rutherford and Isadora move away from the sexual impulse, choosing a spiritual rather than a physical union, and thereby shifting the novel's mode at the last moment from pure comedy to a more elusive domain:

> the Middle Passage . . . in place of my longing for feverish love-making left only a vast stillness that felt remarkably full, a feeling that, just now, I wanted

our futures blended, not our limbs, our histories perfectly twined for all time, not our flesh. Desire was too much of a wound, a rip of insufficiency and incompleteness that kept us, despite our proximity, constantly apart, like metals with an identical charge. . . . Rather, what she and I wanted most after so many adventures was the incandescence, very chaste, of an embrace that would outlast the Atlantic's bone-chilling cold. . . . Isadora drifted toward rest, nestled snugly beside me, where she would remain all night while we, forgetful of ourselves, gently crossed the Flood, and countless seas of suffering. (208–9)

Such a concept of the male-female relation is strikingly similar to that found in the *Upanishads*, one of Johnson's most formative philosophical influences. As Eliade describes the view of marriage expressed in the *Bridadaranyaka Upanishad*, it is a "sacramentalization of physiological life," in which "there is no longer any question of a physiological act, there is a mystical rite; the partners are no longer human beings, they are detached and free, like the gods" (170–71).[18]

This liberation from the merely human domain into something more closely resembling the sacred world is now possible because Rutherford has left behind the trappings of the world: desire, possession, a fixation on the self and its petty cares, a concern with past and future at the exclusion of the present, and particularly the conviction that the creation is separate and multiple, rather than unified and whole. He has absorbed the world-view of the Allmuseri, for whom "the failure to experience the unity of Being everywhere was [their] vision of Hell," and the western "madness of multiplicity . . . drove them wild" (65). By the novel's end, Rutherford's sense of time and of being can be well described as "liturgical": "a sort of eternal mythical present that is periodically reintegrated by means of rites" (Eliade 70)—which is another reason why the merely human world is not enough to satisfy his spiritual longings, since ritual exists precisely to connect the human to the divine. Eliade's expression of this state of being describes Rutherford's experiences on the Middle Passage with uncanny accuracy: "By symbolically participating in the annihilation and re-creation of the world, man too was created anew; he was reborn, for he began a new life" (79). Hence Rutherford at the end has evanesced, for a time at least, from the merely human world, in both its tragic and its comic registers. He "becomes the contemporary of the gods in the measure in which he reactualizes the primordial time in which the divine works were accomplished" (87).

This is the world, both in terms of metaphysics and form, of Romance, in its most ancient sense. Romance, particularly in its most complete realization in the late plays of Shakespeare, presents a world "less festive and more pensive" than comedy, in which the actions "do not avoid tragedies but contain them." The movement is less one of winter to spring, and more "from a lower world of confusion to an upper world of order"—the same ascension from the abyss to serenity that Rutherford enacts (and it is surely no accident that "the usual symbol for the lower or chaotic world is the sea, from which the cast, or an important part of it, is saved"). The emphasis is not so much on a society renewed as on "bodily metamorphosis and a transformation from one kind of life to another," with the conclusions "outraging reality and at the same time introducing us to a world of childlike innocence which has always made more sense than reality" (Frye, *Anatomy* 184). The final pages of *Middle Passage* evoke precisely such a sense of moving from chaos to order, but an order that is liberating, not confining. The life that is promised at the novel's end is a new creation within the novel, a reversal of startling power given the travails chronicled throughout the tale. And yet it is a creation that seems fitting, were the world to dispose of its wanderers and outcasts in a providential way.

In its overall literary structure, *Middle Passage* clearly mirrors the structure of Romance, which depends upon the successful quest for its three-part form: "the stage of the perilous journey and the preliminary minor adventures" (Rutherford's travels up to the capture of the Allmuseri and the beginning of the return crossing); "the crucial struggle, usually some kind of battle in which either the hero or his foe, or both, must die" (Rutherford's confrontations with Falcon, with Diamelo, with the Allmuseri God, and ultimately with himself, ending with his three-day passion and resurrection); "and the exaltation of the hero" (Rutherford's rebirth out of the waters and his concluding spiritual ascension with Isadora). The three-part movement of romance mirrors "the three-day rhythm of death, disappearance, and revival which is found in the myth of Attis and other dying gods, and has been incorporated into our Easter" (Frye, *Anatomy* 187). In other words, by moving his novel towards this mode in its conclusion, Johnson confirms the centrality of the religious impulse to his writing and his thought. He seeks in *Middle Passage* to align his metaphysical argument with the very form of his novel, and as a result the novel's final pages join together both the tragic and the comic to bring about their apotheosis (in the oldest sense of that word: to elevate to divine status, to deify) in the spiritual vision of romance. Such is the climactic moment of romance, according to Frye: "the symbolic presentation of the point at which the undisplaced apocalyptic world and the cyclical world of nature come into alignment, and which we propose to call the point of epiphany" (203). This is why the novel's literal epiphany, the showing-forth of the Allmuseri God, must not be dismissed as a mere literary conceit; rather, the movement towards the divine is the very aim of the book. For, as Eliade argues, and as Johnson, it seems to me, would concur, "to reintegrate the sacred time or origin is equivalent to becoming contemporary with the gods, hence to living in their presence" (91).[19]

How does this help us to understand Johnson's basic effort, to give representation to the great tragedy of the Middle Passage—and to do so in a way that consciously, philosophically, indeed formally resists the mode of the tragic? Here it is crucial to bear in the forefront of our minds the truly radical, experimental quality of Johnson's writing. His is an experimentalism not of technical playfulness, as in much postmodern narrative, but rather of philosophical and fictional possibility. For Johnson, narrative form offers the greatest possibility for both philosophical and political (that is, ethical) growth and instruction. In this he follows Ralph Ellison, who said of *Invisible Man* that its chief significance was both "its experimental attitude, and its attempt to return to the mood of personal moral responsibility for democracy which typified the best of our nineteenth-century fiction" (*Collected Essays* 151). For Johnson, the impulse of both philosophy and fiction—and of course the two domains are inseparable for him[20]—is, to quote an oft-noted phrase in Johnson scholarship, the "liberation of perception," leading to what he has termed "whole sight": the ability to see, not as man sees, not within the narrow confines of the human dilemma, but rather as God sees, the infinitely expanding perspective of the spiritualized cosmos.[21]

This is ultimately the perspective of love, the concept to which Johnson returns throughout all of his writings. At the very center of the novel, Rutherford recounts his experiences with his former owner, Master Chandler, who, as he lies dying—seeking "a solace that eased his pilgrimage through a broken world"—gives voice to the novel's fundamental philosophical premise: "the words of the English mystic William Law: 'Love is infallible; it has no errors, for all errors are the want of love'" (111). This commitment to love, I would argue, constitutes Johnson's rejoinder to those who object that *Middle Passage* lacks a sufficiently rigorous political program, or that he is not angry enough over the legacy of slavery. And this insistence on the primacy of love is not an avoidance of the political—Johnson would have us keep in mind that Christ, like Socrates, was ultimately condemned as an enemy of the state. Rather, Johnson's metaphysics, ethics, aesthetics, and politics share a remarkable unity, one that is matched among the great Modernist authors perhaps only by Ellison himself. For Ellison insisted that the Protean quality of American reality—what he brilliantly described as "the diversity of American life with its extreme fluidity and openness"—could only be captured through "a prose which was flexible, and swift as American change is swift, confronting the inequalities and brutalities of our society forthrightly, yet thrusting forth its images of hope, human fraternity and individual self-realization" (*Collected Essays* 151–52, 155).

This is the very essence of the Ellisonian vision, and it is what Johnson himself praised when he accepted the National Book Award for *Middle Passage* and used his acceptance speech as the platform from which to pay homage to what he described as "Ralph Ellison's remarkable esthetic vision—a vision that has sustained me for over twenty years." In particular, Johnson praised "the intellectual expansiveness and artistic generosity" of *Invisible Man*, and its presentation of "a black American personality as complex, multisided, and synthetic as the American society that produced it." Furthermore, Johnson insisted upon the accuracy of Ellison's "integrative" view of both American society and of the artistic imagination (208–9). For this reason, Johnson's treatment of any aspect of the American reality reaches towards the integrative, the experimental, the form-breaking and form-making, "leaving sociology to the scientists" and striving to express "the truth about the human condition, here and now, and with all the bright magic of a fairy tale" (an Ellison phrase that Johnson quotes in his speech). Johnson calls for "the emergence of a black American fiction that is Ellisonesque in spirit, a fiction of increasing *intellectual* and artistic generosity, one that enables us as a people—as a culture—to move from narrow complaint to broad celebration" (209). Such a conception of the novel is simultaneously aesthetic, religious, and political, for it echoes Ellison's most moving evocation of the American principle—one that Rutherford Calhoun would surely voice at the end of his passage: "The way home we seek is that condition of man's being at home in the world, which is called love, and which we term democracy."

NOTES

1. The Ellison quotation comes from his 1977 essay "The Little Man at Chehaw Station" (*Collected Essays* 500); the Heidegger quotation comes from his essay, "What Are Poets For?," delivered as a lecture in 1926, revised and published in 1950 (*Poetry* 91, 92, 94).

2. With only a few prominent exceptions, such as Robert Hayden's poem "Middle Passage" (quoted as an epigraph to Johnson's novel) and Morrison's novel *Beloved*, it is astonishing how little imaginative work has been published on this central American tragedy. Johnson claimed that at the time of the writing, he knew of fewer than ten books published

on the Middle Passage, which was part of his motivation for the novel: "I wanted to bring all that into the story because people don't know about the middle passage. There's so very little written about it." In a later interview he emphasizes again the surprising originality of the subject: "there was no novel about the slave trade until *Middle Passage*. There was nothing that put people on the boat and took the reader through the daily routine of what happened on the ship with specificity and detail" (Wanner 161, Levasseur 252–53).

3. John Hope Franklin suggests that at least ten million slaves were imported into the New World from 1450 to 1870, and it is quite reasonable to assume at least one death for every living slave brought over (49); in *Africans in America*, Smith states that "half of the more than 20 million Africans captured and sold into slavery never even made it to the ship. Most died on the march to the sea. It is impossible to determine how many more lost their lives during the crossing. Current estimates range from 1 million to 2.2 million" (70).

4. Nash offers an excellent discussion of the complexity of the first cartoon in the context of *Middle Passage* (141–43). The finest overall essay on Johnson's cartoons is Little's chapter, "From the Comic Book to the Comic: Charles Johnson's Variations on Creative Expression" (17–53).

5. See, for example, Little's introductory chapter "The Integrative Impulse" (1–16); Nash's "The Aesthetic Articulated: *Being and Race*" (30–50); and Byrd's "Prologue," in which the concept of the "palimpsest" expresses Johnson's commitment to "a vision of cultural pluralism" as opposed to "the formulaic, ideologically driven representations of the black world that achieved its most concentrated form in the literature of the Black Arts Movement" (*Charles Johnson's Novels* 4–5). Johnson's own most powerful statements on his commitment to racial and cultural pluralism and possibility include the essays "A Phenomenology of the Black Body," "The King We Need: Teachings for a Nation in Search of Itself," and especially "Whole Sight: Notes on New Black Fiction."

6. This is not to suggest that Johnson chooses these forms of writing *for the purpose* of conveying some philosophical or political argument. Indeed, quite the contrary—my sense of *Middle Passage* is that here, perhaps more so than in any of his other novels, Johnson is chiefly concerned with the telling of a good story, and that aim determines, on the whole, the philosophical and formal implications that follow from the story. In this, the novel most resembles among Johnson's other fictions his superb recent book of stories, *Dr. King's Refrigerator and Other Bedtime Stories*.

7. See especially Little's chapter, "Revisions of Self and Society: *Middle Passage* and *Invisible Man*," where he states that "Johnson paints Cartesian dualism as a tragic philosophy, especially in its consequences for human history and human action" (145), and Nash's "'Dualism Is a Bloody Structure of the Mind: *Middle Passage*,'" in which Falcon's "general assertions about dualism" are of a piece with his commitment to "racial separation" and an "essentialist world" (134).

8. It is worth emphasizing that the eros/thanatos conflict that Freud elaborates is nothing more nor less than the opposition of comedy and tragedy.

9. Storhoff is particularly helpful on the Christian and Buddhist symmetries in Johnson's thought; see pp. 13–15 and also 165.

10. See Kakubayashi, "An Historical Study of Harakiri," for a full discussion of the intricacies of this ritual through history, and also Tsunetomo, *The Way of the Samurai*.

Viewing Cringle as a doomed warrior who chooses death over dishonor complements his western characteristics of Christian sacrifice and love of brothers well. I am grateful to Janet Ikeda for her help with these elements in the novel.

11. This stock figure of Roman comedy finds itself in only a slightly altered form in the rich concept of "the mask" in African-American literature. Dunbar's famous lines—"we wear the mask that grins and lies /It hides our cheeks and shades our eyes,— /This debt we pay to human guile; / With torn and bleeding hearts we smile, / And mouth with myriad subtleties" (Dunbar 71)—echo the concept of the scheming servant, as do numerous folk figures from African-American mythology such as Br'er Rabbit and Br'er Bear. This concept can be usefully compared to Du Bois's "double consciousness," a rhetorical figure that would be quite familiar to the great tricksters of comedy such as Lear's Fool or Feste in *Twelfth Night*. A further intriguing comparison could certainly be made to the Esu-Elegbara or Signifying Monkey figure of African and African-American folklore delineated at length by Gates in *The Signifying Monkey*, who stands not only for trickery but, like Rutherford, is also associated ultimately with "generation," "creation," and "translation" (Gates 20). Crucially, these are all figures of improvisation, making them akin to the Blues Hero celebrated by Ralph Ellison and Albert Murray, a figure that has much in common with Johnson's evolving portrait of Rutherford.

12. Passages such as this must surely give the lie to those readers who claim Johnson does not give a sufficiently brutal or graphic account of the horrors of the middle passage. Indeed, there is nothing in Morrison's account of the middle passage to match Johnson's graphic attention to the body's suffering.

13. Compare this to the Invisible Man's anguish in the Hospital, when he awakens and realizes, "My mind was blank, as though I had just begun to live," and senses that "meanings were lost in the vast whiteness in which I myself was lost." When he cannot give his name, "A tremor shook me. . . . I realized that I no longer knew my own name." But, like Rutherford, the Invisible Man realizes that "when I discover who I am, I'll be free" (231–43).

14. Little in particular structures his entire approach to the novel through the comparisons to *Invisible Man*, stating that "*Middle Passage* is Johnson's 1990s homage to Ellison's influence and achievement" (*Charles Johnson's Spiritual Imagination* 136).

15. Hence Harold Bloom describes this lyric as emblematic of "the passion for the Sublime mode, agonistic and transcendental," expressing "a borderline poetry that fears, yet courts madness" (8).

16. In this respect, Johnson's metaphysics seems to me most like that of Joyce in *Finnegans Wake*, where the constant cycles of apocalyptic destruction and of renewal and rebirth occur throughout the book, leading one to conclude "that the imagery of the cycle, with its death followed by renewal and return, is the only imagery that human language, conscious or unconscious, can draw on to express whatever is beyond the cycle" (Frye, "Cycle and Apocalypse" 107). What Joyce famously terms "the chaosmos" (*Finnegans Wake* 118.21) of his book, both cosmos and chaos, suggests that "Joyce's creation is intended to present its readers with a mystery just as insoluble as he considered God's creation to be" (Atherton 229). That Joyce's metaphysical view expressed in word approaches something of Johnson's aim in or behind *Middle Passage* is further suggested when Rutherford describes the sinking of the ship as "this *chaosmos* of roily water and fire, formless mist and men flying

everywhere, the sea and all within it seemed a churning field that threw out forms indistinctly" (183, emphasis added). One might also note the prevalence of the warring brother motif throughout the *Wake*—what one commentator describes as the "great Brother Battle theme that throbs through the entire work" and represents a "battle polarity which is basic to all history" (Campbell and Robinson 11)—a theme that takes hold of Johnson's imagination in *Middle Passage* and is at the heart of his next novel, *Dreamer*.

17. Rutherford says at one point, "I saw something—or thought I did—of myself in him and hated that" (33).

18. The relevance of Eliade's thought in understanding Johnson's work is confirmed by Johnson himself, who wrote upon receiving an outline of this essay:

> I'm intrigued by your reading Mircea Eliade. In the new book I finished a year ago (but have yet to edit), *Clearing the Courtyard: A Phenomenology of Race and Culture for the 21st Century*, I begin a phenomenological section in which I look at black America in 2006 from the standpoint of an Asian observer from (Buddhist) Thailand. I use both Husserl and a quote from Eliade's *Myths, Dreams, and Realities* to ease into this section. Eliade writes: ". . . he who reveals to us the meaning of our mysterious inward pilgrimage must himself be a stranger, of another belief and another race." I've been saving that Eliade quote for 3 decades to use somewhere! (e-mail to Marc Conner, February 16, 2006)

19. This use of the forms and concepts of Romance marks an additional strong similarity in vision between Johnson and Morrison. For, as I have argued elsewhere, the novel that followed *Beloved, Jazz* (1992), moves decisively from an initial tragic paradigm to the forms, symbols, and ultimately the world-view of classical Romance. *Jazz* emphasizes in particular the key elements of reconciliation, grace, and the reunion of old and young that is so characteristic of Romance as we see it in, for example, Shakespeare's *The Winter's Tale*. It is worth considering the curious relevance of Romance to the needs and aims of the African-American novel at the end of the century. See Conner, "Wild Women and Graceful Girls: Toni Morrison's Winter's Tale."

20. He has famously asserted that they are "sister disciplines" (*Being and Race* 32) and insists that "genuine fiction" and "hermeneutic philosophy" are the same thing ("Philosophy and Black Fiction" 82).

21. Johnson explains the concept of "whole sight" in the 1984 essay of that name, where it is primarily directed at expanding perception beyond racial restrictions. Several subsequent writings, particularly "Where Fiction and Philosophy Meet" and the magnificent "Reading the Eightfold Path" give an increasingly rich and complex expression of this idea. "Eightfold Path" concludes with Johnson's description of what a life of whole sight can be: "an adventure of discovery and service: a genuinely creative journey through the mystery of being, which with each step leads to ineffable joy" (*Turning the Wheel* 33). For an expanded discussion of these elements of Johnson's thought, see Conner and Nash, "Charles Johnson and Philosophical Black Fiction," and Nash, "The Application of an Ideal: *Turning the Wheel* as Ontological Program," in this volume.

"GO THERE"
The Critical Pragmatism of Charles Johnson

WILLIAM GLEASON

I read for three reasons: to laugh, to cry, and to learn something.
—CHARLES JOHNSON[1]

Despite the extensive attention paid by scholars to the philosophical underpinnings of the work of Charles Johnson—despite even the grandiose yet entirely fair claim by Johnson himself that "there is more engagement with philosophy—Western and Eastern—in my work than you will find anywhere in the history of black American literature" (Nash, "A Conversation," 222)—certain philosophical traditions crucial to Johnson's writing remain underexplored. Foremost among these is American pragmatism, a tradition whose concerns may at first seem far removed from the emphatically spiritual and idealistic vision foregrounded in Johnson's creative work. And yet when we turn to a different form of Johnson's writing—his voluminous body of critical essays and in particular his book reviews—we find a writer increasingly committed to providing philosophically consistent blueprints for reading, thinking, and living in contemporary American society. These writings function not as apolitical evasions (a charge sometimes laid against Johnson's fictions), but as committed and strategic interventions in vital cultural debates, interventions that owe often surprising debts to the philosophical pragmatism of such largely unacknowledged predecessors as William James, W. E. B. Du Bois, and Alain Locke. This new genealogy, I argue, will also allow us to see more clearly Johnson's interest in writing as a form of political, and not merely spiritual, or abstractly "philosophical," engagement.[2] This genealogy will further help clarify Johnson's relationship to his most important acknowledged predecessor, Ralph Ellison, whose emphatically democratic pragmatism Johnson only gradually comes to embrace. The nature and stakes of that embrace, I will suggest, become most clear through Johnson's essays and reviews, for it is in these forms that Johnson's pragmatic vision emerges in its full complexity. After tracing the development of this vision through Johnson's public commentary, I will conclude with an assessment of the shaping influence of what I term

Johnson's "critical pragmatism" on two of his most recent works, *Dreamer* (1998) and particularly *Soulcatcher and Other Stories* (2001). These dynamic historical fictions advance Johnson's pragmatic program for a contemporary politics of reading by imaginatively representing—often through explicit scenes of directed reading and practical instruction—the pluralist democracy he sees struggling to be born.

In making these claims I do not mean to suggest that pragmatism provides the only lens, or even necessarily the best lens, for viewing Johnson's writing. Nor do I advance a critique of other philosophical approaches to Johnson's work. I wish instead to amplify our understanding of Johnson's philosophical imagination by identifying some of the ways his work resonates with a particular strain of American pragmatism, cosmopolitan and pluralist in its leanings, that has had ongoing significance for many black cultural workers since the turn of the last century. I wish simultaneously to take the first sustained look at a routinely underappreciated mode of writing—namely, book reviewing—to which Johnson has generously dedicated himself for nearly thirty years. The more we learn about Johnson the reviewer, the fuller our understanding of Johnson the reader, writer, and thinker.

BLACK PRAGMATISM

American pragmatism may be said to have its genesis in Emerson but its impetus in William James. As Cornel West and others have argued, Emerson's interest in "action," experience, and the operations of power, coupled with his mistrust of authority, not only "prefigure[d] the dominant themes" of turn-of-the-century American pragmatism but in many ways also made possible the very methods of philosophical inquiry and cultural critique that such founding figures as James and Charles Sanders Peirce would come to deploy (West, *Evasion* 9). James's importance in the genealogy of pragmatism is both as a consolidator of first principles—even though the first principle of pragmatism is that there are no fixed principles—and as an extraordinarily influential teacher. The line that extends from James through pragmatism's other major contributors in the early twentieth century started quite literally at his lectern (he taught, for example, Walter Lippman, as well as authors Gertrude Stein and Robert Frost), but also reached beyond the classroom to mark such important pragmatic thinkers as George Herbert Mead and John Dewey. Indeed, the Emerson-to-James-to-Dewey trajectory is the most frequently given shorthand version of the development of early pragmatism, with Emerson as inspiration, James as founder, and Dewey as most zealous student.

But there is another branch of this genealogical tree that bears further investigation, particularly in the context of African-American literary, cultural, and philosophical history. As Ross Posnock has persuasively demonstrated, one can also trace James's considerable impact on black writers and thinkers of the early-to mid-twentieth century. Here the initial branching shorthand goes something like this: James to Du Bois and Alain Locke. As is well known, Du Bois was one of James's students at Harvard (it was his encounter with James, West suggests, that steered Du Bois from the study of philosophy as then practiced in the academy toward history and sociology); Locke, who also studied at Harvard though not under James, was deeply influenced by James's 1908 Hilbert Lectures at Oxford University, where Locke was at that time the first black Rhodes Scholar.[3]

There are of course important differences between these two figures (and between these two figures and James), and I don't mean to elide those differences here. Both Du Bois and Locke nonetheless embraced a central feature of James's philosophical method—what Posnock calls James's "pragmatic pluralism"—that mark them as sympathetic interpreters of Jamesian pragmatism.[4] Posnock coins the term "pragmatic pluralism" in order to distinguish it from the better known early century call for "cultural pluralism." As formulated in the 1910s by Horace Kallen, another of James's Harvard students, cultural pluralism offered an alternative to the popular melting pot ideology then being urged by many mainstream nativists anxious about the so-called rising tide of foreign immigration. In Kallen's formulation, cultural pluralism called for the recognition and preservation of multiple and discrete ethnic groups in a "pluralist celebration of identity." But James had already repudiated the identity logic that Kallen embraced (even though Kallen did so believing himself a Jamesian pluralist), and black intellectuals like Locke who followed James's pragmatic pluralist lead called vigorously instead for a deracialized and universalist approach to culture best understood, Posnock argues, in the term "cosmopolitanism." It is through the figure of the cosmopolitan—not the leisured tourist, but the person who belongs to the whole world—that African American pragmatists of the early twentieth century projected their complex view of international human identity and human creation, summed up in Locke's credo that "culture has no color" (Posnock 24, 10).

Posnock then expands this African-American pragmatist genealogy to include a corollary line of literary and historical figures dating from the turn of the century to the present day. In addition to Du Bois and Locke, this line includes such writers and thinkers as Reverend Alexander Crummell (one of Du Bois's other crucial mentors), Pauline Hopkins, Jean Toomer, Zora Neale Hurston, Ralph Ellison, and Albert Murray—each an example of what Posnock provocatively calls "antirace race men and race women": figures, in other words, who do not believe in essential racial identities (thus they are "antirace") and yet who nonetheless act in what they perceive as the best interests of the race, instead of sitting idly by. Each of the writers in this genealogy struggles—in a classic Du Boisian double bind—"to assert the freedom of art" from racial representativeness while simultaneously "laboring for race uplift." In *Of One Blood; Or The Hidden Self* (1903), for example, Posnock sees Du Bois's contemporary Hopkins layering an overt fantasy of Pan-African recovery over a latent wish for release from "the Negro problem."[5] Later figures negotiate the terrain of this conflict in diverse ways. Toomer insisted on a cosmic universalism in which "the American race" nonetheless played a signal part.[6] Hurston worked to imagine a "nonproprietary, cosmopolitan understanding of race and identity" while actively seeking to broaden literary depictions of the lives of black Americans.[7] In *Invisible Man*, Ellison's nameless protagonist affirms an invisibility that is also responsibility, embracing ambivalence rather than abdication: "so I denounce and I defend and I hate and I love," he explains (580).[8] In Ellison's later essays, particularly "The Little Man at Chehaw Station" (1978), Posnock discerns a vigorous Jamesian critique of cultural pluralism that "interrogates rather than enshrines identity logic." Five years earlier, at a symposium on Locke at Harvard University, Posnock notes, Ellison and Albert Murray had actively sought to reclaim Locke's "pragmatist legacy" over and against the racial, cultural, and philosophical separatism implicit in the Black Arts movement (187, 189). For Ellison and Murray, as for Locke and James, American culture was to be celebrated as an "appropriation game," a site of "motley mixtures" and "democratic turbulence" rather than "rigid classifications" of race "chauvinism" (185–91).[9]

Even as Posnock carefully traces this genealogy into the present, however, he resists placing Charles Johnson fully within it. And yet few black writers today seem more clearly to belong to this important and influential tradition.[10] Posnock caps his study not with his then-University of Washington colleague, but with the avant-garde artists Samuel Delany and Adrienne Kennedy. Delany and Kennedy are useful figures for Posnock. In them he sees both an acceptance and a remaking of the "antirace race lineage" he traces through *Color and Culture*. For Posnock, Delany and Kennedy escape the Du Boisian double bind by liberating themselves from the responsibility to represent the race in the first place. "What does not endure in Delany and Kennedy," Posnock explains, is the anxious obligation of race work to represent and uplift. That anxiety created for earlier generations an art and affect of ambivalence and division which reflected a struggle for artistic freedom amid racist constraint. With Delany and (especially) Kennedy that constraint and struggle remain. But they also relish fluidity and dispersal as the forms and themes of creative invention untethered to mimetic fidelity. . . . Liberated from responsibility to representation, both political and aesthetic, Delany and Kennedy bring the tensions animating the antirace race lineage to formal and psychic resolution. (262)

To be sure, Johnson is not absent from Posnock's text. In chapter one, "After Identity Politics," Posnock links Johnson with Delany as contemporary writers who regard aesthetic freedom as a birthright, not a battle. "For Johnson, as for Samuel Delany," Posnock observes, "there is no striving to enter the kingdom of culture, one is already in residence." In the book's final chapter, Posnock invokes Johnson's innovative aesthetics to introduce the representational strategies of Delany and Kennedy: "Delany and Kennedy," Posnock writes, "could be said to offer black intellectuals manumission of the burden of representation in a way analogous to Charles Johnson granting the slave narrative 'manumission of first-person viewpoint' in his novel *Oxherding Tale*." Posnock then explicitly collates Johnson's philosophic approach with Delany's and Kennedy's: "In all three writers the revelation of self as collage promotes a salutary distrust of the naturalized conventions—racial, narrative, ontological—that produce intelligibility by inflicting the segregation of discrete boundaries" (28, 262).

After this brief conjunction, however, Johnson is left behind, while Delany and Kennedy take center stage. But they do so primarily as exemplars of genealogic rupture rather than continuity. Were one to seek instead to identify the most salient contemporary practitioner of the cosmopolitan pragmatism articulated by Du Bois, Locke, and Ellison, one would have to work hard *not* to select Johnson.[11] In addition to Johnson's deep and frequently expressed regard for Ellison's aesthetic project, which I will explore in more detail in the following section, what makes Johnson an even more fitting branch on this philosophic family tree is that, unlike Delany and Kennedy, Johnson remains a very public antirace race man. Part of the appeal of Delany and Kennedy as capstone figures for Posnock is their comparative indifference to the larger public stage. "Never ambitious to be public intellectuals in the way their predecessors sought to be or were forced to be," Posnock observes, "Delany and Kennedy have evolved and prospered . . . as experimental writers for largely an avant-garde audience" (293).[12] Johnson on the other hand, though in many ways equally committed to formal experimentation and creative "fluidity," has prospered for a much wider audience. As a result, Johnson's pragmatism, particularly as it has evolved through his role as a prolific essayist and large-market book reviewer, has always had a more public cast. It is for these reasons Johnson stands as the most important late-twentieth/early-twenty-first-century black practitioner of the Jamesian pragmatic pluralism of Du Bois, Locke, and Ellison. Johnson is the inheritor, and also necessarily the updater, not only of their democratic cosmopolitanism, their suspicion of identity logic, and their sense of "overlap as the condition of culture," but also of their roles as public intellectuals (Posnock, 24–25, 18).[13] To be clear: I am not claiming that Johnson is a pure pragmatist (were there such a thing) nor even that he is fundamentally a pragmatist, but more simply (and usefully) that he participates, on several levels and to a much greater degree than we have heretofore recognized, in the "pragmatic turn" of the twentieth century.[14] And nowhere is this participation more clear than in Johnson's book reviews, to which we now turn.

THE REVIEWING ROOM

Johnson has been publishing essays and reviewing books for close to three decades, and these entries make up a substantial portion of his *vita*.[15] He has been a regular contributor to the book review sections of *The Los Angeles Times*, *The New York Times*, and *The Washington Post*, and through these reviews and those for other publications Johnson can claim a readership considerably larger and broader than that expected for his critical essays, which have appeared predominantly in academic journals such as *Obsidian* and *Callaloo*. This is not to say that book review pages in major newspapers aren't themselves directed to a relatively narrow audience; but their presence in periodicals that circulate in the hundreds of thousands rather than the thousands does, at the very least, create the opportunity for more encounters. As such, where Johnson's diction and subject matter in his critical essays tend toward the abstract, the philosophical, and the racial (as in such essays as "Philosophy and Black Fiction" or "A Phenomenology of the Black Body," for example), his approach in the book reviews is in many ways quite different. For one, Johnson is not just a prolific reviewer but also an eclectic one. He does not merely review books by black writers or about "black" subjects, although such works do comprise the largest percentage of his assignments, but rather is called upon for critical responses to works by authors of many races (and whose work does not always directly concern racial questions), covering topics that range similarly widely. Second, regardless of their subject matter, in terms of language Johnson's reviews are more concretely expressed than his essays. This may be part of the expectation, of course, for a newspaper review, but that is in part precisely my point: Johnson has deliberately cultivated this form of writing as one medium for his opinions about art and society, in ways that foreground cultural and political, rather than spiritual (or abstractly "philosophical"), engagements.

Johnson has fully conceptualized the role of his reviews within the larger corpus of his writing. In a 1998 interview with William Nash, Johnson introduces the simile of a multi-roomed house to describe the scope of his life's writings. "I see one's body of work as being like a big house with many rooms," Johnson explains.

> There is a foundation for the house I'm building (*Oxherding Tale*); inside the house are rooms you can wander through or stay awhile in. One has novels. Another has short fiction. In a third you'll find screenplays. A fourth has philosophical essays. A sub-room of that has essays on many other subjects— Indonesia, how to draw political cartoons, etc. Yet another room is devoted to book reviews that (I hope) are position papers on art, as were the reviews of my teacher and friend John Gardner. Yet another room has comic art. On and on through this house, from the basement to the attic, you find art in numerous forms. You find television dramas in one room. Fiction on the martial arts in a sub-room of the bigger room devoted to short stories. This is my conception of what a total body of work is about, one that is evolved over a lifetime, is generous, and offers others a variety of different experiences. (Nash, "A Conversation," 218)

Johnson elaborates on his implicitly political characterization of book reviewing ("position papers on art") in a subsequent interview with Rob Trucks. "The reason I started reviewing," he tells Trucks, "is because I thought the state of it was really kind of bad in respect to Black American writers." This dissatisfaction with contemporary reviews—particularly of his own novels, Johnson admits—eventually helped bring about his major critical statement to date, the 1988 volume *Being and Race: Black Writing Since 1970*. "The third reason [I wrote *Being and Race*]," Johnson explains, "was because I thought some of the reviews of [my] earlier books were just abysmal. I thought that the book reviewers were, aesthetically, just totally at sea with an original work of art. So it's a manifesto of sorts" (Trucks 557, 539).

From the start, Johnson's book reviews evince a similar interventional and instructional pragmatics. "We still ask all the wrong questions about Richard

Wright," Johnson declares in the opening sentence of his very first review, a 1977 analysis of Wright's posthumously published *American Hunger*. Aimed as much at admirers of Wright as Wright's critics, Johnson's inaugural review—which notably invokes William James in its very first paragraph—challenges both the segregatory impulse of contemporary reviewing and the solipsistic aesthetics of recent fiction. Critical interest in Wright (indeed, in "all black writing," Johnson asserts) declines when "black people are not trashing property or promising violence," as though overt racial unrest were the sole legitimate topic of—and the necessary condition for appreciating—black literature. But for Johnson, the relative quiescence of the late 1970s (at least compared to a decade earlier) doesn't mean that the "dreamlike deformations of the black world" Wright famously describes have gone away. Indeed, Johnson maintains, they "still await us when we round the corner in Soweto, Detroit, or Chicago." Nor does it mean that Wright has no other contributions to make to American letters. In fact, and this is the main point of Johnson's review, it is not as a chronicler of deformation but as an "archaeologist of consciousness" that Wright demonstrates his deepest gifts as a writer. The "truly great artist" begins by "tracking down how we feel in our bodies," Johnson insists. "He works from subjectivity outward for a fresh encounter with the world and, if his voice and vision are authentic—true to himself and Being—he revitalizes our perceptions and values." This is the Wright Johnson discerns in his review of *American Hunger*: a "dramatist of black consciousness" seeking to "wrench" an "objective (or intersubjective) truth from subjective life" by grappling simultaneously with the material excesses of American life and the social dimension of writing itself. At stake in such grapplings is the very possibility of imagining a better world than the one we currently inhabit (Johnson 1977, 6–7).

That good writing must reach beyond the "singularity and privacy of the ego" toward intersubjective communication as a precondition for real change in the world is also the primary concern of Johnson's second review, his 1978 critique of Raymond Roussel's *How I Wrote Certain of My Books*. Unlike Wright's struggle toward intersubjectivity in *American Hunger*, Roussel's aesthetic practice produces a hermetic code that forestalls rather than enables meaningful human interaction. Starting from "things taken in isolation, objects wrenched from the web of relations, needs, projects, and desires in which we originally find them in the world," Johnson observes, Roussel constructs stories out of "arbitrary combinations and reshufflings" that divorce words from consciousness. The ultimate effect is a monstrous textual muteness. "Even as he explains . . . how the words tumbled together into a clot of sounds in his novel," Johnson writes, "we see that Roussel's intention was, not to speak—it had never been to speak to us—but to create from words fantastic contraptions like those found in the sci-fi novels of Jules Verne." For Johnson, this "mechanical tomfoolery" ignores the communicative and pedagogic functions of language. "More than anything else," Johnson insists, "words are an opening onto the other's interpretation of the world. They teach the other. They teach ways of seeing, shared vision." The responsibilities Wright sought, one might say, Roussel shirked (Johnson 1978, 11).

Published in successive issues of the same journal, even sharing certain key phrases, Johnson's first two reviews encapsulate and anticipate the primary direction of his future critical corpus: an educational and expressly democratic critique in which Johnson guides readers through the crucial questions of what, how, and why to read.[16] Although Johnson often expresses strong opinions about the books he reviews, his operative mode is not dogmatic but instructional, even teacherly. The importance to Johnson of providing such active and practical direction to readers becomes most clear in the lengthy contribution he makes to a special Symposium on contemporary literature in the *Michigan Quarterly Review* in 1987. In his response to the Symposium's central question "what kind of recent writing interests you especially, and, in your opinion, is most deserving of more attention and more readers?," Johnson declares that the only books worth reading are those that offer "breadth of vision, depth of seeing, [and] the thrill of exploring new territory" through "ambitious, carefully-wrought, innovative, intelligent" fictional technique. These books are worth reading not for stylistic idiosyncrasies in and of themselves—the Raymond Roussel trap—but for the fundamental and necessary relationship between good writing and clear thinking in a democratic society. "What is at stake in the idea of writing as a centuries-old *discipline*," Johnson explains, "is our very capacity to reason, which democracy itself, at least in its classical definition, requires, *i.e.*, a voting public smart enough to recognize rot, rhetoric, and demagoguery when they see it" ("A Symposium" 754). Much like Du Bois (and as we shall see shortly, Locke and especially Ellison), whose notion of cosmopolitan world-belonging depended crucially on a "democratic culture and citizenship grounded in common humanity" (Posnock 13), Johnson sees an invigorated democracy as the potential result of his aesthetic instructions. "Go there," he insists at the end of his essay, referring to the small presses and underground magazines that house today's "most exciting writers of fiction"— and read ("A Symposium" 756).

Much as Johnson places an intellectual value on formal pluralism ("I prefer writers who are conscious of the possibilities of literary form—the innumerable forms and styles of narrative art, each of which can be seen as a distinct method of reasoning," "A Symposium" 755), in his own reviewing practice Johnson's instructional finger points to far more than simply avant garde fiction. It includes, for example, more mainstream works (novels by John Updike, Richard Ford, and Paul Theroux, for example), prominent and often controversial works of non-fiction (including books by Dinesh D'Souza, Stanley Crouch, and Shelby Steele), as well as writings that investigate profoundly anti-democratic ideologies. In a 1988 review of *The Silent Brotherhood: Inside America's Racist Underground*, a history of neo-Nazi skinheads, for example, Johnson insists that "the political importance" of this book "cannot be stressed enough." "A pluralistic vision of America is the goal toward which this country has been trying to move for 20 years," Johnson declares, "but for a few—and even a few is too many—the effort to achieve equality and unity within diversity has transformed their feelings of betrayal into insurrection. [This book] is essential reading for every American. It is a work we cannot ignore if, as a nation, we hope to survive this century."[17] In other reviews Johnson recommends books whose central ideas he rejects, such as *Visions of a Liberated Future*, a collection of writings by poet Larry Neal from the Black Arts Movement of the 1960s and 1970s, a movement to which Johnson, once a believer, is now almost passionately opposed, and in whose aesthetic he sees the polar opposite of his own ideals.[18]

In reviews like these Johnson articulates his own aesthetic in language that recalls the cosmopolitan and universalist concerns of Jamesian pluralism as reshaped by Du Bois, Locke, and eventually Ellison. In a 1992 review of Anthony Appiah's *In My Father's House: Africa in the Philosophy of Culture*, for example, Johnson praises Appiah for delivering "what may very well be one of the handful of theoretical works on race that will help preserve our humanity and guide us gracefully into the next century" (making it, in effect, the necessary corollary text to the book on neo-Nazi skinheads). The most salient point in Appiah's book, Johnson argues, is his observation that " 'We are all already contaminated by each other' in a complex, interdependent human world that is ill-served, finally, by the dead-end effort of engaging in 'the manufacture of Otherness.' "[19] This is a formulation very similar to one that Du Bois himself had made in 1921, when he argued that the " 'Failure to recognize the Universal in the Particular' breeds 'the menace of group exclusiveness and segregation.' " "Each and every one of us, whether we like it or not," Johnson would soon write in an appreciative memorial essay for Ellison in the *Washington Post*, "[is] a cultural mongrel."[20] Indeed of all the writers adduced by Posnock in his expanded genealogy of pluralist cosmopolitanism, Ellison has come to hold the greatest fascination for Johnson. This was not always the case; indeed the evolution of Johnson's attraction to the author of *Invisible Man* is worth tracing for the light it sheds not only on the development of Johnson's artistic goals and public persona but also on the role of Johnson's essays and reviews in his emerging engagement with the legacy of James, Du Bois, and Locke.

Simply put, though Johnson has long admired Ellison's achievement, over time the grounds for that admiration have moved appreciably closer to the core of Ellison's pluralist, democratic pragmatism. Johnson's earliest references to Ellison, though full of praise, emphasize Ellison's "individual vision" and regard *Invisible Man* primarily as a "Freudian tale" or a "tour de force of writing technique."[21] In Johnson's most widely circulated commentary on Ellison before Ellison's death, found in the opening chapter of *Being and Race*, Johnson even finds much to criticize in *Invisible Man*.[22] But starting with his 1990 acceptance speech for his National Book Award for *Middle Passage*—with Ellison present that night in the audience—Johnson begins to emphasize Ellison's "integrative" imagination alongside his "individual" vision, eventually recasting his view of *Invisible Man* as a novel "inspirit[ed]" by, and perhaps even fundamentally about, democracy itself. Johnson draws this new terminology from Ellison's own 1982 introduction to the 30th Anniversary edition of *Invisible Man*. "By a trick of fate (and our racial problems notwithstanding)," Ellison had written, "the human imagination is integrative—and the same is true of the centrifugal force that inspirits the democratic process." In his 1990 acceptance speech, Johnson cites only the "integrative" half of Ellison's observation; in his 1994 "Appreciation" (and thereafter), Johnson gives primary emphasis to Ellison's embrace of democracy. "By any measure," Johnson declared in the 1994 *Washington Post* memorial essay, "*Invisible Man*—the one great work of Ellison, who died Saturday at age 80—is the most complex, multilayered and challenging novel about race and being and the preservation of democratic ideals in American literature." Later in that same essay, Johnson reflects: "perhaps most impressive of all, Ellison's expansive rite-of-passage is the very idea of artistic generosity. Its exuberant, Hegelian movements gracefully blend diverse literary genres and traditions, from Mark Twain to William Faulkner, from the slave narrative to the surrealistic Kafkaesque parable, from black folklore to Freud, forever forcing us to see in the novel's technique the spirit of democracy."[23] Since 1994, Johnson has risen in print several times either to defend Ellison from the charges of political conservatism or (worse) irrelevance, or to link his integrative aesthetics with the work of other prominent black writers, such as James Weldon Johnson and Albert Murray.[24] If this gesture looks familiar, it should: Johnson's gradual embrace of Ellison's pragmatic pluralism mirrors Ellison's and Murray's own reclamation of Alain Locke's pragmatic legacy in the early 1970s.

FICTIONS THAT TEACH

In Johnson's case, this pluralist embrace may be seen to intensify in his fiction as well. While both *Oxherding Tale* (1983) and *Middle Passage* (1990), for example, share black pragmatism's sense of (in Ellison's phrase) the "motley mixture" of American culture—recall the "intricately woven" tapestry of Horace Bannon's tattooed chest or Rutherford Calhoun's realization that he is a "cultural mongrel"—the latter novel, through its central imaginative space, the slave ship *Republic*, meditates even more forcefully on the meanings of democracy. *Dreamer* (1998) raises the stakes yet higher, multiplying images of cosmopolitan interrelatedness with scenes of directed reading and practical instruction in a book deeply concerned with political struggle.[25] Two episodes in particular make this intensity clear. In the first, the narrator Matthew Bishop listens to a speech delivered by King—or is it his double?—in which King explains the fundamental flaw of segregationist logic:

> "No, the segregationists lost before they even began. Nothing stands alone. You know, not one member of the White Citizens' Council can finish breakfast in the morning without relying on the rest of the world. That sponge 'Bull' Connor bathes with came from the Pacific Islands. His towel was spun in Turkey. The coffee Orval Faubus drinks traveled all the way from South America, the tea from China, the cocoa from West Africa. And every time George Wallace or Malcolm X writes his name he's using ink evolved from India and an alphabet inherited from the Romans, who derived it from the Greeks after they'd borrowed it from Phoenicians, who received their symbols from Seirites living on the Sinai peninsula between Egypt and Palestine. . . . After a time, I tell you, a man comes to see only a We, this precious moment as a tissue in time holding past, future, and present, with all of us in the red, everlasting debtors—ontological thieves—in a universe of interrelatedness."
> (139–40)

Typical of Johnson, this detailed enunciation of ontological interrelatedness may be read as a marker of his attraction both to Buddhist interconnectedness and the philosophy of "One in the Many" that critics have already identified in his work. But it may also be read as a sign of Johnson's own ongoing deepening connectedness to American pragmatism, echoing in this case not Ellison but Alexander Crummell, who with James was one of Du Bois's principal teachers. Although Crummell is in some ways a type of racial thinker Johnson is fond of critiquing (he would likely find fault with Crummell's embrace of race-based Pan Africanism), as Posnock shows, Crummell's undiminished enthusiasm for "the heterogeneous and mimetic" could lead him toward ideas—and even linguistic formulations—that one would be hard pressed not to see echoed in Johnson's own work. Like James, Crummell "encouraged in Du Bois a disposition skeptical of any intellectual or cultural edifice which claims absolute originality and purity" (segregationists, beware). "To examine Greek and Roman civilization, noted Crummell, is to encounter not discrete, self-contained worlds but, rather, monuments to man's capacity for 'eclectic' imitation: 'they seized upon all the spoils of time. They became *cosmopolitan thieves*. They stole from every quarter. They pounced, with eagle eye, upon excellence, wherever discovered and seized upon it with rapacity.' "[26] The italics are mine, but the concept, almost down to the rhythm of its syllables (and even allowing for the difference that the terms "ontological" and "cosmopolitan" make) is clearly both Crummell's and Johnson's.

In the second *Dreamer* episode, one of the most famous texts of the twentieth century—Du Bois's own *The Souls of Black Folk*—inadvertently gains a new title. Scanning the shelves of the Black People's Liberation Army Library on a visit to that organization with Amy, another King supporter, Matthew reports:

> I saw seminal works by W. E. B. Du Bois, Martin Delany, Marcus Garvey, and dozens of other cultural nationalists and Marxist revolutionaries from Africa, the Caribbean, and South America . . . [as well as] several volumes by Yahya Zubena, a prominent local activist. . . . Amy pulled down one of Yahya's books and . . . began flipping through its pages and frowning. Truth to tell, I found his work puerile, and while I pretended to peruse a copy of *The Souls of Black Folks*, which I deeply respected, I was actually watching Amy from the corner of my eye, wondering if I'd completely blown my first evening out with her. (168–69)

It's jarring to see Matthew misidentify Du Bois's famous title (which carries no final *s* on *Folk*) even as Matthew professes his deep respect for the work itself. How should we read this curious 's'? Is it a deliberate mistake (and if so, whose: Matthew's or Johnson's?), or simply a typographical error? If deliberate, could the error be intended to slight Du Bois? After all, in this scene he is invoked not as a democratic pluralist but a cultural nationalist, reminding us how important *Souls* was, particularly in the 1930s, to such projects as the black Francophone Negritude of Senghor and Césaire, but also how little stock the integrationist Johnson puts in such ventures. (A few pages later Matthew and Amy will flee the library and its nationalist politics in exasperation, with Johnson surely cheering behind the author's scrim.) Or could the error be intended to slight Matthew by impugning the adequacy of his own project of reading? After all, how much respect can he have for a book whose title he misremembers? (Or is Matthew simply distracted by his preoccupation in this scene with Amy, rather than with politics?) Such questions seem not at all irrelevant in a novel so interested in moments of reading and instruction, from the stack of books (including "Maritain's *Christianity and Democracy*" [24]) on King's nightstand, to the description of his classroom tactics at Morehouse College (according to Julian Bond, Matthew relates, King "often looked up from his notes, closed his copy of Plato's collected dialogues, and brought whole cloth out of his head passages from Socrates' apology" [25]), to Matthew's painstaking review of Chaym Smith's sketches and notebooks the night two Wise Guys take the minister's double for a little ride. But perhaps Johnson's larger point is also Chaym's: "if you want liberation, to be free, you got to get there on your own," Chaym tells Matthew near the novel's midpoint. "All the texts and teachers are just tools. If you want to be free, you're *supposed* to outgrow them" (99).[27] Johnson himself, it turns out, uses both *Folk* and *Folks* when discussing Du Bois's text in his essays and book reviews, suggesting perhaps that even so precise a thinker and writer as he has absorbed Du Bois's lessons without fetishizing his text.[28]

What I am calling Johnson's critical pragmatism, particularly his interest in the complex relationship between reading, instruction, and democracy, is on yet more emphatic display in his recent collection of fiction, *Soulcatcher and Other Stories*. Originally published as part of *Africans in America: America's Journey Through Slavery* (1998), a textbook companion to the PBS series of the same name, Johnson's stories were literally inspired by, and then woven into, the history text. As Johnson explains:

For months, as I worked through spring and summer to complete my fourth novel, huge boxes of research compiled by WGBH's Research Team arrived on my doorstep. That fall, when I finished *Dreamer* and finally could pore over these reams of black-bound books and the drafts of [co-author Patricia]

Smith's poetically written chapters, story possibilities began to percolate in my imagination. Here, in these boxes crammed with primary and secondary source material, I was introduced to facts and historical figures essential for deepening our understanding of America's past and present. . . . Here, in the historical record, was marvelous grist for the mill of fiction.[29]

In a sustained burst of creativity Johnson produced a dozen stories in a single month. The stories not only bore the responsibility of dramatizing the historical record, they faced the simultaneous technical challenge, set by Johnson himself, of telling their tales through twelve different narrative lenses: "I wanted to create, if possible, a diversity of narrative styles that would make each story aesthetically vivid" as well as historically alive (xi). Two years after the appearance of *Africans in America*, Johnson compiled a separate collection of the twelve stories extracted from their textbook context. "Two years ago it was my hope that this repertoire of formal variations would bring a freshness to the illuminating facts in Africans in America," Johnson averred. "And it is my hope today that these stories, now published separately . . . will serve as something of a time machine for readers, transporting them back to an African American past that in every way critically informed the on-going adventure of democracy and the creation of the republic in which we presently live" (xiv, xv).

Befitting their original emplacement within a history textbook, the twelve tales in *Soulcatcher* return even more frequently than *Dreamer* to scenes of reading and instruction. The tale that opens the collection, for example, "The Transmission," begins as a graphic and seemingly dead-end account of the degradations of the Middle Passage:

They were dead, and this was the boat to the Underworld.
　　In the darkness of its belly, the boy—his name was Malawi—lay pressed against its wet, wooden hull, naked and chained to a corpse that only hours before had been his older brother, Oboto. Down there, the air was curdled, thick with the stench of feces and decaying flesh. Already the ship's rats were nibbling at Oboto's cold, stiff fingers. (1)

But the tale, told in third person limited point of view, gradually shifts from speech-numbing horror to story-telling song. For we discover that Malawi's brother, a tribal *griot*-in-training, had before his death begun assiduously to transmit to his younger sibling the "past, rituals, and laws" of their tribe in "songs and riddles" (9), making every moment of contact between them a scene of quietly powerful teaching. The lessons are transmitted *sotto voce*, so as to escape the notice of the white sailors (or "lipless phantoms" [1]), until the story's very end, when Malawi, "hesitantly at first, and then with a little more confidence" (11) sings the song of his own capture and passage for an attentive white outcast, a blue-eyed "hook-nosed" (10) phantom abused by the other sailors. The metaphor of the *griot* as a "living book" is redoubled vividly here, as the brother's teachings help resist horror, spur invention, and finally confer the power to live, in word and flesh, on the previously shocked-speechless Malawi.

Similar dramatizations of the importance of instruction and the power of illumination recur in nearly every tale. In the second story, "Confession," which through third-person monologue explores the liberating pull of slave rebellion, the astonished speaker Tiberius describes the charismatic slave leader Jemmy literally as a light-bringing force. "I never *thought* about bein' free until then," Tiberius reflects. "Never *saw* how things could be different than they was until I listened to Jemmy. Everythin' looked *changed* after he spoke. Like I'd lived alla my life in a cave, believin' the shadows I seen were real until Jemmy held up a light and they all melted away" (19). Though Tiberius's own fate is sealed (the story suggests that he is executed by his captors at the conclusion of his monologue), his Platonic awakening to the desire for freedom resonates as the story's most important dramatization. In the third story, "Poetry and Politics," artistic freedom is the cherished goal. Staging a conversation between Phillis Wheatley and her mistress about Phillis's latest poetic effort—a poorly rendered attempt at protest art—Johnson dramatizes what are surely his own concerns about the perceived necessity for African-American artists to speak truth to power rather than to beauty. In the story's final scene, Wheatley's mistress reads Phillis a letter from George Washington thanking her for her earlier (actual) poem on his virtues, which he praises as "new instance of your genius" but which he elects not to publish for fear of being accused of vanity (32). For Phillis, the final lesson is wrapped in Washington's valediction: "I am, with great respect. . . . Your obedient, humble servant." "He said . . . servant?" Phillis asks her mistress. "This is a complicated time, isn't it?" (32).

In their original publishing context, folded into the pages of the *Africans in America* textbook, these tales of slavery amplify the instructional value of the figures, stories, and documents through which we learn about the past. Within the PBS volume, Johnson's tales typically appear not at the ends of chapters (and thus segregated from the historical material) but in the midst of them, often interrupting the specific account that is then partially reimagined in Johnson's tale.[30] Encountering the tales in their 1998 textbook form thus shapes a markedly different reading experience from the "time machine" approach of the later, stand-alone volume. For example, in *Africans in America*, Johnson's story "Confession" interrupts the textbook's narration of the 1739 Stono Rebellion in South Carolina, in which the slave leader Jemmy has already been introduced as an actual histor-ical figure. Readers of the PBS volume may thus assess Johnson's fictionalization of history in ways that readers of the separate collection may not (at least not as easily). This interplay of text, story, and in some cases physical documents hap-pens, instructively, over and over again. The 1783 pass given to a black soldier who fought for England during the Revolutionary War pictured on page 119, for example, subsequently appears—and is silently read—on page 176 in Johnson's story "A Soldier for the Crown." Richard Allen, whose picture appears on page 222 and whose work on behalf of American blacks in the late-eighteenth- and early-nineteenth-centuries is then discussed on pages 231–38, appears as a central character in Johnson's story "The Plague" that begins on page 239. These are only a few of many such instances in the volume.

What Johnson's originally embedded stories thus help teach is the ability to think critically about both historical and literary materials and to recognize their interrelatedness. This is a point that commentators who focus on the 2001 stand-alone volume sometimes overlook. William Nash, for example, senses in *Soulcatcher* a "confusing" rather than a coherent "thematic picture," noting that while some of the collection's stories embrace Johnsonian "intersubjectivity," oth-ers appear to endorse an un-Johnsonian "black solidarity that leads to sepa-ratism."[31] I would suggest that what appears confusing may be better understood in light of the tales' insistence on trying out new points of view. The intellectual effect of Johnson's stylistic variations is clearer in the stories' original home, where the tales frequently enter into dialogue with each other and their surrounding materials rather than present a single thematic approach. For example, in "Poetry and Politics," Phillis Wheatley explains her reluctance to be a pamphleteer by cit-ing the transitoriness of the medium. "And *why* not a pamphleteer?" her mistress asks. "It's obvious why, isn't it," answers Phillis. "At the end of the day one wraps garbage in newspapers. And while a pamphlet can be valuable and stir people to action, a hundred years hence it may be forgotten—as the injustice it assails is forgotten—or it will be preserved only as a historical document, interesting for what it reveals about a moment long past, but *never* appreciated as art" (Smith, *Africans* 148). And yet later in the textbook, in Johnson's story "The People Speak," it is only through a fictional newspaper article that readers are offered imaginative access to the decision of roughly three thousand black Philadelphians unanimously to reject a proposed African colonization scheme that prominent black leaders in the story support. After reading both tales, one can imagine a fruitful classroom discussion on the merits of Wheatley's confident assertion of the primacy of poetry; and even if Johnson's sympathies may be felt to fall most strongly on Wheatley's side, it seems clear that part of Johnson's aim is precisely to stir this kind of debate. One could imagine the same questions asked about Johnson's aesthetic virtuosity in these stories. Which medium is the most effective for transmitting a particular tale? Could one not turn the glove inside out and rewrite each story in its neighbor's mode? (That is exactly the kind of creative exercise, incidentally, that Johnson gives to his own MFA pupils.[32]) The supposed thematic tension in *Soulcatcher* may in the end have more to do with the insistent turn of the stories' narrative wheel than with any emerging political confusion in Johnson himself. If anything, Johnson's gradually intensifying embrace of Ellison's pragmatic pluralist aesthetics (as we saw earlier in Johnson's reviews and essays) suggests a writer more, not less secure in his political vision, even if that vision requires, as Posnock would suggest, flexibility over fixedness. Indeed by dramatizing critical thinking and authorial choice (or, one might say, constraint), Johnson's virtuosic stories instantiate, at the level of form, the complex decisions and debates necessary for a pluralist democracy to thrive.

CONCLUSION

In arguing for Johnson as the most fitting capstone to a study like Ross Posnock's *Color and Culture*, I have tried to demonstrate why we should consider Johnson the premier inheritor of the Jamesian pragmatic pluralism practiced variously by key black cultural figures of the twentieth century. As an emphatically antirace race man sympathetic to many of the beliefs about culture, race, and human identity shared by such figures as W. E. B. Du Bois, Alain Locke, and particularly Ralph Ellison, Johnson embodies a late-twentieth/early-twenty-first century African-American pragmatism like virtually no other writer today. In arguing for a consideration of Johnson's critical writing, not merely his philosophical essays but particularly his book reviews, I have tried to provide access to an important yet underexplored "room" in Johnson's "house" of writing. Our ongoing efforts to understand and assess Johnson's creative and critical efforts in the coming decades will require more familiarity with the full body of that work.[33]

What I hope I have also shown is that one of Johnson's most significant contributions to contemporary literary and philosophical discourse is his pragmatist—and quite political—interest in the enabling and inherently integrative processes of democracy, processes that for Johnson are best understood and accessed through acts of reading, thinking, and critical interpretation. Johnson's interest in these modes may be clarified not only by Posnock's genealogy in *Color and Culture* but also by Giles Gunn's parallel account of the late-twentieth-century revival of pragmatism in the arts in *Thinking Across the American Grain: Ideology, Intellect, and the New Pragmatism*. In this book, which precedes Posnock's, Gunn distinguishes pragmatism from Marxism on the question of the relation between interpretation and change. "With the Marxists," Gunn asserts, "pragmatism believes that the problem is not simply to interpret the world but actually to change it." Unlike Marxism, however, "pragmatism maintains that we actually begin to change the world the moment we begin to interpret it."[34] Gunn's distinction recalls the stakes of Johnson's very first book review, on Wright's *American Hunger*, in which Johnson (himself a former Marxist) discerns in Wright (who fought against Marxism's dogmatism) a struggle to understand and then disclose "the world's lived structures" to others, a fundamental act of interpretation and communication that necessarily precedes any social change. "The first step in treating any social corruption," Johnson would emphatically conclude in that first review, "is the treatment of the corruption of consciousness" (Johnson 1977, 7). But this move into the body to discover the world is not in itself an apolitical gesture, either for Wright or for Johnson. And despite Johnson's oft-repeated warning that "one of the greatest mistakes that critics and readers make when approaching a novel by a black author is the tendency to read that work as sociology, anthropology, or as a political statement of some sort" (Boccia 200), we cannot be misled into thinking that Johnson's writings—whether fictions, essays, or reviews—embrace philosophy to the exclusion of politics, at least not in the classical sense of the term. Instead, in the end we must say that Johnson cares so deeply about the world and about the role of the critic and the author in responding to that world—and ultimately in changing or revitalizing that world—that he takes up the role of critical pragmatist in the first place. What Johnson originally discerned in Wright, in other words, he ultimately demands of himself. Any writer "true to himself and [to] Being," as Johnson might put it, could do no less (Johnson 1977, 6).

NOTES

1. This essay substantially revises and expands a conference presentation delivered at the Twentieth-Century Literature Conference in Louisville, Kentucky, in February 1999.

I wish to thank fellow panelists Marc Conner and William Nash for their helpful comments on earlier versions of this essay. The epigraph comes from Johnson's "A Symposium on Contemporary American Fiction," 755.

2. Critics have only recently begun to explore the influence of pragmatism in Johnson's work. See, for example, Gary Storhoff's *Understanding Charles Johnson*. Storhoff persuasively argues that American pragmatism "becomes a thematic structure in Johnson's work" (16), best exemplified by Johnson's "fundamentally pragmatic" (149) view of history in *Middle Passage* and the "prophetic pragmatism" (186)—in Cornel West's sense—of Johnson's depiction of Martin Luther King, Jr., in *Dreamer*. For more on West's concept of "prophetic pragmatism," see his *The American Evasion of Philosophy: A Genealogy of Pragmatism* (211–39).

3. On James's influence on Du Bois's disciplinary focus, see West, 113. On Locke's exposure to James's Oxford lectures, see Ross Posnock, *Color and Culture: Black Writers and the Making of the Modern Intellectual* 23.

4. As Posnock notes, conventional assumptions about what might constitute a black pragmatist tradition would likely identify Booker T. Washington, not Du Bois, as the key turn-of-the-century figure. But only if one inappropriately privileges the colloquial over the philosophical sense of pragmatist. "A masterly organizer and disciplinarian, Washington was a pragmatist in the colloquial sense but the virtual antithesis of a philosophical pragmatist," Posnock writes. "Du Bois inverts these distinctions" (36).

5. Posnock 8, 6, 69. In Posnock's account, *Of One Blood* is a foundational antirace race text. "While her uplift fable reflects its historical moment (the Pan-African movement had formally begun in 1900)," Posnock writes, "in dramatizing the latent fantasy of release Hopkins's text is prescient. *Of One Blood* is germinal, for it can be considered the seed of antirace race texts all published in the generation after her own: James Weldon Johnson's *The Autobiography of an Ex-Colored Man* (1912, rpt. 1927), Du Bois's *Dark Princess* (1928), Nella Larsen's *Quicksand* (1928), Jessie Fauset's *Plum Bun* (1929), and Wallace Thurman's *Infants of the Spring* (1932)."

6. Posnock 216–17. For more on Toomer's race-inflected rejection of racial purism, see Hutchinson, "Jean Toomer and American Racial Discourse."

7. Posnock 213. Posnock is particularly discerning in discussing Hurston's Toomer-like refusal to "play by the racial rules of the game" (212) beginning with her 1942 autobiography *Dust Tracks on a Road.*

8. Quoted in Posnock 77.

9. The phrases "appropriation game" and "motley mixtures" are Ellison's; "democratic turbulence," "rigid classifications," and race "chauvinism" are Posnock's.

10. In his *Charles Johnson's Novels: Writing the American Palimpsest*, Rudolph P. Byrd also registers affinities between Johnson's vision of culture, Ellison's pluralism, and Posnock's "cosmopolitanism." Byrd does so, however, without specifically placing Johnson within the pragmatist genealogy Posnock traces. Indeed, Byrd uses the more traditional term "cultural pluralism" rather than Posnock's more precise "pragmatic pluralism" to describe Ellison's and Johnson's conception of culture, a usage that masks Ellison's and Johnson's repudiation of cultural pluralism's implicit identity logic. See 3–4, 196.

11. In identifying Du Bois in particular as an important philosophical predecessor of Johnson, I am aware that Johnson finds certain aspects of Du Boisian thought outmoded.

In his review of Gerald Early's edited collection *Lure and Loathing: Essays on Race, Identity, and the Ambivalence of Assimilation* (Penguin 1993), for example, Johnson questions whether Du Bois's famous formulation of double consciousness "is in fact an accurate account either of the experience of black life in this country or of racial consciousness anywhere" (*The New York Times Book Review*, 23 May 1993, 16). Nonetheless, it is through Johnson's similar embrace of certain fundamental tenets of Jamesian pragmatic pluralism that he can be understood as one of Du Bois's rightful philosophical heirs.

12. It is also worth noting Johnson's early criticism of Delany for failing to connect philosophy with African American culture in his novels. Near the end of his 1980 essay "Philosophy and Black Fiction," Johnson writes: "Don't [Black writers] wonder about religion, political philosophy, the existence of others, the Good, meaning, duty, or thought itself? (Samuel R. Delany, it must be said, struggles with thought and language in such sci-fi fabulations as *Babel-17* and, although his ambition is delightful, it is the world of *Star Wars* aliens, not Black people, where the probing occurs.)" ("Philosophy" 83).

13. Johnson's enthusiastic blurb for the hardcover edition of his colleague Posnock's book all but announces the importance of this tradition for Johnson himself: "Monumentally important in its exploration of the tensions between ethnicity and cosmopolitanism, Professor Posnock's book is the work on black literature that I have been waiting to read for three decades, one that both liberates and enlarges our discussions on racial identity and a century of black intellectual commerce from Du Bois to Samuel Delaney." Johnson is also cited in Posnock's acknowledgments.

14. I make this claim fully aware that at times Johnson seems to disparage pragmatism as a philosophical method. "Most ludicrous of all," he reflects in his 1988 essay, "Where Philosophy and Fiction Meet," "is the depressing fact that America has given but one philosophy to the world: pragmatism." However even here Johnson does not so much criticize pragmatism as lament the absence of a richer array of indigenous philosophical traditions. This same essay, moreover, provides evidence that Johnson knows full well the historical importance of philosophical pragmatism for African American thinkers. "I urged skeptics to remember that a few Harlem Renaissance writers had backgrounds in philosophy," he writes, "and that one of W. E. B. Du Bois's great hopes was to develop a philosophical method for the interpretation of race relations" (92).

15. The online version of Johnson's *vita* runs to more than 45 single-spaced printed pages. As of August 2005, it lists nearly fifty reviews dating from 1977 to 2001. The *vita* may be viewed at: http://depts.washington.edu/engl/people/vita/johnson_cha.html

16. One phrase conspicuously shared by the Wright and Roussel reviews neatly glosses Johnson's goal for his own writing: "Wright sees as perhaps no writer before him—and certainly no few writers since—that if black life . . . can be brought *from concealedness into clarity*, . . . it will create a humanizing vision for the country as a whole" (review of *American Hunger*); "Explaining the being of language requires a phenomenological analysis that shows how each word, like a palimpsest, is a tissue of experiences and meanings— a communal property like an old Protestant church, scarred, remodeled, reworked by thousands who've built upon it as they called their experience of reality *from concealedness to clarity*" (review of *How I Wrote Certain of My Books*). Elsewhere Johnson identifies the bringing of "clarity" from "concealedness" as the phenomenological concept of *alethia*: "a

new disclosure of the Real that brings it from concealedness." See "Philosophy and Black Fiction" 81.

17. Johnson, "White Bandits of the West." Another book Johnson declares "an essential work" whose details he nonetheless finds "sicken[ing]" is Robert B. Edgerton's *Mau Mau: An African Crucible* (The Free Press, 1989). See Johnson, "The Lesson of the Mau Mau."

18. Johnson, "The Prophet of Black Arts." To Neal's credit, Johnson avers, he eventually came to revalue his earlier rejection of writers like Ralph Ellison.

19. Johnson, "Inventing Africa"; the words within double quotation marks are Appiah's, the rest Johnson's.

20. Du Bois's 1921 statement is cited in Posnock, 13. Johnson's "Appreciation" of Ellison, "The Singular Vision of Ralph Ellison," appeared in *The Washington Post*, 18 April 1994, and is collected in *Turning the Wheel*.

21. For Johnson's discussion of Ellison's "individual vision" and "tour de force" writing, see his 1989 essay "Novelists of Memory" (Byrd 100). On *Invisible Man* as a "Freudian tale," see "Where Philosophy and Fiction Meet" (Byrd 93). Although at the end of "Novelists of Memory" Johnson describes contemporary African American literature as "central to the ongoing effort to define . . . the adventure of democracy in the modern age" (107), it would take several more years for Johnson's interest in democracy to crystallize as a recovery of Ellisonian pluralism.

22. Though Johnson avows Ellison's novel is a "masterpiece," he argues that it suffers from inadequate characterization ("Ellison is, one must admit, a sort of intellectual cartoonist when it comes to characterization; his people are, for the most part, principles"), is "top-heavy with symbols," and is "pad[ded] out" narratively. In the Rinehart section, Johnson asserts, Ellison even gets the central philosophical point "wrong, or backward." And finally, at the novel's end, Ellison leaves his protagonist "nowhere to go except outside the lives of others, below the social world, which he lives off parasitically." "Even sadder," Johnson concludes, the novel's "primary metaphor—invisibility—seems to force Ellison into a corner where our links to predecessors and contemporaries have been shattered. True, in the epilogue Ellison reaffirms the 'principles' of [Plato's] *Republic*, or plays with such reaffirmation for a paragraph, but the idea hasn't been dramatically earned" (*Being and Race* 15–17).

23. These sentences from the 1994 *Washington Post* "Appreciation" explicitly revise Johnson's earlier comments on Ellison in his 1989 "Novelists of Memory" essay. The changes primarily introduce pluralist and democratic tropes missing from the earlier essay. For example, Johnson changes the phrase "several literary genres" to "diverse literary genres." He also adds the final clause of the Post passage quoted here ("forever forcing us to see in the novel's technique the spirit of democracy"), which does not appear in the earlier essay. These calculated revisions exemplify Johnson's pronounced shift toward Ellison's democratic pluralism after 1990.

24. See, for example, Johnson's 1995 review of Jerry Gaffo Watts's *Heroism and the Black Intellectual: Ralph Ellison, Politics, and Afro-American Intellectual Life*, in which he chastises Watts for attempting to assess Ellison's politics without any discussion of his art. "Readers hoping for a better understanding of [*Invisible Man*] or of the creative process that made it possible," Johnson writes, "will have to look elsewhere" ("Race, Politics and Ralph Ellison," 15). Other essays that defend Ellison (or single him out for praise) include Johnson's review

of Albert Murray's *The Blue Devils of Nada* and *The Seven League Boots* ("Keeping the Blues Away"); Johnson's essay on James Weldon Johnson for *The New York Times* ("An Ever-Lifting Song of Black America"); Johnson's reply to Norman Podhoretz's critique of *Invisible Man* in *Commentary* (October 1999); and Johnson's essay "Ralph Ellison: Novel Genius" for the *Crisis* (2002), originally delivered as the keynote address for the Symposium Commemorating the Fiftieth Anniversary of Ralph Ellison's *Invisible Man*, Washington and Lee University, February 1, 2002.

25. For more on the importance of images of palimpsestic interwovenness in Johnson's fiction, see Byrd, *Charles Johnson's Novels.* For further discussion of Johnson's deepening interest in social and political engagement in *Dreamer,* see Storhoff, *Understanding Charles Johnson,* 183–216, and Nash, *Charles Johnson's Fiction,* 162–90.

26. Here I am quoting Posnock (except for "eclectic") until the colon; the words that follow are Crummell's. See Posnock 19.

27. At the close of his recent book on Johnson, William Nash offers a provocative reading of the extra 's' on Souls, particularly in light of the pragmatic inheritances I explore in this essay. In response to the 1999 conference paper in which I first questioned the 's,' Nash writes: "I am inclined to read this additional 's' as Johnson's final, fleeting rejection of Du Bois's looming essentialism, a signifying revision of the original that allows the author to claim his own space within this intellectual-activist camp. . . . At the heart of Johnson's vision in *Dreamer* is the multiplicity rather than the commonality of experience among the black community. His recognition of the Cainite-Abelite dichotomy demonstrates this division and suggests the means of overcoming it" (Nash, 190).

28. For example, Johnson uses "Folks" when citing Du Bois's text in his 1987 review of Caryl Phillips's novel, The European Tribe (3), and also his 1993 interview with Jonathan Little (118). In his more recent New York Times essay on James Weldon Johnson, Johnson uses the plural form of "folks" when invoking (though not actually citing) Du Bois's title: "My mother, I believe, knew these idealistic stanzas spoke—and would continue to speak—directly to 'the souls of black folks'" ("An Ever-Lifting Song," AR34). In other of his published writings, Johnson cites the title without the extra 's' on Folk.

29. The "grist" metaphor may make it seem as though Johnson regards history merely as pre-text—factual grain for his fictional machinery—but earlier in the same paragraph Johnson makes clear that what in part appeals to him in the historical record is its already quasi-fictional texture. Johnson recalls: "The research for the PBS series treated major historical moments . . . but in doing so it also unveiled the fascinating and often ambiguous anecdotes, ironies, back-stories, and paradoxes that inevitably arise when human beings for centuries live within an execrable social arrangement they know is unjust and fragile and ultimately doomed" (Johnson, *Soulcatcher* xii).

30. In his otherwise excellent reading of the collection, Storhoff confusingly claims that the tales "are usually featured as interchapters, but occasionally . . . are interpolated within the chapter itself" (*Understanding Charles Johnson,* 219). The reverse would seem to be true. Of the twelve tales in *Soulcatcher,* only two ("The Transmission," "The Soulcatcher") conclude chapters; the rest interrupt them. Of the ten that interrupt, only one ("Murderous Thoughts," which follows a section break), seems to provide the break Storhoff implies in the term "interchapter."

31. Nash, *Charles Johnson's Fiction*, 191. For a different reading of the stories in *Soulcatcher*, see Storhoff, 217–26. Though Storhoff finds the dialogue in the tales occasionally contrived and the stories themselves often "unnecessarily truncated" (218)—owing to the space constraints of the original PBS volume—he nonetheless discerns a consistency of both method and purpose.

32. See, for example, Johnson's essay on his teaching methods, "A Boot Camp for Creative Writing."

33. *I Call Myself an Artist* reprints half a dozen book reviews and works of "cultural criticism," but all the selections are drawn from the 1990s.

34. Giles Gunn, *Thinking Across the Grain* 3–4.

PRAGMATIC ETHICS IN CHARLES JOHNSON'S FICTION

GARY STORHOFF

It is important to understand that I do not write about history. I only write about the present moment.
—CHARLES JOHNSON, *personal communication to the author*

We are discussing no small matter, but how we ought to live.
—PLATO'S *Republic*

Teacher, what good thing must I do?
—MATTHEW 19:16

Charles Johnson is an extraordinarily innovative American writer whose work revolves around profound ethical issues. Because his ethics emerge from the philosophy he studied in graduate school, his ethical outlook is complex and difficult to discern—primarily because his is a dissenting voice from current philosophical schools of ethics.[1] Contemporary Western philosophy usually treats ethics as primarily the moral evaluation of specific actions.[2] However, such an approach is insufficient for a novelist with Johnson's convictions. Johnson's philosophical inclination is the evaluation of the whole person, in evaluating character traits that make an individual good and that lead to a worthwhile life.[3] His ethical vision is broadly ecological and melioristic, consistent with his Buddhism. Undergirding his Buddhist commitment is a systematic and principled pragmatism, though as is typical for Johnson's art, pragmatism is treated with subtlety and qualification.

Indeed, Johnson's pragmatism may reveal as much about his thematic aims as his well known Buddhist commentary. The word "pragmatism," however, should be used advisedly in the context of Johnson's fiction. In its vernacular sense, "pragmatism" implies performing an action that is prudential and adventitious in the most mundane sense: an amoral and self-serving choice that merely increases the bottom line. Pragmatism in this more colloquial sense turns away from moral principle. It is this understanding of pragmatism that Cringle denounces in *Middle Passage* as he describes his father: "Material success is a pretty tyrannical proof for one's point of view. Truth is what *works*, pragmatically, in the sphere of commerce. . . . [Cringle's father] judges everything in terms of profit and how wide an impression it makes in the world" (160). This debased sense of pragmatism Johnson's fiction consistently repudiates; nothing could be further from his vision of the world.

Instead, Johnson's pragmatism belongs to a deeply principled American philosophical tradition, first articulated by Charles Peirce, William James, and Thomas Dewey, and more recently revived by such philosophers as Cornel West. American pragmatism involves the conviction that one must take into account the practice to which a moral position leads, and once that choice is made, revise one's sense of reality within the context of that chosen practice. As West explains, a pragmatist must continually put into practice an interpretation of reality, and only then can we determine, according to West, "the best available, yet revisable theories of reality" (*Evasion* 51). What actions are performed are based on our understanding of reality, but this understanding must be necessarily provisional. As we consider and reconsider our world, testing and retesting, the truth becomes contingent on what is known at the time. As we entertain "revisable theories of reality," we are constantly open to growth. Pragmatism does not connote ethical relativism; instead, contemporary pragmatists like West conjoin humanist ethics with democratic liberalism and an Old Testament sense of social justice. West calls this philosophical amalgam "prophetic pragmatism": "Prophetic pragmatism, with its roots in the American heritage and its hopes for the wretched of the earth, constitutes the best chance of promoting an Emersonian culture of creative democracy by means of critical intelligence and social action" (212). But once one commits to a new practice, one cannot simply return to one's former view of the world, since one has grown away from that formerly held vision of reality—one must have, in West's word, "revised" it. In what follows, I shall attempt first to describe the metaphysics on which Johnson bases his pragmatism, and then explore the effects of pragmatism in his fiction. Johnson's metaphysical moves generate his ethics.

"EMPTY THINGS, COLD, WITHOUT QUALITY, DISTANT": EMPTINESS AND JOHNSON'S ETHICAL OBLIGATION

Johnson's (and West's) project of "revising" our conception of the world is intrinsically Buddhist. Johnson does not assume a timeless, transcendental experience, but rather dramatizes in his fiction the possibility that all human experience is finite, transient, historical, and open to transformation. The seminal Buddhist concept of "dependent origination" ("*partitya samutpada*") explains transience, and how things eventually become what they fleetingly are. According to this concept, all people, thoughts, and objects are incessantly changing because they depend, at the very moment they come into existence and from that point thereafter, on other things, which are also changing because they too are dependent on other things, and so on *ad infinitum*. All things are what they are at any given moment not because it is their essential nature to be such and such, but because other things (also changing) have influenced, shaped, or partially determined whatever exactly they are at the present moment. All things exist in a relational matrix throughout history. No one thing has an essential nature, nor is any thing self-determining; but things depend upon a complex set of relations with other evolving things.

An example of Johnson's symbolic representation of dependent origination occurs in *Faith and the Good Thing*. Lavidia, Faith's mother, has just died, and in her bereavement Faith enters the kitchen. Her mother's death has transformed this simple room:

> Without her the kitchen, the house, the world beyond fell apart. Fruit cabinets on the wall still held sweet jellies preserved in the odd-shaped bottles Lavidia salvaged like a scavenger from house and yard and rummage sales; her stiff mops and silver pail still rested in the corner by brooms she'd assembled by hand. Then what had changed? Certainly not the things themselves. Studying Lavidia's dresses heaped in a wash-tub by the door, her pipes in their dusty rack on the kitchen table, and dry lifeless wigs, Faith felt her answer emerge from the contours of these objects: none of them was for her; they belonged, related to no one. Even Lavidia, perhaps, had not made them her own, because—with her death—they seemed suddenly freed to be as they were. Empty things, cold, without quality, distant. (5)

Mops, brooms, pails, jelly jars, dirty clothes in a wash tub—these mundane, ordinary things are momentously transformed in Faith's perception at her mother's death. Suddenly, these simple things become "as they were." Significantly, the meaning of these objects emerges from their "contours," their form; the distinct form of objects is essential to Johnson for an understanding of their interconnection. Despite their separate forms, Faith suddenly sees that these simple objects lack any independent, autonomous, or self-determining status. Before this epiphanic moment, Faith had known these things within the single, monolithic context of her mother—her character (her parsimoniousness) and her activity (her cooking, cleaning, smoking, and scavenging). But with her mother's death, these objects are released from their familiar monistic context, passing at this moment into other contexts. Their meanings had not been final after all, and Faith lets go of her earlier cognitions; Faith, in West's terms, "revises her theory of reality." Johnson writes, "none of them was for her; they belonged, related to no one." Faith understands that not even Lavidia with all her industriousness had "made them her own"—these things resist Lavidia's (the owner's) imposition of definitive, static, and absolute identity. With her death, they were "freed to be as they were." Thus, not even a jelly jar can be known without a context that itself depends upon other contexts; all things become utterly relational and contextualized for Faith as she meditates on her mother's death. They are, in Johnson's words, "empty things."

Emptiness ("*sunyata*") is perhaps Johnson's central metaphysical concept. As the philosopher Dale S. Wright writes, "the concept 'emptiness' derives from, and eventually encompasses, the key elements in Buddhist contemplative practice: impermanence, dependent origination, and no self. . . . For something to be 'empty' means that, because the entity 'originates dependent' upon other entities, and is transformed in accordance with changes in these external conditions, the entity therefore lacks 'own-being' . . . or 'self-nature' " (Wright 51). For Johnson, an experiential understanding of emptiness leads to a release from the desires for things in the world around us, even a desire for a unique identity. As protagonists are freed from desire in Johnson's fiction, they are liberated from the hold things have over them, including the hold of their own individuality. "Emptiness" in this context does not imply complete negation of existence, the opposite of being or "somethingness"-in-general.[4] Nor does emptiness point to nihilism, a complete negation of meaning itself.

Johnson, in contrast, sees the acceptance of emptiness as ethically redemptive. All things are empty; "emptiness" is a universal descriptor. Its sense is similar to the "nothingness" in Jean-Paul Sartre's *Being and Nothingness*, representing an openness and radical indeterminacy, a rejection of an entirely definite or self-enclosed nature. A specific thing is empty because it "originates dependent" upon other things, but that thing also constantly changes in correlation with all those other changing things. All things—objects, ideas, and sentient beings too—derive their character from the infinite number of factors that precipitate their beginnings and partially shape their transfigurations, which in turn derive their attributes from other factors or contexts throughout history. Thus, no one thing has its own unique identity, or becomes what it is because of its essential nature or its will, its own self-determining drive for actualization. Each thing depends utterly on an infinitely complex network of correlated and interdependent entities.

Johnson's work moves relentlessly toward the concept of emptiness. Even the self—conceived as a ghostly, unchanging essence of an individual usually defined in terms of an individual's societal roles, or (in religious terms) as the soul—does not exist as an independent entity, but is only a bundle of swiftly changing, complementary, and conditional states ("*anatman*"). Nothing in the world, whether mental or physical, has any distinctive identity without its mutual relationships to other elements. Consequently, no one individual can be considered as isolated and unique but is instead an aggregate of experiences shared with others, with the past, and with the earth itself.

The short story "Moving Pictures" from *The Sorcerer's Apprentice* dramatizes the consequences of Johnson's doctrine of no-self. The unnamed protagonist of "Moving Pictures" is a successful Hollywood writer who lives a morally confused life, characterized by an impending divorce, quarrels with his boss, sexual promiscuity, drug abuse, and his children whom he neglects in favor of his career. He is plagued by regrets that he has abandoned his ambitious and complex "Big Book" (a novel) for better-paying, more prestigious, but vacuous Hollywood film writing. He lives in a rat-race world that he attempts to escape one night by going to the movies. The story dramatizes his emotional escape when he weeps for the characters on screen that he himself probably helped to create; that is, he is taken in by the patent sentimentality imaged on the screen—a narrative that he calls an "epistemological Murphy" (117). A "Murphy" is a slang term for a confidence game, a criminal strategy in which a phony story created by con men hooks the victim (in the story, the film's viewer) by exploiting his or her greed. In the story, the protagonist's ego is a con man continually gulled by his own trickery. The action and characters portrayed on the screen evoke the protagonist's own self-pity and remorse over his lost opportunities and wretched circumstances, which he believes he is unable to change. When he returns to his car after viewing the movie, he discovers that his car has been vandalized and he has been robbed. He loses his checkbook, his house key, and—symbolic of his rat race—"the report due tomorrow at nine sharp" (123). With despair, he learns the hard New Testament lesson: "Lay not up for yourselves treasures upon earth, where moth and rust doth corrupt, and where thieves break through and steal" (Matthew 6:12).

The protagonist is "a seeker groping in the darkness for light"—in the double sense that he eagerly looks forward to his escapist pleasure in the theatre, but also that he needs enlightenment. He makes excessive emotional claims on the movie, for he is not impartial, objective, or detached as he watches. Instead, he is emotionally conned by the "epistemological Murphy" that he has in part (but not totally) created for himself, and in viewing the film filtered through his personal biases and emotional requirements, he is not aware that he is producing illusions stimulated by the film's sensory data and mistaking these images for an emotional reality. What should be obvious—that he has created his own narrative, with some assistance from others—remains hidden from him. He is bedeviled by his own desire. His memories create for him a deep sense of craving and desolation that he projects onto the screen. For example, he weeps for his own "sense of ruin" that he felt when he views the movie's cemetery scene, as he recalls his own mother's death and his "irreversible feeling of abandonment" (121). And he weeps for his lack of success with women— first in his past (high school), then with his present trophy wife who "talks now of legal separation and finding herself" (116). In other words, the protagonist's understanding of his world is marked by his emotional cravings (that is, his wants, wishes, felt needs, regrets, and so forth). Further, these desires are contradictory, even mutually exclusive. For example, he wants to be a great man (a great author, a wealthy Hollywood celebrity) pursued by beautiful women, but at the same time he wants to be an infant, cared for by his adoring mother. For this unenlightened protagonist, a response to the movie, like a moral response to the world itself, is filtered through his own self-centered desire, for he believes that his own fulfillment depends upon his ceaseless attempt to achieve his desires. His ignorant cognitions and not the film, then, produce his sorrow.

The protagonist's release (that is, his true enlightenment) would be only through revising his theory of reality to accept the world's emptiness—its impermanence, its radical contingency, and the futility of imposing his emotional requirements upon it. The theatre's screen is in fact "empty" in a Buddhist sense; as a blank screen, it denies the reality that the protagonist projects onto it. The protagonist's immense desire for permanence and stability is belied by the very fact that on the screen—and in the world too—the pictures really *are* "moving"; Johnson's title puns on his theme. Ironically, the lesson should be obvious for the protagonist when he discovers his "empty," vandalized car and how "empty" he feels (123). But "emptiness" in this context is not the paradoxical, Buddhist recognition of the world's fullness and the correlative opportunity to connect with other human beings. Instead, "emptiness" registers the protagonist's refusal to revise his understanding: he brings his "fists down again and again on the Fiat's roof" (124). His spirit-shattering sorrow results directly from his flawed understanding of himself. Of course, the protagonist may yet revise his theory of reality, since he is in charge of his life—"producer, star, director in the longest, most fabulous show of all" (124).

What must the protagonist do to be saved? To answer this question is to distinguish Johnson's ethical fiction from didacticism—a category of writing that Johnson in his interviews and essays disdains. A didactic author is preoccupied with the moral quality of specific actions and the inevitable conflict that arises from a fixed, rigid code of conduct of right versus wrong, good versus evil. But in "Moving Pictures," the protagonist is not an immoral man. In fact, the protagonist's willed conduct is not bad in and of itself. It is not wrong, for example, to write scripts for films (a vocation that on occasion Johnson has undertaken himself); to cry over sentimental movies; to drive a Fiat; or to have a beautiful wife, since some men necessarily marry beautiful women.

Johnson makes the reader understand that our basic ethical issue is different from the didactic concern over right versus wrong. If the protagonist's misery results directly from his self-centered desire, the *ultimate* cause of his suffering is his mistaken view of the self. Put simply, the protagonist must learn to "let go"—relinquish his emotional claims on the world by abandoning his insistence upon a permanent, reliable, resilient, and self-determining identity. To do so, to let go of his illusory self (which is like an internal moving picture), would lead, for Johnson, to an inner transformation that would change his habitual patterns of thought and action. In this sense, Johnson's idea of ethics is more than simply deciding what is right and what is wrong; it is a function of rightly knowing the world and changing one's character.

As Johnson's career evolves, he moves beyond the individualistic focus in "Moving Pictures" to what Thich Nhat Hahn would call "socially engaged Buddhism." In his later works—*Middle Passage* and *Dreamer* especially—Johnson also confronts a flawed theory of reality that leads to desire. Self-centered desire becomes objectified into institutions that need to be challenged collectively; a political system that institutionalizes greed and racism must be confronted on an institutional level as well as on a personal one. But in this "most fabulous show of all," too, Johnson's optimism encourages readers collectively to rewrite the script.

"Popper's Disease" (1982) elaborates Johnson's theme of morality as the function of character. Dr. Henry Popper, whose story is his own autobiography, reveals his dis-ease in writing a science fiction tale about confronting the Monster: a double of himself. Like the Monster, he also feels "the same primordial feeling of *thrownness* that every Negro experiences when hurled into a society that simultaneously supports and . . . annihilates him" (134). Popper invites the reader's suspicion of his status as narrator when he assures us, "I am the most reliable of men" (128), and his self-description bears out this suspicion.

On the surface, Dr. Popper seems to be a genuinely good human being, performing that rarest of medical operations: housecalls. Yet his self-commentary betrays the real motives behind this laudable service. Dr. Popper is burdened with a sense of his identity as an African-American professional. The only black student in his class at Harvard medical school, Harry married his wife Mildred not out of love, but out of self-vindication: "I so doubted myself it seemed miraculous that a woman as beautiful as Mildred, with her light voice and brilliant eyes, would have me" (134). Now, many years later, he is tired of his trophy wife, though he assures us she "still has her looks" (128). She, we discover in the story, has affairs while Dr. Popper is out on his housecalls. He is equally disenchanted with his position in the upper-middle-class, where his white neighbors "cautiously avoid the topic of race" (128). He attends compulsory neighborly "get-togethers," but complains, "I'm not sure I understand them, and sometimes I'm convinced they don't understand me" (129). Indeed, he infers that his neighbors see him (as W. E. B. Du Bois would say), as "a problem," determined by social forces, not by his own hard work and perseverance: "to ask, 'Who am I?' is to ask, 'By what social forces have I been shaped?' " (128). His altruistic housecalls to his patients, then, are revealed to be his way of avoiding his wife, his neighbors, and his possible self-discovery. He is doing the right thing by visiting his patients, but from Johnson's Buddhist perspective he is motivated less by his compassion for others than by his own desires—most notably, to escape a world he dislikes. Perhaps most important of all, Dr. Popper has entirely adopted the same Westernized, materialist "cultural assumptions" as his neighbors: "that history, for example, is linear, not circular, reason is preferable to emotion, and that one event 'causes' another" (129). Understandably, he is deeply unhappy, though his life has been marked by his unrelenting quest for materialist happiness.

Redemption is possible for Dr. Popper if he revises his theory of reality. He understands that there may be an alternative to the constricting social role he has adopted and the worldview he has accepted. For him, the solution may lie in accepting his African heritage that he wants to deny. He senses because of the African culture of his ancestors that there are other ways of imagining human identity and community besides the model of Western individualism: "My ancestors—or so I've read—had a hundred concepts for the African community, but none for the 'individual,' who, as we define him today—the lonely Leibnizean monad—is an invention of the Industrial Age, as romantic love is the product of medieval poets. My ancestors, I've also heard, were pre-Industrial and, therefore, are no test of reality" (134). Although he commits himself to saving only the body, he also senses that there is an "invisible realm of values and belief" that transcends the illnesses of the physical world but may play a part in producing physical illness.

Whether an actual experience or a nightmare, Henry's meeting the Monster forces him to confront his own evasions. The Monster tells Henry the truth about Henry's own existential illness: "It seems we are both strangers here" (141). The Monster is from a planet whose culture resembles Popper's ancestral African one, for in the Monster's culture, "Dualism was death" (144). In a strange reversal, the Monster plays the role of existential rebel on its planet, for it is dying because it has resisted its planet's healthy repudiation of dualism. It suffers from a terminal case of the "Plague," a disease that is more an epistemological disorder than a physical one. The Plague resembles Henry's Westernized worldview; the Plague has led the Monster to insist upon its unique self, its separation from "everything in [its] perceptual field," and a repudiation of literal, concrete meanings. These things outside the self, it tells Popper, "threaten to absorb me, engulf me, annihilate me completely, because I am, in a word, deeply and inexorably *different* from them" (138). As the Monster is dying, it reveals its own ontological solipsism, for Johnson the consequence of its own reluctance to revise its theory of reality. Its last words are, "the idea has just occurred to me that all phenomena are products of my ego" (142), including Popper himself.

The Monster's body disintegrates in death ("Thermogenesis"), and this event gives Popper the opportunity to meditate on his mortality. Henry may yet break down the self-enclosed, self-determining idea of the self that he and the Monster share, but which their dialogue belies. But Henry lacks compassion for the Monster, and he sees this opportunity to help the Monster only as a means of self-exaltation: "The Nobel Prize would be a *gift* to whoever diagnosed, then cured this uncanny disease. It was front-page stuff. Medical history, I hoped, might even rename it after me" (139). At the end of the story he is locked within the space ship and sealed off (just as the Monster was sealed off) in his world, confronting his own demons, his own buried but secretly exalted self. Popper gazes into the Telecipher, which tells the Monster's (and his own) disease: "*It's the Self* and *There is no cure*" (146). Ironically, Dr. Popper's cure may be in front of him, in the Telecipher, the Monster's television-machine that resembles the movie-theatre screen in "Moving Pictures." The Telecipher is Johnson's symbol for the Buddhist concept of emptiness: "Continuous in time, everywhere in space, the field was the idea of polymorphy made fact, its particles mere concretions of energy, as if Being delighted in playing hide-and-seek with itself, dressing up, so to speak, as Everything, then sloughed off particularities when bored with the game" (144–45). As Dr. Popper stares at the Telecipher, ironically cut off from the world he wished to escape anyway, he prepares to understand who he is and what he really wants for himself.

"THE PHILOSOPHY OF AS IF": JOHNSON'S PRAGMATISM IN ACTION

If in *The Sorcerer's Apprentice*, Johnson makes clear the metaphysical necessity of revising our theory of reality, in *Middle Passage*, he dramatizes what social effects may occur with such a revision. The book's setting is on board the ship *Republic* during a shipment of slaves from Africa to their enslavement in the United States. In this novel, Johnson links his theme of personal ethics to the question of America's national moral responsibility: how America's conduct may be performed with the corporate cooperation of its citizens, then constantly revised communally through time. The parallel between American history and a personal biography is inspired by the psychoanalytic theory of repression: that those important experiences (national and personal) which are buried cause "a lot of suffering."[5] Johnson's purpose is to relieve that suffering by exposing what is hidden, what is "beneath the deck" both nationally and personally. Johnson's view of history in this sense is fundamentally pragmatic. Knowledge of the past is important primarily as a means toward a greater end: improving the health of the present. Johnson stresses the freedom and power of the present to use the past, recognizing that the past is always, like the nation itself, a continuous creation in the present moment. In this way, history is a "useful fiction" as we Americans commit "to the business of rebuilding . . . the world" (*Oxherding Tale* 176).

"Useful fiction" is the novel's thematic organizing principle. When the *Republic* is about to go down, Johnson adopts the term when Rutherford Calhoun, the novel's protagonist, tells the fearful, crying child Baleka that all will be well. Though Rutherford has compulsively lied throughout the novel— "I always lied" (90)—this time his (presumed) falsehood has a "useful" significance, since it calms the child. Although he is certain that the *Republic* will sink,

Rutherford lies to Baleka. He explains that "the 'useful fiction' of this lie got the injured through the night and gave the children reason not to hurl themselves overboard" (162). As he reassures the child, Rutherford begins to believe the statement "all will be well" himself: "soon enough I came to desperately believe in it myself, for them I believed we would reach home, and even I was more peaceful" (163).

"Useful fiction" is a term created by Hans Vaihinger in *The Philosophy of "As If"* (1924); Vaihinger's philosophy of "as if" asserts that because we can never rest with ultimate truths, we create for pragmatic purposes partial truths (that is, "useful fictions"), imagined constructions of reality that help guide us in both science and day-to-day life. In Johnson's context, a "useful fiction" is a construction of the world that may not have an absolutely objective referential basis, but which nevertheless provides social guidance and understanding, and promotes compassionate conduct. We abide by this truth "as if" it were true to accomplish our tasks. In the novel, an "as-if" narrative about the world is evaluated in terms of how well it pragmatically satisfies the need for faith in humanity and hope for the future, both individual and collective, and to what degree it contributes to the community's survival. The term "useful fiction" should not be interpreted as the notion that all accounts of our experience are mere falsehoods. Not all fictions are of equal fictionality, and some are superior to others in promoting humane actions. Similarly, a "useful fiction" for Johnson does not denote a simple relativism that denies that any account of experience can be said to be better than any other. Instead, the term "fiction" denies that there exists some ultimate accounting of our world that would be literally true, some final story of our experiences that would conclusively and definitively explain our lives. At least for Baleka and Rutherford, all *is* well at the novel's end. Rutherford's "lie" turns out to be true.

Johnson understands that America needs useful fictions to transform our nation. It is essential to have a useful fiction of what happened in the past—a story that offers meaning and guidance, and provides hope for correction. Ironically, the creation of American history is most vividly fought out not by Americans, but by two Africans, Diamelo and Ngonyama. Each is engaged in making a history, as each captured African attempts to impose a particular and personal interpretation of their experiences. They create competing "useful fictions." Although they are philosophical rivals, they both equally suffer the evils on board during the Middle Passage. Each character is richly entitled to his outrage for what is happening to them, and they both plot the African uprising that concludes the novel. Both could present precisely the same history of the Middle Passage—abuse, humiliations, injustice, deprivation, kidnapping, torture, betrayal, murder. The way they conceptualize their experience, however, is very different; yet neither is "wrong" in the sense that they deliberately distort events or deceive others or themselves about what they have suffered. As Rutherford says about the Allmuseri, "each man had his atrocity to tell" (134). All Africans suffer the evil of slavery, and from Johnson's perspective, the real test of their accounting is not their history's referentiality to past events (very much the same kinds of atrocities), but in their pragmatic consequences for the present moment. The real question of their stories, then, is the "usefulness" of their "fictions"—the karmic possibilities of the faith and commitment their narratives may provide for others.

It is certainly accurate to understand Diamelo within a contemporary context. Jonathan Little writes that Diamelo represents "the late sixties' Black Power movement and contemporary beliefs in Afrocentrism" (Little 148). William Nash agrees: Diamelo represents "an extreme version of the fundamental principles of black cultural nationalism" (Nash 144). Both Little and Nash understand that Johnson opposes Diamelo's extremism. Yet Diamelo's story cannot be dismissed. Diamelo's accusations against the *Republic's* crew correlate with what the reader knows occurred during the Middle Passage, and the "American crimes perpetrated" on Africans on the *Republic* are verifiable historically (134). Diamelo has earned "the purity of his racial outrage" (153) with his own suffering. But in articulating the pain he has experienced, Diamelo cuts himself off from pragmatic action in the present. As Rutherford ruefully points out, "a champion must keep his dragon alive" (154). So it is that Diamelo, in his unceasing rage against those who hurt him, creates impractical—even impossible—rules for the survivors on the drifting ship. He insists that only Allmuseri may be spoken, and that only African maps and Allmuseri medicine may be used. Most impractical of all, the starving survivors were "to dine only on dishes familiar to the Allmuseri" (155). His history leads to no pragmatic benefit on the *Republic*. In fact, Diamelo is responsible for the *Republic's* sinking, when he misfires a cannon that bursts on deck and sets the ship afire. The symbolic point is clear: if the past is something to be pragmatically used to promote faith and encourage self-correction, Diamelo's history, dwelling on hatred and revenge, can lead only to America's destruction.

A wiser perspective seems to be offered by Ngonyama, who separates himself from Diamelo after the revolt. He, to use a Zen phrase, goes "beyond good and evil." Rather than insist on absolute and exact justice, Ngonyama pleads for Cringle's life. Ngonyama's generosity is Johnson's ethical comment on the

Allmuseri suffering on the *Republic*, and by extension on the history of slavery itself. One scene in particular presents Johnson's pragmatic view of American history. This moment occurs when Rutherford is ordered to assist in throwing overboard an Allmuseri corpse. In his ghastly description of the body, Rutherford notes that "the last stages of rigor mortis froze the body hunched forward in a grotesque hunker, like Lot's wife" (121). In throwing the body overboard, Rutherford becomes complicit in the slave trade; no longer uncommitted, he is tied forever to the evil of American history.

His complicity is symbolically expressed with a terrible stigma: a portion of the rotting leg comes off the African's body and stains Rutherford's hand. The stain, of course, is symbolic. Rutherford suddenly understands his entrapment in the system of slavery, and his own participation that stains him (unwillingly, both by his act and by his race). He raises his knife to cut off his stained hand—clearly a Scriptural allusion, "And if thy right hand offend thee, cut it off, and cast it from thee" (Matthew 5:30). But Ngonyama stops Rutherford from his self-mutilation. A wronged man himself, Ngonyama nevertheless forgives Rutherford for his involvement in the slave trade, and by stopping his self-mutilation encourages Rutherford's own self-forgiveness. He silently leads Rutherford to the rail, and says nothing (just as Johnson himself refrains from a moralistic commentary on racism). Instead, Ngonyama allows Rutherford to "decipher" his own interpretation of the event (124).

Unlike Diamelo, Rutherford supposes, Ngonyama understands the radical contingency of human experience. Expressing in his "empty" eyes (124) a compassionate understanding of Rutherford's context for his act, Ngonyama rescues Rutherford from his self-mutilation because he, unlike Rutherford, understands each action as entirely contingent. Ngonyama knows that Rutherford acts only within the context of his limited understanding of slavery and race, his callowness, and his lack of appreciation for the Allmuseri. Because Ngonyama is enlightened, he does not demand perfect retribution, but sees Rutherford's behavior is not self-determined. Rutherford's involvement in slavery originates dependent upon the universe of factors in his life—Rutherford's past, his youth, his race, his American citizenship. Thus, "like Lot's wife" (121), Rutherford must not look back and dwell constantly on his past evil; to do so would transform him into an object, as if he were a pillar of salt. His self-mutilation would pragmatically accomplish nothing. Nor, the reader is led to understand, can America—even in knowing the truth—dwell forever on *its* past evil, but must, using knowledge of it and its effects, change the present and work toward a better future. Rutherford realizes that can he do nothing to change the past.

Nor can he or anyone by themselves control the future. As he says, "the mills of the gods were still grinding, killing and remaking us all, and nothing I or anyone else did might stop the terrible forces and transformations our voyage had set free" (125). Instead, he can only become a better person, more committed to justice and mercy: "I cried for all the sewage I carried in my spirit, my failures and crimes, foolish hopes and vanities, the very faults and structural flaws in the blueprint of my brain" (127). History, if it has any meaning for the present, must lead to changing America's "structural flaws," slavery's baleful effects—among them, racism and discrimination. Individual change may not immediately transform America, just as Rutherford's eventual self-transformation does not save Ngonyama, who goes down with the ship. But Ngonyama dies at the helm, faithfully trying to guide the ship of state.

Among the Americans, Cringle initially resists spiritual transformation. Cringle begins by fearing the Allmuseri, "creatures that defy civilized law" (42), seeing them as the horrific Other. When the slave rebellion occurs, he defies the Allmuseri: "They'll see hell quicker'n they'll see help from me" (134). But his life is saved when Rutherford intercedes on his behalf, asking Ngonyama, "I ask you to make him *your* slave" (136). By actually living the life of a captured African, Cringle begins to understand through his own experience the suffering that the slaves had to endure, and though he attempts to steer the ship towards American ports, he fails because his cosmos is symbolically altered by his servitude: "The heavens are all wrong. That's what baffles me. They've not been in the right place" (158). Accordingly, he begins to revise his own theories of reality. His physical disorientation leads to a decision about what he must do to help the ship's community, since his "civilized laws" (42) are no longer his moral guide. As the ship drifts, his illness becomes worse, but he is capable of overcoming his concern for his own health. Instead, he accepts the necessity of cannibalism, presumably one of the "uncivilized" practices he formerly associated only with Africa, a "bottomless chaos" (42), but now the only pragmatic action to be taken for the benefit of others. He asks that both Americans and Africans eat him so that they can continue to live, in the hopes that they eventually are rescued by another ship.

Cringle's self-sacrificing transformation may represent a symbolic continuation of his civilized perspective, literally "in" Rutherford and the rest of the survivors.[6] Also, his selfless gesture implies in its imagery the Eucharist. However, the impact of Cringle's death is not primarily symbolic but emotional, for Johnson does not shield us from the horror of his death. In Squibb's recounting of the event, which takes place while Rutherford is unconscious,

Cringle instructs Squibb on knifing his vulnerable areas to kill him efficiently: the heart, the jugular vein, and "the soft flesh behind his ear, pokin' straight through the brain" (174). When the Allmuseri butcher Cringle's body, Squibb says, "it hit me, that I'd killed a man" (174). Fully confronting the horror of Cringle's death, the reader can only agree.

"CREATIVE TENSION": MARTIN LUTHER KING, JR., AS JOHNSON'S PROPHETIC PRAGMATIST

The historical King was not a "pragmatist" in the colloquial sense of the word. Indeed, Johnson in *Turning the Wheel* writes that the historical King in one of his speeches denounced " 'pragmatism' applied to questions of right and wrong" (xvi). Yet as John Whalen-Bridge has argued, Johnson's literary purpose is not to simply depict the historical King but to give us a contemporary moral guide. Nor, would I add, is Johnson concerned with "pragmatism" in its vernacular connotation. As we have seen in *Middle Passage*, Johnson evokes a more complex, highly nuanced view of pragmatism, consistent with Cornel West's concept of "prophetic pragmatism." West uses "prophetic" in the Old Testament sense, as in the prophet Elijah confronting a decayed society, seeking radical transformation by forthrightly exposing its moral failures. West, like Johnson throughout the novel, blends political engagement, philosophy, and religion, and they share a common interest in eclectic borrowing, so that any philosophical or religious tradition can help any other. In the novel, King is Johnson's own incarnation of "prophetic pragmatism."

In West's description of American pragmatism, a pragmatist always begins with profound faith, not doubt or skepticism. This faith is held firmly despite the world's radical lack of certainty. Because the world is constantly evolving, there is no absolute principle to be adhered to rigidly, nor is there some underlying, presocial rule in which an ethical person can take refuge. In a world of constant change, there cannot be a recourse to an absolute source of moral truth; instead, ethical action must reflect, according to West, an "experiential" method. An experiential method, as West notes, is "self-correcting," always open to revisions; and it is "communal," for the view of reality it operates on is centered in a community of opinions, a consensus contingent on whatever is known or capable of being known. Our ethical action—as individuals, as a community, and as a nation—is a result of our experiential knowledge, which is necessarily "revisable" (51) as we continually learn that our picture of the world is only partial.

Thus, even the most hallowed religious or moral principles are only assumptions of truth, to be validated by testing and by experience. Johnson in *Turning the Wheel* argues that this pragmatic turn is embraced by the American political structure itself: "America was founded on principles, ideals, and documents . . . that forced it to be forever self-correcting" (*Turning* 173). West writes, "ultimately, convergence and agreement among scientists will disclose reality. Of course, such ultimate agreement never comes; it is simply a regulative ideal and a hope" (51). "Centrality of contingency," West argues, is at the center of American pragmatism. Abstract moral principles like religious or secular laws may offer a guide, but these may be forsaken in specific circumstances. As we saw in *Middle Passage*, suicide, murder, euthanasia, and cannibalism all have precedence over adherence to Cringle's "civilized" principles, given a scrupulous decision that principle in certain circumstances must be overruled. For both Cringle and Squibb, rigid boundaries of personal conscience dissolve in desperate decisions of what must be saved and what lost. These terrible decisions provide the answer to Squibb's hard question, "What was the limit of bein' human?" (*Middle Passage* 174).

In this way for West, prophetic pragmatism is always based on human values, and the "prophetic pragmatist" courageously founds all action upon those human values. Human initiative can transform the world, but such action, issuing from the character of the actor, should have consequences that are equitable, compassionate, and altruistic for the world. But because all knowledge of an action's results are *ex post facto*, the pragmatist must carefully examine all possibilities before any action can be taken, and even then the pattern of action can only be performed in faith and belief. Choosing the moral pattern (Dharma) is always a risk and a struggle; in fact, our only certainty is that we will never be entirely successful in our undertaking, and we may be entirely wrong. Johnson's King makes choices in the context of his faith, but for him, choosing is a terrifying risk, and there are no guarantees that his choice is the correct one. Johnson's aesthetic task in *Dreamer* is to give a sense of King's existential dilemma on a national stage during the 1960s, which may not be immediately clear to a reader in 1998 (*Dreamer*'s publication date). It may be difficult for a reader to recover imaginatively King's formidable obstacles, since King has been sanitized and made devoid of any radical perspectives on American society.[7] He has been turned into the archetypal "nice man." In the novel, however, Johnson portrays a King who is willing to coerce society to undergo the pain of revising itself. In terms of the novel's organizing Scriptural allusion, King is a "paradoxical fusion of Cain and Abel" (125).

King is as much the Cain figure as he is the Abel. He is, of course, "Abel," the accepted, middle-class avatar of virtue that, in Whalen-Bridge's words, "is very much a bodhisattva dedicated to the idea of healing-through-integration" ("Waking Cain" 504). But as a Cain figure, King is also like an Old Testament prophet, for he knows that a spiritual revolution is needed to reverse discrimination, end injustice, and promote a life worth living for all people. To bring his nation to the bitter recognition of moral failure, King must, like Christ, "come to send fire on the earth" (13, Luke 12:49). King must inflict emotional suffering on his fellow (white) citizens with "creative tension," allowing the "long-buried hatreds to surface, where they were exposed for the world to see." As Matthew explains, "King's philosophy not withstanding, 'creative tension' was an act of violence, the murder of a repressive past so that a new order— God's order—could be born" (125).

Johnson's phrase "creative tension" is derived from King's famous "Letter from Birmingham Jail," written on 16 April 1963 while King was incarcerated for civil disobedience in Birmingham, Alabama. In the "Letter," he admonishes those whites who agreed with the aims of the Civil Rights Movement but who opposed King's breaking laws. He criticizes those "who constantly [say], 'I agree with you in the goal you seek, but I cannot agree with your methods' " (King, "Letter" 91). As West's "prophetic pragmatist" would understand (and as King argues in the "Letter"), the "methods" are essential. Those who criticize him are the people, King implies, for whom property rights, laws, and social order (all absolute, abstract principles) are more important than the lived-through, prolonged suffering of African Americans. These people are not necessarily evil, but they value abstract principles over the welfare of others. King makes his indictment clear with a graphic image of a pierced boil:

> We who engage in nonviolent direct action are not the creators of tension. We merely bring to the surface the hidden tension that is already alive. We bring it out into the open where it can be seen and dealt with. Like a boil that can never be cured so long as it is covered up but must be opened with all its pus-flowing ugliness to the natural medicines of air and light, injustice must be exposed, with all the tension its exposure creates, to the light of human conscience and the air of national opinion before it can be cured. ("Letter" 91)

The purpose of King's civil disobedience was to reveal the partly concealed disorder and injustice to whites so that it might be corrected. He rejected opposing violence with violence, since the karmic fruit of such action would be rotten: it would only continue the cycle of suffering and retribution. He understood that social change could only occur when the light shone on darkness and people became ashamed of living in darkness—fear, guilt, bigotry, and the refusal to allow a whole population of Americans to receive their due rights.

Shining the light on evil and piercing the boil of racial injustice, Johnson understands, is painful. Johnson's King is willing, nevertheless, to commit "the murder of a repressive past" (125). For his goal, justice for all, he looks beyond the abstract principles held by those who criticized him, and he brings terrific emotional pain to those who would retain the status quo. In King's aggressive civil disobedience, Johnson fuses the offerings of Cain and Abel because his political activism draws attention to the hateful consequences of static laws. Yet for Johnson, King's "creative tension" is an optimistic social practice, for its faith is that America, despite its past of slavery and racial oppression, is worth fighting for.

In this fight, it is the revolutionary potential of King's faith that inspires and supports him. Johnson shows that it was certainly not obvious in King's time that provoking the reactions of bigots, lancing the boil of national lies, was the best way ultimately to achieve justice. As Whalen-Bridge writes, King "comes to symbolize painful division" ("Waking Cain" 505) even among those closest to him, since even his advisors debate the wisdom of his strategy. On the face of it, his strategy *does* seem unwise. King insists that white people might have to work against their own immediate interests for a greater social good; that they would have to experience temporary pain to achieve less suffering in the future. But King's faith leads him to believe that people of all races live both deeply and shallowly, with multiple allegiances rather than a single allegiance to themselves, and with unconscious commitments to a future life as well as rudimentary concerns for the present. In Johnson's novel, King's faith is that people can change, and that his advisors are wrong. He believes that after his shining the light, people could forgive themselves and one another, make a new start, and join the "beloved community."

Johnson dramatizes the alternative to King's "prophetic pragmatism" in the radical Yahya Zubena's complete absence of faith. Matthew and Amy return to Chicago to attend a lecture given by Zubena at the Black People's Liberation Library. As Nash points out, Zubena is probably based on Eldridge Cleaver (*Charles Johnson's Fiction* 186), and Nash is correct when he writes that Johnson "makes that mouthpiece morally repugnant and intellectually limited" (*Charles Johnson's Fiction* 187). In his lecture, Zubena points to a map of Chicago and, demarcating the areas where African Americans live, he claims that segregation is actually a plot to "contain" the race in case of race-war: "Being concentrated like that means when y'all start rebelling against your miserable conditions . . . all Charlie's got to do is move his tanks and trucks and National Guard troops right down the freeways and Illinois Central tracks to your front door" (172). Zubena requires retaliation. Matthew dismisses Zubena's polemic of hate as "*kitsch*. Revolutionary *kitsch*" (174).

Yet in the mid-1960s, Zubena's diatribe could not have been so glibly dismissed, and Johnson encourages readers to exercise their historical imagination and evoke the 1960s. This was a period, after all, when four African-American children were blown up in a Birmingham church during Sunday School, and civil rights leaders like Medgar Evers were shot in the back late at night as they walked to their front door. In this terrifying time, it certainly was not so obvious that Zubena's call for violent, armed resistance is "kitsch"; in fact, it could have been a provisional "truth"—perhaps a "useful fiction." Johnson makes this interpretation of Zubena possible by showing that it was shared in its time; he grounds the scene in African-American literature of the 1960s, implying that Zubena's political accusations were plausible on some level. As Matthew enters the outer room to hear Zubena's lecture, he notices "a row of works by Chester Himes" (170), an allusion to Himes's novels published during the 1960s about race wars (for example., *Blind Man with a Pistol* and the posthumously published *Plan B*). And Zubena's seemingly paranoiac prediction of African Americans held in concentration camps is an allusion to the genocidal "King Alfred Plan" in John A. Williams's hugely successful novel *The Man Who Cried I Am* (1967). Zubena, then, makes a case that may seem outrageous for a 1998 reader, but that during the 1960s was not entirely unbelievable.

Johnson encourages the reader to ask, what would have been the pragmatic consequence of Zubena's violent philosophy as opposed to King's prophetic pragmatism? Thankfully, through the efforts of King and people like him, the bloodshed and suffering of a race war were averted; Johnson's novel emphasizes King's struggle against not only racist whites, but also violently militant blacks. Nevertheless, in essays Johnson reminds us of the legacy of Zubena's absence of faith. In "The King We Left Behind," Johnson argues that radicals of the 1960s represented by Zubena (such as Cleaver, Huey Newton, and Malcolm X) "are the true spiritual fathers of today's Crips and Bloods" (195). And in *Turning the Wheel*, Johnson (employing specifically the terminology of pragmatism) asserts the immorality of a lack of vision: "*the social payoff* of this grim perception [of victimization], particularly when it smothers all others in a fiction (or life), is . . . immoral. We are responsible for the way the world appears before us, for its depth and richness (if we are open to others) or its poverty (if we are not), and for the impact our vision has on others" (158, emphasis added). Zubena lacks faith and a vision of a life worth living. In contrast, Johnson's King (and the historical King too) lives in faith. Sensing his life might soon end, King chooses Christ who walked before him, suffering for the sake of righteousness, justice, and love. Johnson's novel vividly presents King's example to us, and the force of his writing makes obligatory our love for others. Johnson lets us understand that it is our shame that during these three decades, we have let King down. But Johnson reminds us that each moment we have an opportunity to garner the "social payoff" of spiritual change; that justice and equality are superior to any immediate profit; that love is stronger than death.

King's appeal was for social justice in the United States. His faith was that America could eventually transform itself, but not easily and not without sacrifices—even the sacrifice of his life, taken by the forces of hatred he worked ceaselessly to combat. As a student of King and as a philosopher, Johnson senses that William James and Cornel West are right: that people like King, who are called upon to perform great deeds, must depend not only on a calculus of probable consequences of an action. They, like King, must have bountiful faith, "the substance of things hoped for, the evidence of things unseen" (Hebrews 11:1). This faith in humanity seems unrealistic today, perhaps as much as it did in the 1960s. But Johnson's ultimate purpose is to create King as a moral model for all American citizens. King represents a person who understands that America's social and legal structures and its official consciousness must be utterly transformed by scrupulously moral means, all to be accomplished without despairing or despising the habits of the human heart.

NOTES

1. The argument of this essay draws upon the ideas and concepts expressed in my recent book on Johnson, *Understanding Charles Johnson* (University of South Carolina Press, 2004). For more developed readings of the specific passages in this study, see the following pages of that book: 18–21, 97–100, 136–39, 152–58, 186–94.

2. Technically, "morality" refers to the actual content of right and wrong, while "ethics" refers to the process an individual or a community undergoes (usually cognitive, but often intuitive) in determining right from wrong. Ethics has a long history in philosophy and involves making precise distinctions, though it is an inexact discipline. "Morality" is the result of this arduously complex ethical deliberation. Because of the philosophically relaxed, less restrictive tone of this interdisciplinary essay, the terms "morality" and "ethics" will be used interchangeably.

3. Johnson's approach to ethics resembles "virtue-based ethics," which argues that the proper domain for ethicists is the evaluation of whole persons (as opposed to specific acts, called "act-based ethics"). Act-based ethics is predominant in contemporary philosophy, while virtue-based ethics is more closely associated with ancient philosophy. Emphasizing virtue-based ethics, Johnson's ethics may be considered Aristotelian; a contemporary philosopher who also calls for a return to the classical understanding of ethics is Alisdair MacIntyre.

4. For perhaps the definitive treatment of Buddhist "emptiness," see Streng, *Emptiness: A Study in Religious Meaning*.

5. In an interview, Johnson explains that his artistic purpose in *Middle Passage* is partly therapeutic: "Most of [African American] history is not known, and that's where we get assumptions, prejudices, and misinformation, which causes a lot of suffering. Literature can address some of that" (Levasseur and Rabelais, 265).

6. Molly Travis, for example, calls the cannibalism scene an "intersubjective encounter" (80).

7. See Johnson, "The King We Left Behind" 194.

INVISIBLE THREADS
Charles Johnson and Feminine Civility

JOHN WHALEN-BRIDGE

In this essay I would like to make the case for a kind of feminism in Johnson's work, a feminism that makes visible foundational feminine virtues within African American culture in part by revealing the effects of strong women and in part by rendering the misogynism against which this feminism defines itself. My argument runs against the grain of most though not all work on Johnson. While critics focusing on racial hybridity in Johnson's work have celebrated his integrationalist aesthetic (Little and Storhoff), those who have focused on gender have more often found Johnson's fiction unsatisfactory.[1] Some even draw on terms such as "misogyny" to characterize his plots and comedic stratagems, such as when Travis contrasts Johnson with Toni Morrison to highlight Johnson's exclusion of women as evidence of sexism.[2] Travis reports that "most women with whom I have spoken" about *Middle Passage* (1990) "claim they feel disconnected from the narrative circle because the novel almost totally excludes female characters" (194).[3] Writings by Johnson and Morrison have been frequently compared, and the majority opinion is that Johnson is from Mars, Morrison from Venus.[4]

Less cited and more recent scholars have found the differences between the two authors less important than the similarities. Rushdy's "Properties of Desire" finds that Morrison and Johnson both create works of art that enshrine love (73–75), and Storhoff and Byrd (2005) also emphasize similarities over differences.[5] Whether or not Johnson is masculinist relative to Morrison, I argue that Johnson is a "masculinist" author only in the limited sense that he has, in every novel since *Faith and the Good Thing* (1974), anchored his own struggle to build a fictional world to the imaginings of an incomplete, struggling African-American male character. This narratological limitation could, were one generously inclined, be called "epistemological humility."[6] I would go further, though, and assert an "invisible" feminist undercurrent within Johnson's work, one which is nowhere more evident than in his most recent novel *Dreamer* (1998). Like *Oxherding Tale* (1982), *Middle Passage*, and almost all of the stories of *The Sorcerer's Apprentice* (1988), *Dreamer* develops the quest for wholeness of a young black man, a development that depends to no small extent on his willingness to incorporate values that are widely considered feminine. *Dreamer* is a pilgrim's progress in which the central character, Matthew Bishop, must learn to integrate the ideals of masculinity with the ideals of femininity. Our understanding of Matthew's progress bears on our understanding not only of Matthew or the wider world of black America; rather, Johnson's parable offers lessons applicable to the whole of American culture.

Dreamer has in some ways been an invisible novel.[7] The hardcover first edition of *Dreamer* has a beautiful cover portraying a thoughtful-looking black man whom we assume to be Martin Luther King, Jr., but the image might just as well be King's fictional look-a-like Chaym Smith—*either* way, the person on the cover seems to be the primary subject of the novel, but readers are misled by this appearance, since the novel actually concerns the experiences, perceptions, and growth of Matthew Bishop.[8] This essay will, at the risk of committing Cubism, track Matthew's development by grouping his experiences in the novel into five aspects. First, I argue that Johnson *engenders* the invisibility metaphor of Ralph Ellison, developing Matthew's mother Ellesteen as an "Invisible Woman."[9] Second, I show how Matthew's lack of wholeness follows directly from his own decreasing capacity to "see" his deceased mother, which also signifies his increasingly tenuous grasp upon the communal values she continues to represent in his mind. Third, Matthew finds himself in crisis at the novel's beginning—a crisis that parallels the difficulties Martin Luther King experiences in his ambitious efforts to enlarge the meaning of the civil rights movement. Because he experiences himself as weak and increasingly marginal, and because the rise of Black Power defines his whole mode of existence in terms of emasculation, Matthew is tempted by macho styles of political engagement. His crisis deepens, as political machismo is the antithesis of what his mother stood for. Fourth, Matthew retreats to the Nest with Amy and Chaym. This capacity to retreat and rethink is exactly what is missing from Martin Luther King's life, as his crushing schedule will allow no such extended periods of reflection and reconsideration; while in the Nest, Amy rehearses her family history, detailing the lives of the Evanston black community. This period of retreat allows Matthew to see the invisible world of black America in a way he was not able to previously and thus is essential to Matthew's development. Finally, I examine the possibility that Johnson's progressive and egalitarian sexual politics have largely been misunderstood precisely because he has been keeping faith with a key "Evanstonian" value, namely the belief in the priority of spirituality over politics—which is in no way a denial of political responsibility. A careful understanding of this priority—one that puts reflection and patience before action, however necessary that action—will enable us to see the invisible feminism of Johnson's work.

Johnson's representations of race and gender are shot through with signs (if not representations) of Ellison's "invisibility" metaphor. It may seem like a mixed metaphor, but we must begin by recognizing that invisibility, in *Dreamer*, is a multi-leveled phenomenon. Ellison's *Invisible Man* receives several nods of recognition in Johnson's novel, such as when Chaym opens a can of "Optic White" paint (181). "Invisibility" in Ellison's novel of course refers to seeing a body without seeing a person; a racist person, circumscribed by stereotypical preconceptions, fails to recognize humanity and individuality in that body. Racist thinking and sexist thinking are the obvious causes of invisibility, but Johnson develops the invisibility metaphor in two further ways in *Dreamer* when he narrates what might be called "classist invisibility," in two very different senses. First, Chaym is uncomfortable with middle class blacks and is envious of their relative visibility: "God loves these Negroes!" he exclaims, as lower-class Cain looks with anger at middle-class Abel. But "classist" also extends beyond economic and sociological categories and leads to a second kind of invisibility. Martin Luther King is in a *class* by himself, and Chaym resents being outclassed by King. The power of King's performance, despite what Chaym might think when he comments on God's love for middle class blacks, is not merely due to class privilege. Illustrious figures like King receive attention, while the significance of lesser people tends to be overlooked, and Matthew would be a case in point. Many characters within the King circle feel themselves to be invisible compared to the great man himself, especially the novel's narrator Matthew. He does not personally resent King (as does Chaym in the first half of the novel), but Matthew is aware that people hear "movement" and think "King," whereas there are numerous unrecognized foot soldiers who make King possible.

A third kind of invisibility that Johnson develops is the inability to recognize King himself. Like Ellison's Invisible Man, King is all too visible on the American scene, and everyone in the novel is focused on him, but Charles Johnson complains, both within the pages of *Dreamer* and without, that King's superficial appeal receives attention while his radical criticisms of American society are ignored. Johnson makes exactly this complaint in his essay "The King We Left Behind." In contrast to the hagiographic superficiality of America's celebration of Martin Luther King's birthday each year, *Dreamer* as a work of art provides readers with the structured experiences that help correct our failure to understand the contributions of women to the civil rights movement and to the creation of

Beloved Community more generally, but any reader would quickly have to admit that the novel proceeds from an androcentric story-world. That is to say, women are largely background figures: they play supporting roles to male actors. While King is enduring death threats, his "wife and children were staying at the home of Mahalia Jackson until the shooting died down" (21). This tiny sketch of the King family perhaps foreshadows King's funeral, at which women will sing and mourn.[10] The overwhelming emphasis of the narrative frame—Martin Luther King's life and Matthew's meditations about it—brings us largely into a world inhabited and controlled by men. The visible surface of *Dreamer* is an androcentric one, and it is one of the paradoxes of invisibility that Johnson understates the role of women in the changes that occur within Matthew's psyche.

Beneath the novel's androcentric surface is another narrative, one concerning the women who are "invisible" to history but who are consistently celebrated in *Dreamer*. Of special importance is Matthew's own mother, Ellesteen Bishop, who is presented not merely as an interesting background figure in King's movement, but rather as a person who is *necessary* to that movement. Readers familiar with the novel may remember that Matthew thinks of her on one occasion early in the book, but she actually appears nearly a dozen times and is arguably the thread that holds all the narrative parts together.

Matthew's mother is the Invisible Woman, the secret center of *Dreamer*. She is very much the unsung hero, and Matthew's increasingly attenuated relation to her memory leaves him feeling depleted: "History knew nothing of Ellesteen Bishop. Since her death it was as if she had never lived, and now only existed in memory, in me during those times when I thought of her, which were less and less each year, and when I ceased to be, it seemed to me, all vestiges of her would vanish as well. (Often I tried to reconstruct her face, and found I could not remember, say, her ears. How could I forget my mother's ears?)" (26). Ellesteen is invisible to everyone but Matthew, and her image recedes even to his mind's eye. That we only know about Ellesteen Bishop through her son Matthew, who experiences himself as an invisible man, of sorts, one "so anonymous most people forgot I was there" (25), doubles her negation.

The ways in which his mother's identity have been historically negated are directly related to Matthew's own sense of lack. His own anonymity and his mother's invisibility are frequently linked: as a foot-soldier in King's *satyagraha* army, Matthew is running dangerously low on morale, and King forgets his name and tells him flat out that he is "replaceable" in the struggle against racism. Much of what is deficient in Matthew can be traced back to the loss of his mother. When King asks him, "You're in school, then?" Matthew replies,

"I was . . . until last year. I left when my mother passed" (27). Matthew never knew his father and has just lost his mother, and he is in some ways treading water at this time in his life.

The pain of Matthew's loss is compounded by the fact that his mother was his primary connection to faith, and so his self-doubt has multiplied with her passing: "I fumbled through my coat, hoping I still had the three-by-four-inch copy of the King James Bible, a gift long ago from my mother, which I carried as a kind of talisman for times of trouble, or just to study when I rode the subway. Not that I really felt much anymore when I fingered the Book's tissue-thin pages. Try as I might, I no longer could breathe life into the vision the Bible embodied—or, for that matter, into any system of meaning" (53–54). The context of this meditation is most significant: Matthew tries to help someone in a riot who, in turn, almost kills him. He naively calls a man "brother," and the man responds by trying to split his head open. It is a moment of supreme disillusion, about which earthier-than-thou Chaym gloats. Matthew's loss of faith is contrasted directly with his mother's never-failing faith, which is not just a Christian faith, but also, it would seem, a belief in the promises and potentials of liberal America. Matthew is struck especially by the place of King in her imagination: "In her mind, the minister was a saint. She'd kept his portrait right besides those of Jesus and John Fitzgerald Kennedy. . . . More than anything I wanted to help the Movement that had meant so much to her, to do something for *him*, since I was, as I said, a man of no consequence at all" (26). Thus, Matthew is connected to King primarily because of his feelings for his mother. It is a continuing, functional link, and not just an historical accident, as Matthew continues to operate from a second-hand religious and even political faith. This second-hand faith, however, has severe limitations. Matthew attempts to pray at several junctures, especially when Chaym is shot by a man who believes him to be Martin Luther King, but he is completely unable to. Though Chaym and Ellesteen Bishop are as different as any two characters Johnson has written about, they become connected at those moments when Matthew attempts to pray, for he is unable to pray (in his mother's way) precisely because he shares Chaym's doubts about prayer—Chaym doubts that *his* prayers matter, relative to other prayers. Praying that Chaym might survive, Matthew thinks about his attempts to pray as his mother died: ". . . he did not answer when I whispered his name; he remained as remote and unreachable as my mother had been when she was dying in a hospital bed at Cook County and I stayed beside her cooling body night and day. . . . I prayed . . . I begged the god she'd given me when I was a child to return to me whole the only person in this world who'd cared if I lived or died, but He did not accept the offering of my tears . . ." (149). While Matthew cannot partake of Chaym's ruthless cynicism and so cannot draw any sort of power from Chaym's adamant unbelief, he nonetheless shifts into what might be called a "Cainite" viewpoint after his mother's death, since he believes God does not answer his prayers. Perhaps it would be better to say that he is *in danger of* adopting a Cainite resentment about his gifts not being properly valued. Only in one scene (the "Pit Stop" incident) does Matthew indulge in the sort of anger that characterizes so much of Chaym's activity in the novel.

Matthew, however, rarely acts out in the manner of Chaym, and in part this is because of the "Victorian" personality that survives his loss of belief: "An old fuddy-duddy at (now) age twenty-five when American culture in the mid-'60s was becoming so fluid . . . I was cursed with a shy, Victorian personality" (164). Matthew lacks masculine charisma, especially compared to Chaym, and this, it seems to him at the time, is why Amy rejects him. Matthew Bishop and Martin Luther King both are criticized within the novel for being less masculine than they ought to be; both are charged with having relatively *effeminate* approaches to racial suffering. Chaym admonishes Matthew for his lack of masculine credentials: "You ain't never gonna have fame or fortune. Maybe not even a girl. I'll bet you ain't had pussy since pussy had you. When you die, it'll be like you never lived" (65). Ridiculing Matthew's lack of masculine self-possession and self-assertion, Chaym explicitly assesses Matthew in terms of his sexual experience, all the while laying out his own credentials in the form of a richly antagonistic and ribald speech that Matthew at one point calls "*niggerese.*" One can be a fumbling Victorian fuddy-duddy and not get the girl or, Matthew's experiences suggest, one can talk like Chaym and perhaps have more success. Johnson's King says, after first meeting his magical doppelganger, "you keep that man away from my wife, you hear?" (43). This sentence also shows King's recognition that Chaym's angry, embittered style is *sexy* in the way that *satyagraha* is not. Matthew, thus, is a character in search of wholeness, and the choices available to him are, at the novel's beginning, quite scarce. King is kind to him but has very little time for him, his mother meant everything to him but is now gone . . . and then Chaym—the antithesis of his mother's civilized, feminine manners—shows up at the door asking to replace Martin Luther King as a body-double.

While Chaym Smith never aligns himself directly with Black Power, he does represent some of the dangers of what may be called "toxic masculinity," a repressive mode that can thrive in the soil of either macho individualism or the more communal Black Nationalism as exemplified in the novel by Yahya Zubena. Chaym, speaking as either a friend or a tempter, says, "You interest me, Bishop. You've got promise" (43). Since his mother died, no one besides Chaym has pushed Matthew into a fully-embodied engagement with ideas and or has applauded his development.[11] Chaym Smith, who differs from Ellesteen Bishop in so many ways, resembles her in one key way: he takes a personal interest in Matthew's well-being. He calls him "Bishop."

When Amy and Matthew drive Chaym south to "the Nest" to take him away from the pressures of the city and perhaps prepare him to double as Martin Luther King, the group makes a stop at a greasy spoon called the "Pit Stop," where they come across a casually racist waitress named Arlene. (She refers at one point to "Martin Luther Coon.") Ordinarily, someone like Matthew would ignore racist slights or provocative behavior in the disciplined manner required by Gandhi and King of "truth-force" workers, but Chaym seems to be exerting an influence on Matthew, albeit one Matthew might not consciously recognize. As his anger at Arlene's attitude increases, he remembers "that my mother's expression was sad but stoic as she looked into the distance with her chin lifted, both hands folded in front of her, and I saw that for me she would suffer a thousand indignities and denials of her personhood so that I would not go hungry, dying this way everyday, one little piece at a time" (72).[12] Chaym's indulgent anger and Ellesteen's sad stoicism are antithetical responses, but it would seem Matthew must confront and admit the anger Chaym insists runs beneath the surface before Matthew can proceed beyond it—part of Matthew's progress involves moving through such apparently regressive stages.

As Matthew's anger builds up, so does the image of his mother in his mind; she functions almost as a kind of superego instruction, staying his hand as he becomes increasingly impatient with the unmindful Arlene: "My belly was still knotted. I'd wanted to slap her, but I remembered how my mother told me to behave in public, and how polite and civilized and patient the minister was himself—always a credit to the race—when confronting white people with an I.Q. the size of their shoes" (71). Associated with his mother are the ideas that one must be patient in the face of provocation and, especially, the pressure to be a "credit to the race." To be a "credit" of this sort requires the inhibition of his anger, and it is noteworthy that this ethos is constantly associated not only with King but with Matthew's mother: to be a "credit" in this way is to voluntarily surrender a portion of his manhood, to be a mama's boy.

The deepening awareness of his mother's humiliation and sacrifice takes Matthew to a deeper place, one more Dionysian than he ordinarily could go.

Matthew keeps control of himself until the moment when Arlene puts change on the counter rather than make physical contact by putting it in his palm: "I thrust my palm toward her for the coins, and had perfect control of myself, the magnanimity and external calm my mother had insisted upon, and which the Movement's leaders so nobly embodied, until she slapped the money on the counter, and something inside me (I don't know what) snapped (I don't know how), flooding me with hatred so hot, like a drug, I was nearly blinded by it as I threw the food in her face" (73). Chaym is delighted: " 'You left her toasted, roasted, and with an apple in her mouth. It was choice' " (73). In the next chapter, italicized to signify that it is a part of King's inner world that Matthew could not know directly, King *wondered if the Negro church would ever be more Apollonian, as intellectually respectable as it was Dionysian and emotionally intense*" (79). Chapters three and four, counter-pointing Matthew's Pit Stop against King's prayer and memory of his "Kitchen Conversion" experience (83), may signal an ironic juxtaposition, or maybe that Matthew needs a conversion of sorts—a more Dionysian one—before he can make genuine progress. Amy tells Matthew at one point that he talks "like a damned thesaurus" (150). Matthew feels ashamed after his emotional outburst "as if I'd failed the minister, my mother, my self," but Chaym cackles and compares him to " 'William F. Buckley on bad acid' " (74).

Throughout this episode, Matthew thinks constantly of his mother, of "the memory of trips my mother and I made to visit relatives in South Carolina" (71) in which they had to go to the back doors of restaurants for food because of Jim Crow laws and practices. His explosive anger shows the cost of being black in a racist society and the difficulty of maintaining a stoic response, but the scene is hardly an advertisement for anger. What can be said for sure is that Matthew knows the temptations of violent anger firsthand after the Pit Stop, whereas his previous experiences (*sans* Chaym), his ideas, and responses are all somewhat second-hand, like alternative words plucked from a thesaurus.

Chaym expresses nothing but disdain for the values represented by well-behaved, patient African Americans such as Matthew's mother. When Amy starts to recount with pride the achievements of her family and the black community of which they formed an important part, "Smith responded to Amy's family history with a contemptuous *pfft!* from his pursed lips" (89). Chaym has no use for the quiet, proud-yet-humble Negro tradition of the Griffith family. When it seems he will finally get a chance to address a church full of King's followers, he says to Matthew and Amy, "Everything here seems so . . . *finished.* God loves these Negroes. What do I *say* to them?" (130). Matthew shouts

"Nothing!" signifying the voicelessness of the Chaym Smiths in this middle class world. Chaym is uncomfortable with polish, finish, finery: in a word, "grace." It is a relatively feminine quality.

Chaym fills the void left by Matthew's mother, at least temporarily, which is not to say he is similar to her in any respect. One quality they share, Matthew realizes, is bitterness. To understand Chaym's Cainite bitterness, we must remember that he has attempted, against great odds, to forge domestic happiness, but his attempt to make a home for the prostitute Juanita and her sons fails miserably: "The near hysteria he felt when he realized his life was a nightmare, a ghastly joke on everything he once dreamed of becoming" (38). He probably murders Juanita but cannot remember. Chaym, suffering from partial amnesia, finds himself in the middle of a nightmare that is in every sense the antithesis of King's "I Have a Dream" idealism. These events happen in 1963, the year of the Kennedy assassination and thus the year in which many Americans stopped believing in American national innocence. Chaym's situation figures the troubled state of African-American families—those outside of the protected vale of the middle class. Chaym, like Matthew Bishop, is a fatherless man, hence his contempt for Amy's proud recitations of her family's values. He compensates for this failure with fierce cynicism and combative humor, and he develops the Cainite worldview as a way to accommodate his abject sense of himself. Matthew summarizes Chaym's position this way: "Outcasts, I'd learned from Chaym (though perhaps he failed at this himself), learned not to ask for much, yet were there if the Abelites were in need" (123). "Cainite" outcasts feel inferior and are "wannabes" who will never fit in, and the appropriate response, to Chaym, is to have no illusions about the nature of the (dog eat dog) world. Chaym's worldview offers a temptation: protect oneself from the risk of disappointment with preemptive bitterness. Chaym, it must be noted, is a complex character—he is not *only* a Cainite, murderous, drug-using man, but he has, at times, fallen from his highest potential into the "pit" of anger, and he consequently distills a worldview Matthew ultimately rejects, as does Chaym himself.[13]

Angry pride of the sort Matthew demonstrates in the Pit Stop becomes an important factor in Martin Luther King's decline in *Dreamer*, as those who have become impatient with his patient, Gandhian approach seek out more macho alternatives. King's compromise "Summit Agreement" is not manly enough: "To their eyes, the Summit Agreement was a sellout. . . . Many proclaimed they were tired of being led by middle-class Negroes and rejected the Agreement terms. A new black cat was on the scene, they said, represented by the fierce black masculinity of Stokely, who told it like it was—and by ex-cons in the Black Panther Party" (152). King is being outflanked on the masculinity front. Forced by political weakness into unsatisfactory compromise, his political capital plummets. The criticisms of his movement and its methods spike up. His weakness is associated with "middle-class" communities, whereas the primary opponents of his ways are associated with macho gangsterish types. In attacking King, the rising Black Pride movement is thus attacking middle-class, feminine values. The rise of Black Pride values are at the expense of the "Negro values" embodied by Matthew's mother and Amy's Evanston relatives. With these changes, figures of moderation such as King are called "Uncle Tom," as his way of compromise and non-violence is branded less masculine than Stokely Carmichael's macho alternative.[14]

The temptations of hyper-masculinity extend throughout the novel and peak in the portrait of the black nationalist Yahya Zubena, who seems to be a fictionalized version of Eldridge Cleaver.[15] Speaking to an all-black audience, he brags of "rape, *dozens* of rapes" before "he moved on to assault white women" (168). As Cleaver brags about rape as a political tool in *Soul on Ice*, so has Yahya committed such crimes. When Yahya spews hatred about King and Amy and Matthew wish to leave, Yahya says to Amy and Matthew: "I'd appreciate it if you'd let me finish talking to the *real* black people in the room." Authentic black culture, according to Yahya, is macho and violent. African American authors who seem "too white" (meaning too middle-class) are, by this logic, sell-outs or Uncle Toms. This macho sexual style affects Matthew's love life negatively just as it affects King's attempt to lead Americans to a Beloved Community through non-violent means. Amy says to Matthew after the Yahya meeting, "I've *dated* guys like him. . . . They're the reason I wasn't seeing *any*body when we met." Amy is temporarily affected by the attitudes of such men (before she meets Yahya), and she explains that she initially rebuffed Matthew precisely because she had come to believe all men were like that. In an intriguing ironic reversal, Matthew originally supposes that he is not man enough to win Amy's heart, but then he finally does win her trust and her love when she realizes, instead, that he is *not* overly manly in the manner of Yahya and similar men Amy has met. To be "more like Dr. King," thus, does not mean to be more famous or to have more status, but to have a more balanced self in terms of "masculine" strength and "feminine" civility. As we shall see, the Evanston sections of the novel complicate and undermine this gendered dualism.

As if the presentation of hyper-masculine anger as a Cainite, destructive force with contempt for feminine values were not sufficient enough, one final touch closes off this series of images. Extremes meet when the marchers in King's movement come up against white racists who are also characterized by stereo-typically masculine traits: "The boys had greasy, slicked-back hair and packs of cigarettes rolled up in their T-shirt sleeves at shoulder level like refugees from movies starring Marlon Brando and Sal Mineo" (117). Not only do these hyper-masculine white racists taunt and throw bricks, they do so, partly, in imitation of role models from popular culture, connecting racism, sexism, and popular culture. Johnson is extremely critical of popular culture and regularly refers to "post-cultural America." In this conjuncture of popular culture, racism, and macho pride, Johnson imagines the very antithesis of Beloved Community. The angry whites who parody Brando are infected by toxic masculinity, whereas Matthew becomes increasingly drawn to the world of mothers, sisters, lovers, and dreamers. Consequently, Evanston, at least as he remembers it or hears about it from Amy, is something of a utopian space in *Dreamer*.

While masculine anger is a temptation that holds less and less appeal for Matthew, the *relatively* feminine world inhabited by his deceased mother and the lost world of Amy's Evanston relatives becomes increasingly important in *Dreamer*: "Amy . . . seemed aglow whenever she looked at the grandmother who'd taught her Scripture and how to be a woman, how to crochet, that she could use a string and an old tin can for fishing . . . and that at all times she must remember others" (30–31). These are the kinds of stories Chaym sneers at, saying, "I need to shit" (91) when Amy enthuses about her elders. Amy endures these sneers and finishes her story. To say the least, Amy finds it diffi-cult to be around Chaym, and Matthew concurs much of the time.

Matthew's education regarding Evanston values begins even before the trip to the Nest. His own distance from those values is measured by his distance from Amy, whom he is attracted to from the first: "I felt her presence before my eyes found that imprint of the simple cross under her white blouse, her denim skirt, and the Afro, an aureole black as crow's feathers, framing her face" (28). Matthew does not say anything disrespectful, but his view of her follows from an acquisi-tive desire that breaks her into attractive segments. He does not mean any harm, but his approach earns him rejection. He asks her to join him for a meal, and she says, "I don't eat" (31). His view, whether she intuits it or not, reduces her to Body—and so she denies Body in her response. Her response shows her to be a strong character, a remarkable mixture of bluntness and consideration. Significantly, Amy's "civilized composure" helps Matthew to handle the rejection without bitterness. Matthew is highly impressed, in fact, at how "she was doing her best to be gracious—to salvage the situation for me and herself—after the minor mess I'd created. And it was strange, I realized, how at that moment my emotions were a pastiche of pain and wonder at her civilized composure" (94). This "civilized" response to his desire expresses the Evanston community values such as self-reliance, moral clarity, and a complete refusal of resentment.

Amy never says she dislikes Matthew, though she is initially put off by his thesaurus-talk and his plastic pencil-holder shirt-pocket-protector. Exchanges with Amy teach Matthew that his situation with her is not merely personal but also communal. His meditations on communal values return him, time and again, to thoughts about his mother Ellesteen: "it was all that painful history behind us, the centuries of black men and women hurting and betraying and possibly hating each other since the days of slavery when a Negro risked death if he defended his family; the damage wrought by centuries of discrimination was always there, right at the heart of something as private as passion" (170). Amy and Matthew are inhibited by vicious historical pressures leading to mistrust and competition between black men and women. This discovery is a breakthrough for Matthew who had been marking every sign of disinclination from Amy as a *personal* judgment. What if Abel's gifts to God were preferred to Cain's because of the contingencies of communal need? Amy's civility and kindness contribute to Matthew's ability to resist the bitterness that is a constant temptation.

It is tempting to interpret Matthew's cry-of-the-heart as a masculine over-generalization about the faults of Women. Nash has interpreted this very rich passage as an indication of the unresolved "conflicts inherent in Johnson's view of women and his sense of what racism has done to the black family. The first element appears more subtly in the flaws in Amy's character; she is every inch the 'typical' shrinking fainthearted female for most of the novel. But here the critique takes on a new edge" (*Charles Johnson's Fiction* 179). "Johnson's view of women" is the thin edge of the wedge. Nash believes the idea that "only a black American woman could place that burden on a man" is not only Matthew's final philosophical position but Johnson's as well: "One sees a version of this dynamic in each of Johnson's earlier novels, but nowhere has he more bitterly or more pointedly critiqued black women than he does here. On its own, I find this assertion most troubling, as it points to a still-unresolved conflict between Johnson's theory and his practice" (180). Nash's interpretation of this passage is especially interesting, since Nash is clearly (as Travis is not) a sympathetic reader. By assigning Matthew's "bitterness" to Johnson, and by then interpreting the bitterness to express disappointment in feminine frailty, Nash misses the real object of Matthew's anger. Matthew is *discouraged* by Amy's rejection, but whatever bitterness he feels is directed toward his father rather

than the woman he wishes were his lover. The "painful history" passage continues as follows: "It was about my mother Ellesteen's bitterness toward my
father, that pathetic bastard, after he took off and left her to raise me alone.
Oh yes, all *that* was in the car between us, unspoken and perhaps unspeakable"
(180). To separate Cainite and Abelite consciousness absolutely, as if these
opposite abstractions could ever be found in unadulterated form within an
embodied self, is to submit to a nostalgic idealism. It is important to remember that Matthew does *not* accept Chaym's worldview in which foolish Abel
loses to streetwise Cain.[16] Chaym does in fact bring Matthew to recognize that
repressing resentment is not *transcending* it. Through a recognition—but not a
fetishization—of a bitterness he in fact shares with many others, Matthew can
broaden his "imagined community" of Evanston such that it will include
Chaym and others like him.[17] Matthew's interior journey—his soul-healing
reconnection with the values of his mother—corresponds to his exterior journey, his pilgrimage, we might say, to Evanston. As Nash argues, Ellesteen *does*
experience bitterness, even if she does not submit to it (*Charles Johnson's
Fiction* 169). The moment in the Pit Stop allows Matthew to recognize his
mother's pain, and this developing and deepening connection with the memory of his mother makes Matthew all the more receptive to what Amy will tell
him about her family.[18]

In the Nest, Matthew reconnects with values and beliefs that were unavail-
able to him before Chaym's provocations and Amy's evocations of these missing,
even ghostly, aspects of his communal past.[19] The retreat to the Nest, in the
manner of a religious retreat, allows for a spiritual integration, one in which
Chaym's overt and immoderate masculine behavior is an important component.
Chaym's hypermasculinity, paradoxically, answers Matthew's sense of lack, and
thus enables Matthew to get out of his rut. The mixture of characters and influences has the shape of a Zen *koan*: as there is no sound from just one hand clap-
ping, so there is no *nirvana* without *samsara*. Abstract entities (heaven and hell,
black and white, male and female, grace and disgrace) exist, in the embodied
world, in a relational manner. There is no male without female, and there is no
Ellesteen without Chaym. Matthew's confrontation and dialogue with Chaym
enable the *restoration*—to use a word suggestive of the politically utopian dimension of King's "dream"—of Ellesteen. Matthew's forgotten mother is initially
described as "regal, aristocratic," and "a sister to Mother Pollard" who famously
said during the Montgomery bus boycott, " 'My feets is tired but my soul is
rested' " (26).[20] Johnson's phrasing connects Matthew's mother to a social web,
one that was essential to the civil rights movement.

As Matthew points out, Mother Pollard was the chief example of the invisible female presence within the movement, invisible in a relative way even though recognized by King: "It was that woman and my mother King had in mind when in his 1955 speech at the Holt Street Baptist Church he said, 'When the history books are written in future generations, the historians will have to pause and say, There lived a great people—a black people—who injected new meaning into the veins of civilization'" (26). The historical Martin Luther King enjoyed telling this story, and one cannot say Mother Pollard is unknown—but she is known far less well than Sister Rosa Parks, and this relative invisibility, insofar as it can lead to temptations of various sorts, is extremely important to the developing story in *Dreamer*, a novel that seeks to point out and so to correct such "oversights" as much as possible. To King Mother Pollard was "amazingly intelligent and possessed a deep understanding of the meaning of the movement" ("Antidotes" 517). Perhaps she was the model for Mama Pearl, who is described as "everybody's grandmother" (*Dreamer* 30).[21] These two women embody Grandmother Wisdom of the sort absent from Matthew's life since his mother's death. Critics who have focused exclusively on Johnson's androcentric fictions have failed to notice his *constant* appreciation of maternal wisdom, going back to the Swamp Woman of *Faith and the Good Thing*, who is even described as "the Last Gnostic" (17).

Evanston represents the closest thing to a "Beloved Community" that we find in any of Johnson's novels (excepting perhaps that of the Allmuseri before they came to America), and Matthew's primary link to this sort of community, now that his mother has passed on, is Amy. Amy speaks often of Mama Pearl, who was "once an employee of Fanny's Restaurant in Evanston" (125), and so Amy "knew something of the town's older black residents, mostly craftsmen." She proudly rehearses the virtues of black self-reliance and impulse-control, as she "loved seeing her kin making their own clothes and bartering with other black people in the area for the little they could not produce themselves" (88). This is a world composed of both men and women, but the women are quite prominent. Scanning the crowd before Chaym is to appear in lieu of King, Matthew sees men in their best (only) suits, and notices "their wives, bearing names such as Adella, Inell, and Luberta, sitting quietly beside them in light cotton dresses, some wearing gloves despite the heat of bodies packed so close together on benches" (132). The propriety and dignity of these women, the finesse and polish with which they conduct themselves, unnerve Chaym.

Women in *Dreamer* are often celebrated as "mother" or "sister" or "lover," suggesting the possibility that Matthew—and perhaps Johnson—understands and values women primarily in relation to the men they support, but the presupposition that women are support personnel applies less and less as we go deeper into black churches such as Calvary AME in Evanston (Mama Pearl's church, where King preaches in chapter seven) and Bethel AME (the church of the Griffith family headed by Rev. Littlewood, as described in chapter eight). There we find that women are not merely extensions of male power and privilege. The black physician Dr. Jennifer Hale appears *only* in relation to the community as a whole, not any particular man in it, and is described as "the person who saw them before their own mothers and spanked wind into their lungs" (126). Cain is the first builder of cities in the Bible, but Dr. Hale is one of two city-builders in *Dreamer*: "By mobilizing blacks and whites of conscience, Hale became one of the principal players in first envisioning, then coaxing into being, Center Hospital; and by doing this, Amy said, she saved countless black lives as well as created jobs for other doctors, nurses, and dentists of color" (126). Like Mother Pollard and Ellesteen Bishop, this invisible heroine is briefly sung in the pages of *Dreamer*.

The Evanston "beloved community" is a world eclipsed by the macho political swaggering of the mid-1960s (in Johnson's fictional reconstruction), but the good place Johnson imagines is by no means an equal-and-opposite world in which feminine qualities eclipse masculinity: it is a good place because gender roles are predicated on mutuality. The communal heroes Matthew identifies are always associated with civility but are not without masculinity: the businessman and community leader Robert Jackson is a pillar of this community as well. These men may be feminized when held side-by-side to the heroes of Black Pride, but only because they have not attempted to purify themselves of traits and characteristics that may seem, conventionally, to be feminine.[22] Like Matthew's mother, these people "belonged to the same era, Dr. Hale and contractor Jackson—a breed of black men and women, like King's parents and Amy's great-grandfather, so toughened by prejudice, by the rule of having to do twice as much as whites to get half as far, that they regarded no problem as insurmountable" (126).

While the Calvary AME church appears robust (to the frightened Chaym, at least), the Bethel AME church is in decline. The Griffith family tombstones are untended and weed-covered, and the church itself is in a state of disrepair. One cause of this decline is that old-fashioned church-going is not sexy enough for the present world: "Its parishioners were plain, country people, primarily elderly women who worked as domestics in white homes in the area, a few retired men living on their pensions, and small children dragged to services by their grand-parents." The lineage of "Negro" Americans, sustained in large part by these churches, has been disrupted by the political developments of 1960s America. The Bethel church in particular has been thinned out: "It was not an activist church. Its ranks of teenagers and those in their twenties thinned after the rise of the Black Power movement. They never returned" (155–56). The remnants of this church community are not all female, but the reference to Black Power and the description of the congregation suggest that *men* have gone elsewhere: "There were no more than fifty people in the room. Older women in simple, bright summer dresses held their hymnbooks, fanning with folded copies of the church's newsletter, 'The Trumpet'" (156). The grandmotherliness of Mama Pearl, Mother Pollard, and Ellesteen Bishop are at this point merely quaint remnants, like an old musical instrument that no one plays anymore. Like the Allmuseri, the beloved communities of Evanston are things of the past.

Johnson's ideal tribes, whether from Africa or Illinois, are at once "past" and "lost," but they also exist in the present as potential pathways. No character in the novel figures "potential" as much as Chaym, who insists to Matthew (in a way that parallel's King's own understanding) that "everything is emptiness."[23] Emptiness, in this Buddhist sense, refers to the lack of self-inherent identity, or, one could say, teleological direction: sometimes Chaym does poorly, and occasionally he "doeth well" (236), and it is his emptiness, his existential freedom from any particular, permanent meaning, that creates the possibility of his doing well. We should not conclude that Chaym reverts to evil just because he cooperates with the FBI in the novel's closing pages rather than go to prison. We might have admired him better had he chosen to sacrifice himself. If, on the other hand, we judge Chaym solely by his last (and worst) action, then we miss the drama, the potential, and the deepest significance of his life: namely, that he is the ground through which the Evanston *ethos* may renew itself. As Matthew must retreat, understand his sources and resources, and *then* return in a stronger position, the shocked lineage-holders of Evanston values at novel's end must learn to incorporate those they have excluded such as that very "embodiment of the blues," Chaym Smith (33).

Chaym appears most frequently as the antithesis of Evanston values, and so it may seem like a violation of his nature that he should—temporarily—re-embody those values. But Chaym is exactly the sort of border-crossing iconoclast who can show the way when conventional thinking suggests no way forward. Chaym in this way is a shocking figure, as shocking as Lazarus, who returns from the dead even after his body has begun to stink. After he takes a bullet meant for King, he stands for the possibility of rebirth, resurrection, of returning when return seems impossible: "Indeed, he might *have* died on us a time or two and, like Lazarus, returned to life in a country where the customs and language were only faintly remembered" (153). After his near-fatal wound, Chaym stops at the Bethel AME and helps Reverend Littlewood rejuvenate the place. He denies that he has become religious, but he becomes able, once again, to serve others before himself.

Through the novel Matthew witnesses Chaym's anger, his transformation, and his recession. Matthew's insight into Chaym's anger deepens his insight into his mother's own bitterness, and Chaym's moment of self-sacrifice, paralleling Ellesteen's stoic self-sacrifice, allows Matthew (and even Chaym, temporarily) to partake of the Evanston experience. As a result, Matthew and Amy grow closer. Early in the story, she tells him "I don't eat" (31) when he asks for a date, and she says "please don't do it again" when they fall into a kiss (93). Matthew measures himself in large part by her feelings toward him, thinking "in a movie I'd make a good prop" (165), and he mentions that he "always felt she was testing me" (169). His separation from Amy often figures his alienation from parts of himself; only by confronting the fears and resentments that underlie his sense of inadequacy can he "doeth well." This growth becomes clear when Matthew and Chaym meet for the last time. Matthew is finally able to return to prayer, something he has not been able to do since his mother died, not because he wills himself to do it, but because Chaym asks him to: "I felt something slam inside my chest, then hot tears were hopping down my cheeks, and instead of offering words I wept for my counterfeit, fatherless status, gave myself over to it shamelessly, and by the end of my halting, stumbling appeal I felt emptied, no longer trying to bring a distant God's grace to my finite desires as His cast-aside son, but only wishing *Thy will be done*" (214). It could be claimed that this ability to pray, which has eluded Matthew from the novel's first page, is a sign of personal growth, but the essential lesson of the novel is that there is *no* personal growth, strictly speaking. We are bound together, and the threads that connect us signify the available alternatives to self-assertion and Cainite craving. At novel's end, his fingers interlaced with those of Amy, Matthew can think, pray, and march forward.

When Amy asks him where he thinks Chaym is, Matthew says "Everywhere . . ." (235), and there is a quiet irony—even an invisible presence—in this answer. Matthew is saying we are all one and that Chaym walks among us as one might say "Christ is in every human heart"—a broad, dull sentiment that does not go far in answering Amy's question. In a more insidious way, saying Chaym—who has probably betrayed King—is "everywhere" bears witness to a culture that has abandoned King.[24] "Everywhere" has a third connotation, allied to the first, but with a pronounced communal resonance. Sitting in Rev. Coleman's Calvary church waiting for King to preach, Matthew remembers a verse from his childhood:

Nevermore thou needest seek me
I am with thee everywhere:
Raise the stone and thou shalt find Me
Cleave the wood and I am there. (133)

"This," Matthew thinks, "was what Calvary's congregation believed. What I had been taught from the time I could walk." The word "everywhere" connects Matthew to divinity, but only by way of his childhood, and therefore his mother.

Johnson readers have on the whole been quite comfortable with Johnson's staging of racial hybridity, of a "fluidity" (Parrish 97) that we have embraced in casually transgressive ways.[25] Invisible to even Johnson's most sympathetic readers have been the interdependence of gender roles, Johnson's criticisms of masculine arrogance, and the longstanding celebration of feminine dignity in his work. These qualities quickly become visible if we focus, even briefly, on Ellesteen Bishop, a minor but hardly insignificant character who illuminates our understanding not only of Matthew Bishop but also of Chaym Smith and Martin Luther King. I would like to close by taking this examination of the politics of representation in Johnson's work in another direction, one that connects the concern with his philosophical and religious commitments.

One of the puzzles of Johnson's work is that his praxis in the realm of identity politics—marked by innumerable interventions in literary, philosophical, and pop-cultural discussion about the representation of black manhood—is seemingly at odds with his Buddhist profession of "no-self." No-self, to bend the concept slightly in the direction of this paper, refers to the philosophical claim that human beings (and other objects) have no self-inherent identities but are rather patterns-in-flux or, to put it another way, conditioned and provisional identities that pose as unalterable "souls" that transcend the alterability of the physical world and all other manner of mutability. The centuries-old attack on Buddhist philosophy as no more than nihilistic denial of the possibility of meaningful existence would have us think that Buddhism is too subversive of human standpoints to allow one to take any position whatsoever in questions of social justice, but this is a politically motivated misunderstanding of Buddhism. Gender identities, like racial identities, arise from what is called "co-dependent origination" in the language of Buddhist ontology, which means that human "being" is not individual but is thoroughly and radically intersubjective. As the 13th-century founder of Soto Zen, Dogen wrote in the fascicle "Only a Buddha and a Buddha," "Buddha-dharma cannot be known by a person" (Tanahashi 161).[26] Only a Buddha and a Buddha can know a Buddha because realization cannot be *self*-centered. It is between people, a shared recognition of shared Being (and it extends beyond *human* being, according to Dogen). There is no single enlightened person, only enlightened relationships or communities, and these could be called "Beloved Community," ones that practice Vietnamese Buddhist teacher Thich Nhat Hahn's ideal of "interbeing" at the social level.[27] The appeal of this sort of thinking for writers who not only oppose racism but seek a language and a social existence beyond racism or anti-racism (which reifies racial categories insofar as it reinstates them through our compulsive struggles to exorcize them) is clear from this passage from Dogen's fascicle: "Being unstained is like meeting a person and not considering what he looks like" (Watson 162). To see someone but not be distracted by what he or she looks like is both the vision *of* and the vision *in* beloved community. Johnson's fictional celebration of women such as Ellesteen Bishop and the "unselfconscious" and "egoless" Mama Pearl (29) marks the path connecting Buddhist no-self and the relatively/conditionally feminine (and, Matthew Bishop would agree, implicitly feminist) African American tradition of civility.

NOTES

1. Hayward's "Something to Serve: Constructs of the Feminine in Charles Johnson's *Oxherding Tale*," anticipates my argument in some ways but is at the same time a highly ambivalent approach to Johnson's views of the Feminine. Arguing that Johnson works with sexual dichotomies that reduce female experience and the significance of women in (primarily male) history, Hayward recognizes that Johnson is anything but uncritical of these reductions. However, Hayward is quite critical of Johnson's treatment of Minty's fate, though she stops just short of calling it "intentionally misogynistic" (699).

2. Feminist criticism of Johnson often sets Johnson against Morrison. Yet African American literary criticism owes much to the comparisons between the two. Morrison has not made public comments about Johnson, but Johnson and Stanley Crouch have each criticized Morrison, especially in Crouch's important review of *Oxherding Tale* and Johnson's interview with Little. Several critics have explored this rift, subsequently. The unfortunate but conveniently binaristic side-effect of these comparisons, however, has been the contrastive fixation of Morrison as feminist and Johnson, therefore, as a misogynist. (See in particular Muther and Thaden for readings of Johnson's work as misogynistic.)

3. Travis argues that Johnson's Ellisonian integration aligns him with white/masculine centers of power (195), in order to insinuate that Johnson's focus on masculinity is therefore anti-feminist. Travis thus ignores the political range of the black men Johnson celebrates. Comparing the textual strategies of *Middle Passage* with those of *Beloved* (1988), Travis argues that Johnson intentionally "seeks to transcend race and to suppress the feminine" (181) in ways that alleviate white readerly critical anxieties.

4. O'Keefe concludes that Morrison is the greater artist and the finer moral intelligence, while Parrish contests this alignment, saying that Morrison and Johnson approach similar cultural and even aesthetic ends through clearly distinct artistic means. Parrish finds Travis's view "too extreme" (82) and celebrates Johnson's conception of "an African-American identity" that is "irretrievably mixed with other American identities, a happy mongrel" (81). O'Keefe, like Parrish, is less interested in staging Morrison's victory over Johnson but maintains a focus on the sexual politics of Johnson's narrative choices: "A key difference" between *Beloved* and Johnson's novel is that *Middle Passage* focuses on Rutherford almost to the exclusion of Isadora, whereas *Beloved* places Paul D's story next to Sethe's in a way that allows readers to experience the human relationship more fully. O'Keefe claims that Johnson's novel is linear and detached, whereas Morrison's is emotionally involved and non-linear. See Conner's essay on *Middle Passage* in this volume for a more balanced discussion of the Johnson-Morrison relation.

5. Byrd compares *Oxherding Tale*'s Reb with Morrison's Paul D to show that both authors similarly reveal the damage done by slavery to black manhood (*Charles Johnson's Novels* 74).

6. Johnson has defined this phrase as follows: "I see the Other as a great and grand mystery, one that is ultimately ineffable—even holy. Which demands (on my side) a humble listening to how the Other speaks and appears, and always a sense (for me) that my knowing is provisional, incomplete, partial since the Other is process, a becoming that is open-ended in its being, or meaning. That's how I was using the phrase 'epistemological humility'" (Whalen-Bridge, "Shoulder" 306). Johnson has kindly provided a history of this term, tracing it to Husserl and Merleau-Ponty via Herbert Speigelberg:

> Going through my yellowed notes and brittle pages in notebooks kept for the last 30 years yesternight, I saw the phrase in one of them (notes I took in the '70s when studying at Stony Brook) and tracked it down to Volume Two of Herbert Spiegelberg's essential and definitive *The Phenomenological Movement: A Historical Introduction*. It appears on p.539 in his chapter on Merleau-Ponty (naturally). Here's the context: "It was only as a result of his growing sense of the scope and difficulties of his task that Husserl had arrived at an increasingly more modest estimate of the chances of phenomenology to reach absolute and final insight: what could at best be hoped for were approximations to an infinite goal. Such statements of *epistemological humility* and even resignation obviously fit in much better with Merleau-Ponty's conception of truth as in the making and as essentially historical than did Husserl's earlier battle for absolute knowledge against the attacks of historicism and other relativisms." (My italics). So that juicy, capacious phrase ain't mine. And I swear I can't remember when I started incorporating it into my writing and reflection. Nevertheless, I want to set the record straight: the phrase

was coined by that magnificent scholar of phenomenology, Herbert Spiegelberg. (E-mail to John Whalen-Bridge, 26 September 2004.)

7. *Dreamer* has received very little critical attention to date, and most critical writing so far has focused on the Cain/Abel metaphor rather than gender constructions in the novel. Little, Whalen-Bridge, and Nash have published essays on *Dreamer*. Only Nash has discussed gender in *Dreamer* with any thoroughness.

8. One could argue that King is changed by Chaym just as Chaym is changed by King—but not very convincingly: King is a saintly, over-pressured, underappreciated character from first to last. Amy Griffith and Mama Pearl are rich characters, but they do not develop significantly. They add texture to the novel and provide the means for other characters to develop. Matthew changes most significantly, and Chaym, who appears to slide back into his original type, can never really go back: his cooperation with the F.B.I. in the novel's conclusion is tragic rather than cynical. His horrible failure has a dignity that could not have been attained by the Chaym that we first meet. So it must be admitted that the novel dwells on the subjectivity of men. The novel presents the ways in which the world prioritizes men over women critically, and Martin Luther King in particular criticizes the predominance of values associated with masculinity.

9. Ellison, Evanston, Ellesteen: Marc Conner has pointed out to me that "Ellesteen" is not far off from "Ellison." This phonemic family resemblance becomes more compelling as we notice the pattern of Ellisonian qualities that adhere to Bishop's developing relationship to his lost mother. (E-mail to John Whalen-Bridge. 1 December 2004.)

10. It is also possible that Johnson is developing King as a Christ figure in this passage: Jesus sought moments of contemplation away from the crowd, and women were by his side until his death and mourned his loss at both cross and tomb. I thank Jeff Partridge for suggesting this possibility.

11. While King makes brief recommendations to Matthew regarding his course of study, Johnson emphasizes that King, who cannot remember Matthew's name then, is extremely busy and has very little time for Matthew.

12. Johnson writes in an e-mail, "when Matthew describes his mother and the 'thousand indignities and denials of her *personhood*,' that's a direct reference to King's embrace of Brightman's major work, 'Person and Reality,' the theological philosophy of 'Personalism.' It was one of the few (perhaps only) places in the novel where I could concretize that obscure and now forgotten philosophy, Personalism, in terms of King's application of it 'in the field,' one might say" (26 September 2004).

13. Nash perpetuates the Cain/Abel split, such as when he writes "all of these people are Abelites in some sense" and that the Evanston community is a "chosen" (people)—it is Chaym's greatest error to *believe* in a "chosen" people; Matthew tries on the idea for size but ultimately puts it aside. Nash gets it just right when he connects Johnson's "enemy within," meaning a negative conception of blackness, with the "Cainite consciousness" that afflicts Chaym (*Charles Johnson's Fiction* 169, 172).

14. Yahya Zubena says, at Amy's mention of King's name, "I guess we got some Uncle Tom nigguhs here," and he also refers to them as "house niggers" who do not understand "the necessity of revolutionary violence" (173). That Yahya attacks Amy when she attempts

to speak her views, that King is called an "Uncle Tom," and that the house/field binary is deployed to disparage middle class blacks as more effeminate than lower class blacks, all bespeak the absolutism of Yahya's gendered Manichaeism. As he splits "ice people" from "sun people," so too does he morally cleave masculinity and femininity.

15. I thank Linda Selzer for suggesting this point.

16. Matthew describes Chaym's "fascinating" theory as an "airtight, one-dimensional interpretation of history, one in which there was no room for ambiguity" (173–74).

17. The phrasing "unspoken and perhaps unspeakable" resonates keenly with Toni Morrison's phrase "unspeakable things unspoken." Reading about Ellesteen Bishop's pain at being left to fend for herself, one may think of Eva's bitterness about being left by BoyBoy in *Sula*. Male African Americans have also expressed great bitterness about negative literary representations of black men, and Cainite rivalry may flavor this conversation more than a little: Johnson attacked Morrison's *Beloved* as lacking intellectual depth in the Little interview (106–7), and numerous critics have staged battles between the two authors in critical articles. Against this backdrop, Matthew's awareness of "unspoken and perhaps unspeakable" forces impinging upon human relationships—put in this highly resonant form—strikes me as a civil nod toward Morrison.

18. Matthew cannot in any way identify with the hyper-masculinity of Yahya Zubena, but the example of Chaym Smith is accessible to him: it would seem that Johnson admits the deficits and hungers of African American manhood but warns readers about the risks of revitalization along gender lines: there is, one might say, a thin line between being a strong man and being a bully.

19. Nash compares the Griffith world to "the prelapsarian Allmuseri of *Middle Passage*" until the rise of urban America reduces it to a "kingdom in ruins" (170).

20. See Cozzens for a handy contextualization of Mother Pollard. See also King, "Antidotes for Fear," 517.

21. That Mama Pearl is "everybody's grandmother" echoes the dedication of Alice Walker's "Everyday Use": "For Your Grandmama" (2469).

22. Johnson has written repeatedly about his Uncle Will Johnson's milk bottles. One wonders if MLK and "milk" are being pressed together so as to squeeze the milk of human kindness out of the initials MLK. See *Dreamer* (127–28) in relation to "*The Second Front*" and Johnson's discussion of his Uncle Will and the resurfacing of milk bottles in "An American Milk Bottle" in *Turning the Wheel*.

23. I have discussed relations between "emptiness" and integration in my "Waking Cain."

24. Again I thank Jeff Partridge: Chaym, in being "everywhere," can also be compared to Judas.

25. Parrish states that "Johnson . . . imagines African-American identity to be irretrievably mixed with other American identities, a happy mongrel" (82).

26. I am not, in this section, arguing that Johnson has been especially influenced by Dogen and Lin-chi, only that their expositions of no-self can help us appreciate Johnson's own Buddhistic approaches to character and identity politics. Among the Buddhist authorities Johnson cites in *Turning the Wheel* are Alan W. Watts, Hui-neng, Stephen Batchelor, Nyanaponika Thera and Maurice Walshe's translations of Buddha's discourses, Gunapala Dharmasiri, Thich Nhat Hahn, Huang Po, Jack Kornfield, the Diamond Sutra, Isshu

Miura and Ruth Fuller Sasaki, Shantideva, Philip Kapleau, Chogyam Trungpa Rinpoche, and Irving Babbitt's translation of the *Dhammapada*.

27. It may seem that Buddhism is somehow too exotic for import to the context of American racial politics and artistic traditions, but contemporary Buddist scholars and teachers think otherwise:. See Thich Nhat Hanh's essay "Interbeing" (*Being Peace* 83–102) for an anticipatory exploration of the mingling of Buddhism and "the scientific way of looking at things" and the "spirit of free inquiry" in the West. More than any other teacher, Thich Nhat Hanh has been associated with the politically active tradition of "Engaged Buddhism."

"AT THE NUMINOUS HEART OF BEING"
Dreamer *and Christian Theology*

MARC C. CONNER

. . . whether there be knowledge, it shall vanish away.
—1 CORINTHIANS 13:8

Christianity is the deepest wound that can be inflicted upon a man.
—KIERKEGAARD

When John Gardner first read the manuscript of *Oxherding Tale* in 1980, he exclaimed, "This is a new Charles Johnson" (Johnson, "Introduction," xvii). The response to Johnson's 1998 novel, *Dreamer*, could well be the same: the novel announces a dramatic shift in Johnson's primary concerns, in terms of the aesthetics, the politics, and the philosophical dilemmas that the novel engages. Most strikingly, *Dreamer* reveals a new religious investigation for Johnson, one that both complements and complicates his earlier explorations of spirituality and the ethical life. The radical difference of *Dreamer* is first suggested in the epigraphs that open the novel: one attributed to Meister Eckhart, the 13th-century Dominican theologian and mystic; one to Martin Luther King, Jr.; and two to the Book of Genesis. Readers familiar with Johnson's previous novels may wonder, where are the references to eastern philosophy and religion? Wither the Vedas, the Oxherding Pictures, the Upanishads? The immediate focus of *Dreamer*, even before the novel proper begins, is strikingly Christian. This focus will dominate the novel, which, although it certainly continues Johnson's investigations into multiple world religions, and particularly Zen Buddhism, primarily grapples with the Christian theological tradition.

This is more than just an expansion of Johnson's spiritual interests into another world tradition. (For of course Christianity has been present in his earlier writings—one thinks of Faith's investigations into Christianity in *Faith and the Good Thing*, or Andrew and Peggy's wedding in *Oxherding Tale*, or Cringle's adherence to a code of Christian morality in *Middle Passage*.) Rather, *Dreamer* shows Johnson revising his own concept of the "philosophical novel" that has constituted his earlier work, all of which fosters a reading attitude of philosophical plenitude. As Johnson has stated, his fiction seriously engages "those old virtues from the pre-Socratic era: the good, the true, and the beautiful. Those are very, very important to me—however we might interpret them, however we might try to seek them" (Davies 154). Johnson encourages the reader to seek these things as well through the serious and rigorous practice of philosophy. But *Dreamer* frustrates the approaches of Johnson's earlier fiction, by self-consciously calling into question the very enterprise of philosophy— part of the wisdom of *Dreamer* is the weakness of the philosophical method, the limits of human wisdom.

The emphasis on Christianity with which the novel begins is also the note on which it ends. On the novel's penultimate page, Matthew offers his despairing response to King's death: "The Way of agapic love, with its bottomless demands, had proven too hard for this nation. Hatred and competition were easier. Exalting the ethnic ego proved far less challenging than King's belief in the beloved community" (*Dreamer* 235). This elegiac statement brings together the novel's two primary concerns: agapic love and the beloved community. "Agape" can certainly stand for the central concern of this novel: described as the "defining word for Christian life and teaching," it functions in the New Testament as the "affirmation of the 'Great Commandment' as the love of God and of one's neighbor," and even functions theologically as the very personification of God in John's Gospel (Freedman 27–28). It is the selfless, self-giving love of God and of one's fellow humans, a "fraternal charity" (*New Catholic Encyclopedia*, 169). Indeed, this concept has been central to Johnson's thought in recent years. In a lecture on Christianity and Buddhism, delivered to the Harvard Divinity School in April of 2003, Johnson emphasizes Tillich's conception of Agape as the defining force in Christian thought. Tillich writes, "In the New Testament the Greek word agape is used in a new sense for that kind of love that God has for man, the higher for the lower, and that all men should have for one another, whether they are friends or enemies, accepted or rejected, liked or disliked. Agape in this sense accepts the unacceptable and tries to transform it. . . . Agape accepts and tries to transform in the direction of what is meant by the 'Kingdom of God' " (Tillich 70–71).[1] In a novel that opens with direct reference to the Cain and Abel story, such a concept of love offers a powerful contrary to the motif of brother-killing.

Certainly this idea of selfless love corresponds with some of Johnson's major ideas in his other novels: the *karuna* (compassion), and *metri* or *metta* (loving-kindness), and the *anatman* (selflessness, literally, "no-self") of Buddhism so frequently emphasized throughout his fiction (*Dictionary of Buddhism* 20, 155–56, 184). But I've grown dissatisfied with the idea that *Dreamer* expresses the same views as Johnson's other novels, but now in a Christian context—old wine in a new wineskin. John Whalen-Bridge makes this argument in a compelling manner, describing the novel as "Johnson's Buddhist revision of the *Genesis* story" ("Waking Cain" 513), and shows the ways in which the novel's Christian positions are similar to Buddhist teachings. While I certainly acknowledge these similarities, my argument is that Johnson is more concerned with the ways in which Christian thought is *not* identical with Buddhist or other traditions—he is concerned in *Dreamer* with those aspects of Christianity that his previous religious-philosophical investigations have not sufficiently explored. Put differently, *Dreamer* suggests that there are new elements at work in Johnson's thought and writing, that Johnson has engaged Christianity in his fourth novel precisely because his previous philosophical explorations have proven insufficient, or in need of supplement.[2]

What makes these concerns particularly pressing is the presence of many highly autobiographical elements in *Dreamer.* Johnson has written in many aspects of his own life and family history, and particularly the world of his boyhood, to a degree unprecedented in his earlier work (which indeed seems to me by comparison to be somewhat impersonal at times, as if the author is keeping the characters at a distance—the relation between the author and his characters in *Dreamer*, by contrast, is intimate, invested). In the novel, Johnson writes much of his personal family history, particularly the history of the fathers and their efforts to establish in Evanston, Illinois a haven of self-reliant African-American life. As Will Nash points out, Johnson "is telling his personal history" here (*Charles Johnson's Fiction* 172), and this becomes both Johnson's homage to the community that helped foster his own creative self, and also one of several models in the novel of the ideal human community. The result is that *Dreamer* is Johnson's most profoundly personal novel, constituting a major new step in his efforts to conceive and evoke the meaningful life.

The Christianity that Johnson investigates in *Dreamer* is rich, elusive, and complicated. As in his earlier novels, Johnson approaches this major world religion with all the rigors of philosophy, trying to understand its origins, its epistemologies, its ethics, its metaphysics. The novel's epigraphs point towards two of the oldest stories in the Judeo-Christian tradition, the Cain and Abel story and the story of Joseph and his Brothers. If, as Matthew speculates, he was just possibly "composing a Gospel" in his telling of King's life (102), why does the novel preface this "gospel" with these two Old Testament archetypes?

How do the Cain and Abel and the Joseph stories inform this novel—and for that matter, how do they relate to the Gospel stories themselves?[3]

Central to both stories is the motif of the warring brothers. Cain kills Abel because God prefers Abel's sacrifice to Cain's; Joseph's brothers sell Joseph into slavery because his dreams suggest that he will reign over them. Each story is an example of denying the fraternal link, the bond of sympathy and common cause implied in brotherhood, expressed in Cain's famous denial: "Am I my brother's keeper?" (Gen 4:9).[4] The stories suggest that jealousy, rivalry, ruthless competition—particularly for the approval of the totemic father, whether God the father in Genesis 4 or Jacob the tribal father in Genesis 37–50—seem to reside at the very heart of humankind. Both stories also show the consequences of brotherly strife: wandering, homelessness, the condition of the outcast. For his crime, Cain is cast out of the human community: "a fugitive and a vagabond shalt thou be in the earth" (4:12); similarly, Joseph is thrown into the wild, and soon his brothers too will have to leave the home of their father in search of sustenance in a time of famine. But both stories also reveal a corresponding mercy that brings a measure of comfort to the outcast. God places the mark of protection upon Cain, who then goes forth to become the builder of cities and father of many descendants. Similarly, Joseph ultimately responds to his begging brothers with mercy and generosity, and saves his father's house by bringing them to Egypt and his protection. Each story, then, enacts the characteristic action of Genesis that follows the original sin in chapter 3, when God punishes Adam and Eve but also clothes and protects them, demonstrating, in the words of one commentator, "God's providential care for all mankind" (Neil 22). The dual attitude of God's justice and mercy, punishing and protecting, condemning and restoring, will form one of the fundamental structures of the Bible, reaching its climax in the Passion and Resurrection narratives of the Gospels.

But what makes these stories of warring brothers and of justice and mercy so relevant and powerful to the nearly contemporary world of America that Johnson evokes in *Dreamer*? Put differently, what does the Cain and Abel story give to Johnson that he finds of especial force and power in interpreting the world of *Dreamer*? The primary importance lies in the novel's depiction of a world in strife, a world in which blood-hatred dominates. On the novel's opening page, the narrator Matthew says of King that "violence followed him like a biblical curse," that the world King is attempting to heal consists of "families divided, fathers at the throats of their sons, brothers spilling each other's blood" (13). *Dreamer* opens on the very verge of the apocalypse threatened in the Gospels, the Book of Revelations, and, most powerfully, the prophecy of Isaiah: "Through the wrath of the Lord of hosts is the land darkened, and the people shall be as the fuel of the fire: *no man shall spare his brother*" (Isaiah 9:19, emphasis added).[5] This is precisely the world for which the Cain and Abel story stands as the founding myth. As Leon Kass argues in his sweeping study of Genesis, the Cain-Abel story "shows the reader what unregulated human life is like" (123)—shows "the possibility that enmity—yes, enmity to the point of fratricide—might be the *natural* condition of brothers" (124). Kass argues that "Cain is truly the human prototype" (126), that he sets the pattern for all humankind of enmity, pride, self-reliance, and a refusal to acknowledge one's dependence as a created being. Through his murder of his brother, "the cosmos itself has been violated; the crime is a crime against 'blood'—against both life and kin; the whole earth, polluted and stained with bloodshed, cries in anguish and for retribution" (142–43). As a result, "civilization as it comes into being, starting from his founding act, is tainted" (145). This corresponds to Johnson's depiction of the America of the late 1960s, recalling Yeats's great apocalyptic lines: "the blood-dimmed tide is loosed/and everywhere the ceremony of innocence is drowned."

Chaym Smith embodies this position, and he articulates it as well. When he saves Matthew from being killed by the very person Matthew is trying to help, Chaym mocks Matthew's altruism: " 'Did I hear you call him *brother*?' Smith chortled, his head tipping back. 'You didn't even know his name! Did you call him that 'cause he was black, or was that a church thing? You ever *thought* about what brothers are really like? Romulus and Remus, say. Or Jacob and Esau? How they can hate each other, especially if one is doing better? See, if I were you, I'd forget about that brotherhood malarkey, and remember what they said during the French Revolution. *Fraternite ou la mort*' " (55).[6] The philosophy of brotherhood, Chaym concludes, resolves itself into the statement, "*be my brother or I'll kill you!*" (55). This is precisely the Cain position, argues Kass: "Fully understood, 'Am I my brother's keeper?' turns out, in fact, to be the maxim of a would-be murderer, an expression of fratricidal intent. For to deny responsibility for your brother is, tacitly, to profess indifference to his fate" (142).

Thus *Dreamer* conjures the Cain and Abel story in order to portray a world given over to murder, hatred, and violence. The effect is at times Old Testament-like in its depictions of rage, as in the riot scene on the north side of Chicago, when Matthew observes of the racist white crowd that "there was something biblical, mythic, and ritualistic in their hatred of their darker brothers, something in the blood, as if to found and sustain a city, a sacrificial slaughter must take place" (117). This recalls one of the great legacies of the Cain figure, as Quinones explains: "Cain, who aspires to possession, to rights, to identity, is the founder of the first city" (26). The story suggests that civilization itself is founded upon an unspeakable act, the killing of the brother, an act that effectively mars the unity of existence. In Quinones's words, "the great purpose of the Cain and Abel story has always been . . . to address a breach in existence, a fracture at the heart of things" (3).

Chaym explains this "breach" as a condition of unfairness, resulting from the arbitrary and unjust preference of God for one brother over another. This theory of unfairness is also his explanation for racial discrimination, as he explains to Matthew: " 'What you got to face, Bishop . . . is the possibility that we are, as a tribe, descended from the first of two brothers whose best just couldn't hack it. And, it wasn't *his* fault. See, if you check that Bible of yours, you'll find the world didn't begin with love. It kicked off with killing and righteous hatred and *ressentiment*. Envy, I'm saying, *is* the Negro disease. We got the stain, the mark. Nothing else really explains our situation, far as I can see' " (66). This ancient, and erroneous, concept that the African peoples are descended from Cain[7] serves as Chaym's justification for his own resentment at the world and his refusal to acknowledge his own dependence. But Johnson does not allow this reading of the Cain story—nor of contemporary African-American racial politics—to stand for very long. For Chaym confronts in Martin Luther King, Jr., a figure who resists the stance of anger and retribution, and a figure who, crucially, seems to be Chaym's very twin. King not only refutes Chaym's reading of the world's injustice, but offers a far different philosophical approach to the problems of difference and division. This fits with Kass's deeper reading of the Cain and Abel story, which teaches, not that one brother is unfairly favored by God, but rather that, through "the existence of one's brother," one realizes that "one is not the sole meaning of one's origins" (128).

For in fact, the figure of Cain stands not for justified indignation at what Quinones describes as God's unfair "arbitrariness of preference" (11), but rather for the human, all-too-human refusal to acknowledge one's status as a created being, and, crucially, one's involvement in the rest of the creation. This stance of radical self-reliance underlies the problem of Cain's unacceptable sacrifice: as Kass argues, Cain's sacrifice—indeed, his *will* to sacrifice—stems from the assumption that God is "just like" Cain, that He desires to eat, that what He wants is the same as what His created man wants. Such assumptions "are in fact expressions of human pride and presumption, masquerading as true submission" (134–35). Consequently, when Cain's offering is dismissed, Cain responds with outrage and anger precisely because of his wounded pride: "Cain desires to be first and best, and to be so recognized," Kass explains, and when "the world does not affirm his lofty self-image" (an image of himself as God-like), his response of anger "expresses the world's first sense of justice—or rather, injustice: 'I did not get what I deserved; I was wronged'" (137).[8]

This is precisely the attitude of Chaym Smith throughout the first half of *Dreamer*, expressed most poignantly when he delves further into King's family life and realizes his own lack of family and love: "He said, 'I woulda given anything for a loving, decent childhood like that. Parents like that.' He peered up to me, but his eyes were still filled with all he'd seen. 'Bishop, it ain't right not having anybody who cared'" (107). Chaym's early arguments to Matthew about this status of inequality, of ineradicable difference, assert the injustice of this, the unfairness of the seemingly arbitrary preference of the world. But, as Kass points out, this position—from Genesis 4 onwards—represents a strange notion of justice: "Through Cain's anger, the text conveys its first instruction regarding man's interest in justice. Justice is, to begin with, not an altruistic matter of doing right by others, but *a selfish matter of not letting others do wrong to oneself.* A concern for justice begins in the passion to get what one deserves and to get even when one feels cheated or slighted" (137, emphasis added). It is in this regard that Cain is seen as "humanly prototypical" (Kass 139): the affront to his offering is perceived as "contempt for his own person," provoking his response in which, as Rousseau phrases it, "*in a manner proportionate to the stock he set by himself, vengeance became terrible, and men bloodthirsty and cruel*" (Kass 138–39). Crucially, this refutation of one's unique status in the creation is precisely the effect of confronting the fact of one's brother: "The existence of one's brother is painful proof that one is not the sole meaning of one's origins" (Kass 128). Thus the Cain/Chaym position is not a Promethean cry for justice, but rather the far less heroic complaint that one's apparent god-like status is not recognized—it is far more akin to the child's burst of temper when the grown-up world sets limits on its desires.[9]

This explains much of Chaym's transformations in the second half of the novel. As he works to learn everything about King, in order to become an ever more perfect mimic of him, Chaym confesses that his subject is elusive: "'I been trying to get a handle on him,'" he states to Matthew, "'but sometimes it's like he ain't there. Like he's an instrument, not the music itself—a conduit for something else that's always just outta reach'" (111). Chaym's inability to "get a handle" on King results from Chaym's inability to submerge his own self in the greater work of the creation—he cannot conceive a world-view in which his own interests are not addressed. King, however, strives towards a spiritual philosophy in which the self vanishes before the concerns of the other. As Matthew explains, King's ideals of nonviolence, of agapic love, and of integration all amount to the same essential philosophic position: "Others *first*. Always" (108). But Johnson is careful not to rest in an easy opposition of Chaym vs. King, Cain vs. Abel; for in fact the spiritual philosophy that King articulates goes beyond this opposition. King becomes, as Matthew phrases it, "the almost paradoxical fusion of Cain and Abel" (125). He embodies, in other words, the transcendence (in the specifically Hegelian sense of *aufgehoben*, to overcome but also to preserve) of both models of human brotherhood—much as the subject of the Gospels does. When Christ states, "greater love hath no man than this, that a man lay down his life for his friends" (Jn 15:13), he articulates an ideal of discipleship—we might say, brotherhood—in which the other comes first. Similarly, the "new commandment" given by Christ— "That ye love one another; as I have loved you, that ye also love one another" (Jn 13:34)—expresses the same doctrine of selfless love to replace brotherly resentment and competition.

In other words, Johnson's uses of Old Testament archetypes are an intentional re-reading of the Gospels themselves—the Gospels read through the lens of the war of brothers found so early in the Bible. Indeed, the Bible itself suggests that this is the relation between the Gospel accounts and the stories told throughout the Patriarchs: both a parallel and a surpassing, or what Frank Kermode describes as "fulfillment, fullness of time" in which "Old Testament types are crowned by their antitypes" (Kermode 376). For whereas many world mythologies place these warring brother stories at the level of the creation, in Genesis they are subservient to the Creation account, which is accomplished by God's speaking power alone, a speaking power specifically invoked again in the opening hymn of John's Gospel. The warring brothers do not engender creative power in the Old Testament; instead they reinforce the urgent message of Genesis 1–3—and of the New Testament—that creative power resides solely in God. This is why the latter-born consistently inherits the father's blessing: Abel, Isaac, Jacob, and Joseph (and later, of course, David) all receive God's favor partly to show that blessings come not because of one's status in the line of human generation, but through the providential will of the Creator. Indeed these stories all serve to emphasize—to a community in exile, a community apparently of outcasts and the disfavored (precisely the audience of the Hebrew scriptures[10])—that only in this creative power can a harmonious life be found. And this is precisely where *Dreamer* locates its exploration of Christianity: as a fugitive religion, a way of faith for a people in exile.

The strongest presentation of this exiled community occurs in chapter seven, the Evanston church scenes. Here we see a community, Calvary AME, which exists outside of, or unnoticed by, history: "Its rich, never recorded history was hidden inside, stored within every parishioner" (124). It is not embroiled in the Civil Rights movement: "Most black residents were too busy making a living and caring for their children to take a day off for civil disobedience" (124). This may sound like apoliticism, turning a blind eye to the great tide of history and hiding in one's relatively safe enclave. But we need to look more closely at how the residents *devote* themselves during this turbulent time: they are "mostly craftsmen" (125), literally in their trades (plumbers, electricians, builders), but also figuratively in the way they turn their lives into craft. These are builders who have begun their work, as did Cain, as "outcasts"; and yet their ethic of work is utterly opposed to the self-elevating, prideful work of Cain. Rather, the community Matthew describes embodies both self-reliance and disciplined commitment to community—"the paradoxical fusion of Cain and Abel," and the true expression of Emerson's ideal of self-reliance.[11]

This Evanston community is figured as an approximation of the Land of Canaan, the place to which the first exiles, like the Hebrews after the Exodus, settled after the captivity of the deep South. "While not the fabled Promised Land," Matthew reports, it "was a curious pocket of tranquility compared to the Black Belt" (125). Among the original "Founders" is one Robert Jackson, who came to Evanston from South Carolina, founded his own milk company to service the black community, started his own construction business, employed many of his nieces and nephews, and eventually built Calvary AME itself. Johnson expounds upon Jackson's work ethic, humility, discipline, and in particular his commitment to home and family, and compares him to King's own parents and to Amy's admirable grandfather—that older generation that serves as a bulwark and a beacon for ethical behavior in the present.[12] Jackson succeeded in helping to rear a generation of children who believed in themselves, in their community, and particularly in the power of an education as the best solutions to "the economic inequities they saw in the world." Jackson achieves this "by fulfilling his duties as a householder" (129). The idea of "the householder" is Johnson's central ethical concept, what Andrew in *Oxherding Tale* comes to see as his "dharma," that is, " 'that which one ought to perform by virtue of the place one occupies in the social order' " (*The Bhagavad Gita*, quoted in Little, 87). "The Householder" is the second of the four stages of life reaching towards liberation in Hindu thought, described by Suzuki as the stage wherein one learns "the sacred rites that uphold the world . . . to marry, procreate, and serve society." As Little explains, in this stage "one must realize that one's duty, or *dharma*, is not only to oneself, but also to the wider community" (87). In other words, it expresses the very unity of self and other that Johnson also sees in Emerson. In *Dreamer*, this Eastern concept is expressed as the way of life of an exemplary Christian in an exemplary Christian community.

At this point, the novel reaches its most autobiographical stage for Johnson. For Robert Jackson is an embodiment of Johnson's own great-uncle, William Johnson, who followed a parallel course from South Carolina to Evanston, founding the Johnson Dairy Company, starting his own construction business, and serving as the bulwark in his community (and Johnson's family, for which he stood as "patriarch") for decades. Johnson has written extensively about this father-figure in several important essays, even using many of the same sentences in both *Dreamer* and in the essays to describe both figures. And Johnson particularly champions the work ethic of his great-uncle, describing him as "[a]lways an optimist, a man who preferred hard work and getting his hands dirty to complaining, building to bellyaching" (*Turning* 170). The principles Johnson associates with this patriarch are virtually identical to those espoused by Ellison in the epilogue to *Invisible Man*: "He understood—and made *us* see through his personal example—that while black people had endured often mind-numbing oppression, America was founded on principles, ideals, and documents (the Declaration of Independence and the Constitution) that forced it to be forever self-correcting. That, he knew, was the ground that nurtured black Americans. The opportunities denied him would be there for us, he said. But *only* if we were educated and hardworking" (*Turning* 173).[13]

Robert Jackson/William Johnson serves as a political allegory within the novel, connecting King's civil rights efforts with contemporary debates about affirmative action.[14] But I am less interested in the political messages that might be implied in this depiction, and more in the ethical emphasis Johnson associates with this householder. For Johnson brings his reflections on his great-uncle to a climax by insisting that the primary lesson he taught was the primacy of family: "We must relearn what our elders knew regarding the primacy of the family (or extended family) as the social entity best suited for ensuring the survival of its members and providing examples of acceptable behavior for its children," for "whatever renewal and progress black people in America can hope for must come from *within*" ("*Second Front*" 183). Is this not precisely the lesson *not* understood by Cain? Seen in this context, the Cain-Abel story becomes a parable of the devastation resulting from rejecting the familial link. Certainly it is in this sense that Johnson invokes the story at this point in *Dreamer*. For when Chaym realizes what sort of congregation he must face as King's stand-in at Calvary AME, he collapses in anxiety. " 'What do I *say* to them?' " he asks, and when Matthew responds, " 'Nothing!' " Chaym responds with precisely Cain's resentment towards Abel (King) and the world he represents: " 'Shit, as long as *he's* alive, I guess I'll always be nothing' " (130).

Chaym cannot imagine having anything to say to these people, for whom God obviously feels "love." Yet the ethos of the Householder may well contain the proper response to the trauma of being a Cainite. For the Calvary community began as Cainites—wanderers, outcasts, preterite—and have become Abelites, suggesting again that this is not a division or opposition, but the product of choices and beliefs, the combination of ethics and theology—stages on life's way, as Kierkegaard might put it. Indeed, Johnson resists the easy opposition of Cain vs. Abel so that he can define that brotherhood relation as more dialectic, constantly shifting, suggesting that at any moment one might be more Cain-like or more Abel-like, depending on circumstances, historical forces, trauma, degree of faith . . . perhaps even race.

As Chaym "begins to unravel" "inside a tiny kitchen" (131—setting up an ironic contrast with the dramatic kitchen conversion sequence of King himself later), the reader is immersed in Matthew's powerful reaction to and meditation upon this Church, and all it represents (and here, I suspect, we see Johnson at his most autobiographical). Matthew enters the church and "the feeling that always flooded through me when I entered Negro churches came over me again—the sense, right or wrong, that for the briefest of moments I was safe from the ravages, the irreality, the racial stupidities of the world outside Calvary's doors" (133). In a remarkable, sustained passage, Matthew offers a litany of the values, traditions, and histories he associates with this church, giving a rich depiction of the novel's vision of ethical Christianity:

> . . . no harm could befall anyone here where so much of value was pre-served, meaning made manifest in the minutest details by black people who came to this place, sacred and set off from the chaos of the streets out-side, to find husbands and wives, to baptize their children, and to bury their dead before gathering at the home of the deceased, sharing memories of her with the survivors, and being fed by her friends and neighbors who filled the kitchen table with food as a reminder that the bereaved must take nourishment, no matter if they were hungry or not, and walk on, and know

that death was not final, because Jesus conquered that once and for all, so yes, eat and be joyful even in mourning because no Christian should ever forget the good news of the gospel, and no believer in Him ever feel alone or have cause for despair. (133)[15]

This lyric encomium to the powerful Christianity at the heart of African-American culture has no precedent in Johnson's work. His considerations of Christianity heretofore have been either philosophical abstractions, or incidental steps (generally to be discarded or overcome) in a character's larger religious journey. But here, he returns to the faith tradition in which he was raised, and which he associates with his own parents,[16] both to praise and, crucially, to investigate its philosophical and even political soundness.

Thus Matthew's reflections move to the root meanings of "religion"—"Latin *religare*, 'to bind,' or bring together those things broken, torn asunder" (133)—a definition that sounds precisely like the contrary of Cain's resentment and prideful outrage. Instead of radical self-sufficiency and rejection of the Creator, a stance that as we have seen produces a rift in the very fabric of being, "religion" in this sense offers connection and continuity, reconciliation and communal dependence. Matthew goes on to consider all the nurturing—spiritual, intellectual, and artistic—that has gone on in this faith tradition. He concludes the meditation by realizing that this tradition offers a bedrock of belief and ethics that goes far beyond any limited, human political program, thinking of the "clergy, stewards, and trustees who, if they knew nothing else, understood that they served their people best by reminding them again and again that *their political and racial struggles were but the backdrop against which a far greater spiritual odyssey was unfolding*, and that no worldly triumph deserved hallelujahs if in their secular victories they somehow lost their souls" (134, emphasis added).

This remarkable passage constitutes the climax of Johnson's depiction in *Dreamer* of *ethical Christianity*, Christianity as a map for right living, for "doing well" (to invoke the novel's oft-repeated failure of Cain: "If thou doest well, shalt thou not be accepted?" God asks him [Gen 4:7]). This expresses in living culture the two great commandments of the Gospels, commandments that are both theological and ethical (crucially, the ethics *follow from* the theology): "Thou shalt love the Lord thy God with all thy heart, and with all thy soul, and with all thy mind, and Thou shalt love thy neighbour as thyself" (Mt 22:37–39). This is the very essence of King's teachings as highlighted by Johnson throughout the novel, and certainly constitutes part of the novel's reaction to the Cainite position. However, this is only one part of the diptych

Johnson presents of Christianity. The other part is *existential Christianity*, a rich and complex grappling with the fundamental tenets of lived Christian thought over two millenia. In combining these two aspects of Christianity, Johnson brings together the ethical and the existential, meeting the philosophical challenge of Jean-Paul Sartre to wed existentialism and politics,[17] and in particular the challenge of Emmanuel Levinas, to wed existentialism and the ethical encounter with the other.[18] This becomes *Dreamer's* central philosophical undertaking, a project that is simultaneously theological, political, and, I would argue, personal for Johnson.

Existential Christianity takes up the classic Sartrean definition of existentialism, that "existence precedes essence . . . that subjectivity must be the starting point" (Sartre 13), but with a particular understanding of what Rudolf Bultmann terms *Fragestellung*, literally, "the putting of the question." As John Macquarrie explains, for Bultmann, " 'the right philosophy'—and that, we take it, means the philosophical outlook proper to theological study—'is quite simply that philosophical work which endeavours to develop in suitable concepts the understanding of existence that is given with human existence' " (Macquarrie 10). In other words, it marks a philosophical enterprise in which the specifically human questions of existence are investigated with the utmost concern. Existential Christian theology puts the question of being—what Heidegger describes as the state of "astonishment," the "disposition in which and for which the Being of being unfolds" (*What is Philosophy?* 85)—as follows: *how are the statements of the New Testament significant for my existence, and for human existence as a whole?* Hence Bultmann takes Paul's conversion experience—Paul's "entering into a new understanding of himself"—as paradigmatic for "a new understanding of man's own existence in relation to God" (Macquarrie 11–12). Existential New Testament thinking seeks to learn how a meditation upon our uniquely human existence points us towards an understanding of existence itself, understood as the manifestation of the Christian God. This approach focuses, as Jacques Maritain emphasizes, "on the act of existence as the enactment of being" (Herberg 3), understood in Tillich's famous formula: "the being of God is being-itself" (Herberg 256).

The concerns, the perspective, even the language of Christian existential thought open up Johnson's fundamental queries in *Dreamer* in powerful and illuminating ways. Bultmann's concept of the putting of the question—*how are the statements of the New Testament significant for my existence?*—describes the essence of King's dilemmas regarding right action, of Matthew's uneasy relation to Biblical revelation, and ultimately of Chaym's effort to grapple with the Biblical message. Furthermore, the question of one's existence and its relation to the divine is at the very heart of those troubling epigraphs of warring brothers with which the novel begins. The very crisis of Cain is his need to justify his own being in relation to the being of God—we could say that this crisis is central to all of Johnson's thought and writing. Indeed, when we consider the highly autobiographical nature of *Dreamer*, we might suspect that this may be the very challenge with which Johnson himself approaches the material of this novel.

Johnson has emphasized the personal nature of this engagement with the Christian tradition, and his desire in *Dreamer* both to study, and praise, its teaching: "During the 7 years I worked on [*Dreamer*], my 'To-Do' blackboard here in a corner of my study had a note I made to myself (one I stared at for 7 years) that *Dreamer* should not only be a celebration of Martin Luther King Jr., but also a spirited praise song to the 2,000 years of Christian theology that produced King and his vision. Thus, through King I hoped to access everything from Jesus' philosophy to medievals like St. Anselm and Aquinas, St. Francis and Luther" (E-mail 17 May 2003). This confirms that the central project of this ambitious, complex novel is Johnson's exploration of the Christian *kerygma*, the proclamation of a new understanding of Being itself in the face of which the human subject is radically transformed—new wine, new wineskins.

The most powerful and provoking illustration of Johnson's engagement with Christian existential thought in *Dreamer* is King's kitchen conversion scene in chapter 4. This chapter opens with King thinking about the challenges of the Way of nonviolence as "an experiment with truth. It was a truth-seeking process" (75). This thought leads him to think of Aquinas—not an accidental connection, for Jacques Maritain asserts that "Thomism, properly understood, is the 'only authentic existentialism'" (Herberg 3). King's mind then recalls his greatest crisis of faith, "that terrible night in Montgomery when his faith, lukewarm since childhood, became real" (78). This prompts a recollection of seeing parishioners seized by the spirit, the awe-filled emotional enthusiasm that grips the body and takes one out of oneself in ec-static spasms—the sort of experience King, an intellectual philosopher, hoped never to have himself (78–79). He muses that despite his rigorous philosophical and theological training, "even a jackleg preacher incapable of writing his own name had direct knowledge of the peace that passeth understanding he had only experienced in books" (80).

At this point, King's thoughts reach despair, as recollection of his spiritual impotence reminds him of his crisis of faith when the death threats became too much, and he felt he had to abandon the movement: "He knew he could not go on. The forces gathered against him were too many and great. . . . He could turn to no one for help. . . . He felt caged. Chained. In bondage and no longer belonging to himself" (80–81). This moment marks for King—and for Johnson too, I suspect—the failure (or at least the limits) of philosophy: for all his training in the grand western tradition, King is unable to think his way to divine understanding. Such a realization, Kass argues, epitomizes the teachings of the Book of Genesis, which insist that "obedience to God, not the independent and rational pursuit of wisdom, is the true and righteous human way" (58).[19] This is a remarkable moment for Johnson, self-described author of the "philosophical novel" ("Foreword" xi), to render a powerful scene the essence of which is the insufficiency of philosophy, the limits of human wisdom. In the face of this insurmountable challenge, King feels his sense of self-belonging slipping. This is the crucial step in his liberation, his entry into selflessness—a gesture common to all of Johnson's novels (Andrew reaches this crisis in *Oxherding Tale*, Rutherford in *Middle Passage*), but here rendered in an explicitly Christian context, which, given the powerfully autobiographical strain of the novel, signals Johnson's own engagement with this failure, or limitation, of the human intellect.

With King's mind "whirring widdershins" (implying movement in contrary directions, against the course of the sun, an unlucky way—the way of self-ful-ness), he moves to ultimate questions of human freedom, the very existence of God, the meaninglessness of life . . . and here, in the most powerful demonstration of the limits of philosophy, he finally gives it all up: "At last he began to pray. To whom—or what—he could not say. Not asking for anything then. Not fighting, only confessing, 'Lord, I have nothing left . . .'" (82). And the result is the dissolution of the thinking, seeking self: "the very belief in an 'I' that suffered and strained to affect the world, dissolved. . . . Awake, he saw that he was not the doer." At this point he hears the "*vox dei*," either within him or without (it makes no difference now), saying "Not I, but the Father within me doeth the works . . . I seek not my will but the will of the Father who sent me" (82–83, quoting from the Gospel of John 5:30).[20]

Johnson is fond of Husserl's notion of the bracketed experience—what he describes in *Being and Race* as "the phenomenological *epoche*, or 'bracketing' of all presuppositions in order to seize a fresh, original vision" (5)—and this could well describe King's awakening here. But perhaps a more accurate interpretation of this experience would invoke Rudolf Otto: King faces what Otto describes as "*the mysterium tremendum*: the hushed, trembling, and speechless humility of the creature in the presence of—whom or what? That which is a *mystery* inexpressible and above all creatures" (12–13). Clearly this experience is inaccessible to philosophy; like the God of the Bible, Hebrew and Christian, it thwarts human inquiry. It is not a thing *known* (hence Johnson, and King, here rejects Gnosticism), it is rather *a submission to the unknowable*.[21]

Johnson explores precisely this mystery in his penetrating meditation on the Book of Proverbs, where he states that the "axiom" that "encapsulates the pith of all the other proverbs" is the "mantra" of the first chapter: "The fear of the Lord is the beginning of knowledge" (*Turning* 63, Pvbs 1:7).[22] Johnson concludes that essay by affirming the central truth of the Old Testament: "Always life's true wealth in Proverbs is found in God, in wisdom and love" (65). The New Testament corollary would be Paul's dismissal of all merely human knowledge in the First Letter to the Corinthians: "and though I have the gift of prophecy, and understand all mysteries and all knowledge . . . but have not love, I am nothing . . . whether there is knowledge, it will vanish away" (1 Cor 13:2, 8).

King then moves from the dissolution of the self to the understanding of human empathy, the interrelatedness of all things and persons, a crucial step in Johnson's ethical vision. This is precisely the concern voiced by the New Testament theologians in the Existential tradition. As Herberg explains, "Maritain's 'Christian democracy,' Berdyaev's 'personalist socialism,' Buber's 'true community,' and Tillich's 'religious socialism' " all reflect "a social concern that is most characteristic of the fundamental outlook they share" (4). Indeed, Johnson, in his discussion of Proverbs, also arrives at the conclusion that the Pilgrim or seeker ultimately labors for others, offering "work and indefatigable service to the things loved" (*Turning* 65). All of which raises the pressing question of *Dreamer*: can Johnson yoke existential and ethical Christianity, with their apparently opposite impulses—the former inward, towards the self, and the latter outward, towards the community?

It is here that we see the true significance of King to Johnson's vision. Matthew witnesses the joining of these two elements in the depiction of Christianity at Calvary AME, when King delivers his sermon. Matthew notes that King's "grace or spiritual wealth" emerges because "he could give of himself endlessly"; King is "hugely present," but "at his center I felt a cemetery." King reminds Matthew of "my own staggering shortcomings as a man." King announces that he is focused on "only one problem: What is God?" (139) *This* is the aspect of King that so fascinates Johnson: not the social activist, not the political revolutionary, but the pilgrim seeking the presence of God, for this is the novel's—and Charles Johnson's—quest, as well.[23]

From this foundation of mystery and submission, Johnson moves forward into his essential ethical arguments about America, African-America, and humanity writ large. The central element of this teaching is the primacy of the concept of family. The most striking aspect of Johnson's portrait of King, it seems to me, is not King as activist, not even King as philosopher, but King in "the roles he cherished the most, those of father and husband" (187). He is able to "at last be himself" only after "the strange alchemy of marriage," in which his ego disappears and he sees himself as "a man working in concert with another for the welfare of his family, which reinforced his passion for politics and social justice" (193). This, I would argue, is the novel's "political" impulse: marriage and family first; politics and social justice follow. When we consider Johnson's autobiographical relation to the Evanston material, we see that this wisdom is precisely the wisdom of his own fathers. While meditating on the milk bottle of his great-uncle, and the paternal legacy these enduring men left their children, Johnson concludes that this is precisely what is missing in American culture today, reaffirming "what our elders knew regarding the primacy of family" that we observed earlier.[24]

Johnson's grand insight in *Dreamer* consists in his realization that his developing ethical and spiritual ideal of the Householder is also the heart of Christian theology, as expressed by Christ and by King. In his Calvary sermon King concludes, " 'after a time, I tell you, a man comes to see only a We. . . . Every man and woman is a speculum. Our mirror. Our twin' " (140). This is the ultimate response, of course, to the Cain-Abel paradox with which the novel begins, for the resolution of this opposition is precisely brother love. Cain's failure is his refusal to be his Brother's Keeper. Thus King cites 1 John 4:20 in his Letter from Birmingham City Jail: "If a man say, I love God, and hateth his brother, he is a liar: for he that loveth not his brother whom he hath seen, how can he love God whom he hath not seen?" (218). Not accidentally, I would argue, this echoes the central idea of one of the greatest Christian Existentialist theologians of the 20th century, Karl Rahner. Rahner writes: "The love of God is still borne by that opening in trusting love to the whole of reality which takes place in the love of neighbour. It is radically true, i.e. by an ontological and not merely 'moral' or psychological necessity, that whoever does not love the brother whom he 'sees,' also cannot love God whom he does not see, and that one can love God whom one does not see only *by* loving one's visible brother lovingly" (244). Eventually, the person of true vision comes to see not me, but we, "our twin" in all others. As King concludes his Calvary sermon, he asserts that this vision leads to a concerned response to "all the countless outcasts," which results in the realization that "at the numinous heart of being, there is a Heart, a Father." This restoration of the Father assuages the most pressing need felt by all Cain figures—the perceived rejection by their father. As Nash states, "much of the Cainite bitterness . . . arises from the sense of spiritual and social illegitimacy" (180) of these fatherless figures. It is in this respect that I see *Dreamer* as striking perhaps the most profoundly hopeful note in all of Johnson's work. He locates in his exploration of the Christian theological tradition the theology, the ethics, even the politics of this novel: a movement from me to we, which generates concern for the homeless wanderers, which leads one to God, "at the numinous heart of being."

NOTES

1. Johnson quotes part of this definition in his lecture ("Tillich," n.p.).

2. Ultimately, Whalen-Bridge's argument—which is admirably complex and insightful—comes close to this position, when he asserts that "neither a strictly Christian nor a strictly Buddhist interpretation of the novel will work" (514). Yet he does see the novel as seeking "the primary integration . . . between Eastern and Western standpoints from which to view political struggle" (505), whereas I will emphasize here Johnson's radical investigation of the Christian theological tradition.

3. Though both stories are featured in the novel's epigraphs, the Cain and Abel story seems much more important to the novel than the Joseph story. The latter is employed mainly to invoke the figure of the dreamer, and the interpreter of dreams, and has further importance to the extent that it parallels the Cain/Abel story.

4. I follow the novel in taking all Biblical quotations from the King James Version of the Bible.

5. See, for example, Luke 23 ("For, behold, the days are coming, in the which they shall say, Blessed are the barren, and the wombs that never bare, and the paps which never gave suck. Then shall they begin to say to the mountains, Fall on us; and to the hills, Cover us"); Mark 13 ("For nation shall rise against nation, and kingdom against kingdom: and there shall be earthquakes in divers places, and there shall be famines and troubles: these are the beginnings of sorrows . . . the brother shall betray the brother to death, and the father the son; and children shall rise up against their parents, and shall cause them to be put to death"); and Revelations 16 ("And there were voices, and thunders, and lightnings; and there was a great earthquake, such as was not since men were upon the earth, so mighty an earthquake, and so great. And the great city was divided into three parts, and the cities of the nations fell").

6. On the relations between brotherhood, death, and the French Revolution, see Ricardo Quinones's study, *The Brotherhood of Cain*. Johnson acknowledges this text in his foreword to the novel, and also alludes to it when Matthew states that "because Smith always seemed so obsessed with the story of Adam's two sons, I sat reading a book on them" (160)—a book that clearly refers to Quinones's, even though that work would not be

published until over 20 years had passed from the time of *Dreamer* (the sort of anachronism in which Johnson always delights).

7. Nash shows the complex derivation of "the mark of Cain" as a racial signifier, and argues that Johnson not only rejects this "racialist interpretation of the original story," but offers a re-reading of the mark as "the damaging dualist worldview" that fragments and damages humanity (*Charles Johnson's Fiction* 138–39).

8. Paul Ricouer, in his probing study "Ethical and Theological Considerations on the Golden Rule," similarly emphasizes "our radical dependence on a power that precedes us, envelops us, and supports us. This sense is supraethical par excellence." Ricoeur goes on to note that "the sense of our radical dependence on a higher power thus may be reflected in a love for the creature, for every creature, in every creature—and the love of neighbor can become an expression of this supramoral love for all creatures" (Ricouer 1995, 297–98). Ricouer's tenets reflect the main reading I will propose in the pages that follow.

9. Kass elaborates on Cain's desire for godlike status: Cain "was the first to be interested in bridging the gap—in his case, by gifts—between the human and the divine, an impulse we have shown to be largely presumptuous or hubristic. This prototypical human being begets a line leading to civilization, the arts, and the heroes—all manifestations of an impulse toward self-sufficiency, an impulse that culminates in a desire to jump the gap entirely, in a wish to *become* a god" (147). This view seems to me eminently analogous to the implications of Johnson's novel, which critique precisely our desires to be god-like, to assume mastery of our own existence. In this, I differ somewhat from Nash's reading, which sees Johnson as attempting to view this story "through the lens of inequity," and thereby valorize Cain and interrogate "Abel's filial responsibility" (*Charles Johnson's Fiction* 166).

10. The multiple sources and periods of composition of the Torah suggest that these writings took their final shape during the period of the Babylonian Exile, when the J, E, and D documents were edited together and the P document was composed, and the time of the rebuilding of the Temple, when these narrative strands were all connected—in other words, during a time of exile and return. See Davies, pp.16–20.

11. Near the end of "Self-Reliance," Emerson states that "It is easy in the world to live after the world's opinion; it is easy in solitude to live after our own; but the great man is he who in the mist of the crowd keeps with perfect sweetness the independence of solitude" (Emerson 263). Thus the apparent opposition of "self-reliance" and "the world" is in fact false for Emerson—precisely the reading that Johnson himself gives of this crucial precursor: "Over and against this false dualism [Emerson] sets a vision of divinely-infused human agency that spiritualizes our secular works and recalls the motto of Benedictine monks, *Laborare est orare* ('to labor is to pray') as well as the mindfulness of Zen Buddhists" (Johnson, "Emerson"). In this essay, Johnson describes an intellectual genealogy from Emerson to Toomer to Ellison to King (and, I would say, to Johnson himself) that seeks to overcome the dualism of self and other in all its manifestations. Nash interrogates Johnson's responses to and revisions of Emerson in insightful ways (*Charles Johnson's Fiction* 124–25, 163, 177), as does Gleason in his essay in this volume.

12. As Nash rightly points out, Johnson's portraits of this "entire generation of African Americans who rose above racist oppression without ever losing sight of, or pride in, their

black identity . . . provide a compelling answer to the novel's basic question: 'How shall I live?' " (*Charles Johnson's Fiction* 169).

13. Compare this to the Invisible Man's grandfather's belief in "the principle" of the nation: *Invisible Man* p.574.

14. For Johnson's further thought on the relations between King's teachings and affirmative action, see "Dr. King's Refrigerator" and "Executive Decision" in *Dr. King's Refrigerator and Other Bedtime Stories*.

15. This passage offers a forceful contrast to another litany, the "litany of things" strewn on the sidewalk of the old dispossessed couple evicted in *Invisible Man* (267–84). As I have argued elsewhere, in *Invisible Man* "the Eviction scene is the pivot of the entire novel, and presents its defining metaphor: the plight of the evicted, the homeless, the dispossessed" (Conner, "Litany" 177). Johnson's remarkable contrary vision is one of both physical and spiritual home and belonging, the "at-home-ness" so often desired but rarely achieved in modern literature. Johnson refers to this part of Ellison's novel as "the masterful Harlem eviction scene in which the possessions of an old black couple thrown onto the street become a doorway for experiencing black history from the Civil War forward" (*Turning* 109).

16. See, for example, Michael Boccia's interview in McWilliams, 196–97.

17. As one scholar describes Sartre's intellectual development, his "constant concern" from 1940 onward is "the predicament of the lone individual confronted with history as a massive ineluctable challenge to freedom and responsibility." This constitutes a shift from Sartre's earlier "apolitical" views to a focus on "choices . . . of a broadly social and political import" (Wood 83).

18. Levinas boldly revises Existentialism by insisting that prior to the understanding of Being comes the awareness of the other, that is, ethics precedes existence: "Preexisting the disclosure of being in general taken as basis of knowledge and as meaning of being is the relation with the existent that expresses himself; *preexisting the plane of ontology is the ethical plane*" (201, emphasis added). I find Johnson's engagement with both the existential and ethical implications of Christianity to be profoundly sympathetic with Levinas's thought. As one of his commentators states, Levinas's ultimate question regards our relation with the other: "How can I coexist with him and still leave his otherness intact?" (Wild 13). This surely is the very question at the heart of the Cain and Abel story. We might add to this Paul Ricoeur's eloquent reflection on Levinas's theory of the encounter with the Other: "this face is that of a master of justice, of a master who *instructs* and who does so only in the ethical mode: this face forbids murder and commands justice" (Ricoeur 1992, 189).

19. Or as Kass describes this in a more pithy fashion, "the wisdom of Jerusalem is not the wisdom of Athens" (4).

20. It is important to note that Matthew reaches a similar moment of crisis and self-abandonment to a higher power, when Chaym finally leaves him and Matthew gives himself over to selfless prayer: "I felt something slam inside my chest, then hot tears were hopping down my cheeks, and instead of offering words I wept for my counterfeit, fatherless status, gave myself over to it shamelessly, and by the end of my halting, stumbling appeal I felt emptied, no longer trying to bring a distant God's grace to my finite desires as His cast-aside son, but only wishing *Thy will be done*" (214).

21. This is why King's epiphany is aural, a heard voice, not a perceived vision. As Kass argues, in Genesis "the path to wisdom and happiness lies not through wondrous sights seen by the eye but through awesome command heard by the ear" (3). The New Testament parallel would be Christ's repeated injunction in the Parables: "He that hath ears to hear, let him hear" (Lk 14:35).

22. By "fear" is understood proper reverence, appropriate awe: "reverential fear and respect for God on account of his sovereignty, goodness and justice toward men. This is the foundation of religion" (New American Bible 702).

23. Johnson has written that "I deliberately rendered King as a philosophical and spiritual figure more than I played up his activism" (e-mail 29 May 2003).

24. This is the wisdom of "the householder," as discussed before, and it confirms that Johnson's central effort (as in his essay on Proverbs) is a spiritual and ethical teaching, as opposed to any specific political model or message. My reading of the novel thus differs somewhat from that of Whalen-Bridge, who views the novel as "Johnson's most politically engaged novel to date" (504), and also from that of Nash, to the extent that he claims Johnson "advances [a] social-activist response" to the question of "How shall I live?" (*Charles Johnson's Fiction* 177). Whereas Nash argues that *Dreamer* presents "Johnson's newly awakened activist impulse," and his "frank admission of the need for action" in the political realm (190), I see Johnson's career as progressing more along the lines of Walt Whitman's, into increasingly spiritual domains. I would stress, however, that these differences in interpretation are more complementary than contrary.

THE APPLICATION OF AN IDEAL
Turning the Wheel *as Ontological Program*

WILLIAM R. NASH

In "Shoulder to the Wheel" (2003), an interview with my fellow Johnson scholar (and good friend) John Whalen-Bridge, Charles Johnson explains what led him to publish *Turning the Wheel: Essays on Buddhism and Writing* (2003). The author notes, "in this phase of my life, what I call Act Three, I finally had to declare myself someone devoted to the dharma" ("Shoulder" 301). The work certainly does that; indeed, this collection of sixteen essays (seven on Buddhism, nine on writing) marks the fullest overt written articulation of elements that Johnson has "tuck[ed] into" his fiction from the publication of *Faith and the Good Thing* (1974) on through his most recent novel, *Dreamer* (1998). In foregrounding his dedication to the dharma and offering his views on how one enacts its most basic principles, Johnson realizes a program for the application of an ideal that has driven his work since 1974: the notion that race is an illusion.

The work comes at an opportune time. *Turning the Wheel* emerged into an especially welcoming environment for American writers of color to discuss their interests in Buddhism, as the past five years have brought significant advances in this area. Johnson published selections from *Turning the Wheel* in *Tricycle* in 2000; Angel Kyodo Williams published *Being Black: Zen and the Art of Living With Fearlessness and Grace* (2000); Jan Willis published *Dreaming Me* (2001), her stirring memoir of her journey from a protestant upbringing in pre–Civil Rights era Alabama to her present life as a noted scholar of Tibetan Buddhism and a practicing "Baptist-Buddhist"; and Hilda Gutierrez Baldoquin edited a landmark volume, *Dharma, Color, and Culture: New Voices in Western Buddhism* (2004), which includes a reprint of Johnson's essay "Reading the Eightfold Path" from *Turning the Wheel*. While these works do not share completely unified goals or uniform success of execution, the authors of these various works all address the particular usefulness of Buddhist practice, with its emphasis on seeing past apparent differences to the interconnectedness of all sentient beings, as a counter to the ravages of American racism.

At the heart of this common resistance lies one of the most important foundations of Buddhist thought. Regardless of sect, all Buddhists embrace

Shakyamuni Buddha's teaching of the Four Noble Truths, which one might translate as follows:

1. *Suffering exists.*
2. *Suffering arises from attachment to desires.*
3. *Suffering ceases when attachment to desire ceases.*
4. *Freedom from suffering is possible by practicing the Eightfold Path.*

In the context of American racism, the First Noble Truth is self-explanatory—certainly "suffering" is a fair term for living under the weight of systemic, systematic injustice, violence, and oppression.[1] The Second Noble Truth also resonates in this context, although one must take care to define "desires" clearly. The greatest desire, the most destructive illusion to which we become attached, is the notion of a concrete "self," a discrete entity with firm boundaries that separate and protect us from others. That desire for selfhood figures powerfully in othered individuals' quest for citizenship and acceptance as so-called real Americans.

With that definition in hand, one can confront the last two Noble Truths; at this point, the terrain becomes much more complex. Does the Third Noble Truth somehow effectively suggest that Americans of color must stop wanting to be full-fledged citizens, that they must instead accept and submit to their otherness? Not exactly. In the terms of these American Buddhists of color authors, the response is not resignation, but rather recognition that otherness is a constructed, lived illusion.

Beautiful rhetoric, one might say, but the *suffering* is real, and the historical record is replete with examples of *enforced* otherness—one need only look at the famous Civil Rights-era photographs of Alabama law enforcement officials setting dogs on African-American children to see that. How, then, in the face of these actions (and countless others like them), can one view otherness as an illusion? Here, as perhaps in all places, the devil is undeniably in the details. Attacking innocent children, or dragging a black man to death behind a pickup truck, as was done all too recently in Texas, is the *living* of the illusion. Johnson says of the contemporary racial climate that for people of color, this illusion is "one they're pulled into, whether they want to participate in it or not, the moment they walk out their door" ("Shoulder" 307).

So, what does one do in the face of this hostility? Or, to paraphrase Ralph Waldo Emerson's famous question in the essay "Fate," how shall one live?[2] In answer to that query, each of these authors points to the Fourth Noble Truth, and each recognizes that the living of what Johnson calls a "complete ethical system" is indeed the Way to liberation from racialized suffering (McWilliams, "An Interview" 297). Willis and Baldoquin certainly embrace this reading of the Eightfold Path. In Johnson's case, liberation is not an end in itself, however; he pushes the reader farther, stating "the question, I think, is what does a Buddhist do *after* awakening. . . . If he decides to stay in the world, the marketplace, in order to teach, as Shakyamuni did, or serve in some capacity, he does so—and lives daily—with nonattachment and *metta* [loving kindness towards all sentient beings]" ("Shoulder," 314). In *Turning the Wheel*, Johnson offers a series of reflections on his attempts at awakened living.

With that, Johnson fulfills the promise appearing in the final pages of *Dreamer*. That work turns on the notion that "doing well," a formulation initially articulated in the Biblical story of Cain and Abel, is the path to universal acceptance into the "beloved community" that Martin Luther King, Jr. sought.[3] I see him emphasizing, at the end of *Dreamer*, the need for individuals to pursue "doing well" fully and passionately. As narrator Matthew Bishop walks in Dr. King's funeral cortege, he stands on the verge of despair, realizing that he "believed in each of us there was a wound, an emptiness that could not be filled in our lifetime"; and yet, as he comes to this awareness, he also sees that "we could not stop if we wanted to, or go backward." In an eerie echo of this insight, someone behind him remarks, at that precise moment, " 'keep moving forward. If we stop, we'll fall and be trampled' " (236). And so, facing the internal void and unable to turn away, one must pursue the right course of action, which here Johnson identifies as "doing well."

Right action, of course, resonates with "Right Conduct," which is the fourth stage of the Eightfold Path, if one imposes a linear structure on them.[4] Recognizing this, one can then turn to the opening essay of *Turning the Wheel*. "Reading the Eightfold Path" outlines and provides a philosophical interpretation of each step of the Buddhist Way towards enlightenment. It also advances a social program of living that answers the call to action that Johnson sounds through this anonymous speaker at the end of *Dreamer*. Indeed, the essays that *Turning the Wheel* comprises systematically propose a means by which a seeker, specifically an African-American seeker, *more* specifically an African-American writer, can "keep moving" and serve the ideal of the beloved community. In so doing, they also provide, by example and directly, suggestions for how his readers might themselves turn the wheel of the Dharma.

At the heart of "Reading the Eightfold Path" is the notion of *svadharma*, or "personal responsibility." As Johnson succinctly states, "Followers of the Buddhadharma, fully aware of impermanence, dualism, and relativity, yet also aware of the ubiquity of suffering, are obliged at some point to oppose the origins of *duhka* ('suffering') in the social world" (26). For the best American example of this opposition, Johnson turns once again to the subject of *Dreamer* and states that American Buddhists

> will, I believe, share the dreams stated by Dr. Martin Luther King Jr. in his Nobel Prize acceptance speech in 1964, where he said "Civilization and violence are antithetical concepts. . . . Nonviolence is the answer to the crucial political and moral question of our time. . . . The foundation of such a method is love. . . . I have the audacity to believe that peoples everywhere can have three meals a day for their bodies, education and culture for their minds, and dignity, equality, and freedom for their spirits. I believe that what self-centered men have torn down men other-centered can build up."
>
>   To work for *this*, to find an occupation that realizes this, is to fulfill the step [of the Eightfold Path] called Perfect Livelihood. (26)

What Johnson calls for with this description is a form of "engaged Buddhism," a variant on the teachings of Thich Nhat Hahn, the Vietnamese monk who led the Vietnamese Buddhist Coalition at the Paris Peace accords and whom King nominated for the Nobel Peace Prize in 1967.[5] Furthermore, he specifically weds this mode of being to Dr. King's vision and reinforces the call for action that he sounds in *Dreamer*. In Johnson's view, the responsibility of the enlightened one is not merely to sit quietly beneath the bodhi tree; rather, to invoke a formulation that drives his second novel, *Oxherding Tale* (1982), the enlightened one must needs "return to the village with bliss-bestowing hands," sharing what he has learned in his own quest with those villagers who suffer without knowing why.

The specter of *Oxherding Tale* proves extremely important here, in that it evokes both Johnson's movement toward and his shying away from activism in his earlier fiction.[6] In each of his novels, Johnson plays with the bodhisattva role, offering the lessons of enlightenment in the various guises of *bildungsroman*, slave narrative, sea story, and fictionalized biography. All of his books are, in one way or another, about the need for individuals, especially black individuals in America, to free themselves from their illusions of separation and to work together to build and maintain a more harmonious life-world. To a person, his protagonists experience great suffering and grope their way towards the cessation of that pain. And, in every case, they find what they are seeking, and more besides. Faith Cross, Andrew Hawkins, Rutherford Calhoun, and Matthew Bishop each experiences a profound awakening to the interconnectedness of all beings. For them as individuals, these are powerful, liberating moments. In all of Johnson's novels, save *Faith and the Good Thing*, that awareness leads the seeker to a concomitant realization of the power of love as a means of overcoming suffering, a step further on the Path of Right Relationship.

That these *individuals* experience enlightenment leads me to the related question: what about the rest of the community—not just the fictional community, but also the extratextual community of readers? Does this lesson about love and "interbeing" translate to them?[7] As I read the novels, the answer is "not quite." Johnson certainly makes a strong case for these principles being broadly applicable; however, he also introduces a counterclaim in the fiction that limits the accessibility of the interbeing ideal.

The counterclaim that intrudes in each of his novels, however, manifests itself in a pressing sense of the sustained injustice that African Americans have faced throughout the nation's history. Throughout his fiction, the tension between his Buddhist ideals and his sense of the frustrating racial realities of American life keeps Johnson from ever fully achieving a satisfactory application of his philosophical and social ideal, which is to both address and eschew the systematic and systemic violation of American black being. With *Turning the Wheel*, Johnson finds the medium that allows him to fully address the questions of what it means to be black in America and to demonstrate the liberation available to African Americans in the dharma.

Two essays in the first section most effectively illustrate the point. The first, "Accepting the Invitation," is a brief meditation on why Buddhists should vote. Johnson notes that the Eightfold Path, specifically the "injunction for Right Conduct," calls Buddhists "to translate the Dharma into specific acts of social responsibility." He continues, "in a democratic republic, that surely means voting for those initiatives we believe will reduce suffering and violence, ignorance, and hatred" (44). He weds this call for spiritually enlightened social engagement to a brief but forceful account of the injustices black Americans suffered in the era before the Voting Rights Act of 1965 was passed. The message is clear: African Americans are a group of people who have known suffering and who have had to work especially hard for their enfranchisement. As a result, they have a particular duty (*svadharma*) to embrace the responsibility that attends finally gaining the ballot. Furthermore, in the religious-philosophical system that calls on blacks to embrace a particular attitude towards voting, there lies a means of addressing the broader conception of racially inflected suffering that this group faces. Keep moving, the essay says, echoing the end of *Dreamer*; and, as you move, here is a religious-philosophical roadmap that will show you the Way to freedom.

The second essay, "A Sangha by Another Name," pushes this notion even farther, arguing that Buddhism is an effective, perhaps even an ideal, response to the challenges inherent in being black in America. The essay opens with the following assertion: "The black experience in America, like the teachings of Shakyamuni Buddha, begins with suffering" (46). I find this assertion striking for two reasons. First, because it equates black life in America so directly to Buddhist philosophy, a correlation that is still sufficiently rare in the national public discourse to command special attention. Second, because it marks perhaps the only instance in Charles Johnson's corpus where one can find the phrase "the black experience" used in anything other than a mocking or dismissive manner—throughout his critical oeuvre and in interviews and discussions, he consistently prefers the formulation "experiences of blackness," which allows for the richness and breadth of black life and defies any attempts at viewing the black community as a monolith.

Indeed, Johnson has spent his creative career decrying the notion that there can meaningfully be anything called *the* black experience, given that individuals have such varying responses to even the same stimuli. But here, in this instance, Johnson finds the formulation useful; and as he explains it, I understand his usage. Certainly it seems reasonable to characterize the slave trade and the enforced cultural re-education of newly made African-Americans as experiences marked by suffering. In that vein, it seems worth pausing to note that some of Johnson's earlier humorous representations of the slave trade (most notably a cartoon from his first published collection *Black Humor* [1970]) have raised objections from scholars unsettled by the notion that one might find anything to joke about in the hold of a slaver. And yet, given how Johnson makes a powerful teaching tool of humor, the drawings demand reassessment of the importance of suffering in African-American life and lead one to reject the victimization model of black identity.

In "Sangha," the vision of black suffering and struggle is much more conventional, because he cannot explain his notions about the cessation of suffering without emphasizing that idea of group suffering as a starting point. Johnson's shift away from one of his most adamantly-held positions in service of this greater social and moral good resonates with a similar shift in ideas that one sees running throughout *Dreamer*, where he makes strong steps towards the fully-realized social program he presents in *Turning the Wheel*. To get people thinking about how to correct injustice, he has use for the notion of a monolithic character for African Americans' experiences that he presents in the opening of "A Sangha by Another Name."

Perhaps paradoxically, Johnson's recognition of suffering as the hallmark of black life doorways not into a sustained lament over the narrowness of black being, which I would argue is the usual resolution of such a set of claims; instead, it opens onto the Way, the path that Johnson believes will lead African Americans through suffering into enlightenment. As he says in the closing sentence of the essay, "through the Dharma, the black American quest for 'freedom' realizes its profoundest, truest, and most revolutionary meaning" (57). Johnson has hinted at this notion before, to be sure; indeed, it is a version of this realization that carries Andrew Hawkins to "*moksha*," or enlightenment, in the last chapter of *Oxherding Tale*. In that instance, however, the enlightenment is very particularized, the end of one man's journey and not a broadly applicable notion. What Johnson aims at in "A Sangha by Another Name" (the title is a reference to Johnson's view of King and his "beloved community") is precisely that universal vision. What is more, he attributes flashes of that vision to a range of predecessors in the African American literary tradition, including W. E. B. Du Bois and Jean Toomer, a move that simultaneously legitimizes the notion by grounding Johnson firmly in an established tradition and expands its scope by offering an alternative reading of that canon.

In a recent interview with John Malkin, Johnson likens his creative process to the practice of meditation. This link in many ways explains the second half of *Turning the Wheel*, entitled "On Writing." In these nine essays, Johnson complements his alternative reading of the African-American tradition in "A Sangha by Another Name" with a combination of essays that redefine the writer's role. He also illustrates how authors concerned with racial issues, and black writers in particular, can first achieve enlightenment and liberation through their work and then share those insights with readers. With these goals in mind, the several essays on writing and on particular works of literature demonstrate something of the application of Johnson's Buddhist ideal.

Two of these essays are particularly noteworthy for their interlocking commentary on how writers and readers can escape the limitations of racialized thinking that plague Americans: "The Beginner's Mind" and "The Role of the Black Intellectual in the Twenty-first Century." The former, which is largely a tribute to Johnson's mentor, John Gardner, demonstrates the level of careful observation and "clean," or value-neutral, observant thought that the reader must bring to each experience in order to wring the most from it. The latter provides a program for black writers and for readers of all ethnicities; I read it as a literary attempt to erase the "mark of Cain," or, in the terms of *Dreamer*, to "do well."

The reference to "the mark of Cain" is, of course, an allusion to the widely held belief that African Americans bear the curse of their blackness as a sign of their heritage as Cain's descendants.[8] In this essay, Johnson argues that black intellectuals have been similarly marked, in the sense that their perceived racial identity is the litmus test by which editors and readers judge their ability to comment meaningfully on any subject. Throughout the twentieth century, he argues, the range of African Americans' contributions to public intellectual discourse was largely, if not exclusively, limited to questions of race, regardless of what an individual's field of expertise might be. As he notes acerbically, "twentieth-century black 'intellectuals' were granted authority by the white world on but one worldly subject: *themselves*" (85). He goes on to explain that for him, the term "intellectual" has the negative pre-twentieth century connotations that signify a tendency towards reducing phenomena to reason and, more broadly, towards speaking boldly and expansively on all racial subjects regardless of what one might or might not know about the issues at hand.

One quickly sees the limitations of this pigeonholing of the African American mind: the speaker who comments about everything related to race risks ending up full of sound and fury, signifying nothing. As Johnson puts it, "the result is often comic when the 'intellectual-celebrity' steps out of the field where he or she has genuine authority (artists, for example, who talk about the fields of economics or politics when they are amateurs; or, if you like, [Toni] Morrison's recent statement that William Jefferson Clinton is our first 'black' president, which was probably news to everyone in Clinton's family)" (87). Extending the point, sometimes the results are comic even when figures speak *inside* their discipline but stretch for connections to contemporary events, a move that increases their prominence in the public eye.[9]

Certainly this emphasis on public commentary limits an intellectual's ability to make a meaningful contribution to a particular discipline. In Johnson's terms, it is this that distinguishes the public figure from the scholar. Johnson reserves the latter term for people who add to the body of knowledge associated with their disciplines in a manner that distinguishes them and materially advances the subject at hand. By way of illustrating the point, Johnson notes W. E. B. Du Bois's phenomenal contributions to sociology and John Hope Franklin's accomplishments as an historian. In speaking of Du Bois, he also notes the broader benefits of the life of the mind to both the scholar and the community. First, he says, such real scholarship is "a *moral* work," one that fully engages every element of the scholar's being and thereby ennobles and transforms him or her. Second, he notes that emphasizing the success of such role models could inspire future generations of African Americans to achieve ever-greater scholarly heights (92). If the community can do that, he argues, then it can reverse the trend that restricts black thinkers to commentary on racial matters.

One might wonder what this essay has to do with Buddhism, and at first glance it might well seem disjointed. I would argue, however, that there are at least two powerful links that illuminate the Way buried in this essay and, by extension, in all of Johnson's "On Writing" essays. First of all, the black scholar who embraces the methods of his or her chosen field and pursues knowledge for the pure (or almost pure) love of it embodies the ideal of one who lives his or her *svadharma*. The standard by which the public intellectual must necessarily measure his or her success is public recognition; one cannot expect that it is possible to garner (and arguably to pursue) fame without becoming tainted by it. This is especially true in an environment that increasingly demands public displays of insight, or PDI's, from African American pundits regardless of what they might or might not reasonably know about a given issue.

By contrast, the scholar may pursue knowledge for its own sake, performing biochemistry experiments because she wants to know how certain crystals grow or studying Sanskrit so that he might better read traditional texts. This dharma-driven pursuit of information yields, arguably, not just knowledge but also *wisdom*. Punditry, by contrast, dresses information (and sometimes mis-information) in the cloak of wisdom, with regard for little more than the impact that the commentary will have on the speaker, not the perceiver. Since what passes for insight is often not the Truth (in the metaphysical sense), then it cannot really set either the speaker or the perceiver free. In sharp contrast to that, Johnson offers a Way that frees not only the present individuals but also subsequent generations of the community. The scholar, in short, is the Buddha returning to the village with bliss-bestowing hands.

Or perhaps one should say "*a* Buddha," with the acknowledgment of the creative writer as another such figure. One of the pieces in "On Writing" is a paean to Ralph Ellison; two others are introductions that Johnson composed for new editions of Sinclair Lewis's *Kingsblood Royal* (1947) and Harriet Beecher Stowe's *Uncle Tom's Cabin* (1852). A third, "Progress in Literature," makes the case for the importance of writing and reading (e.g., "literature is dangerous *ontologically* because reading is the most radical and liberating of all enterprises . . . the triumph of individual consciousness and human freedom" [131–33]). He continues, compellingly arguing the public's need, even its responsibility, to support the independent venues for innovative experimental fiction as a means of defending against the same sort of cultural ghettoization he decries in "The Role of the Black Intellectual." This time, however, the restrictions he warns against fall on the reader, not the writer. Getting free of these confining attitudes is, in

Johnson's view, clearly noble work, a step on the Way towards the elimination of suffering that is the goal of all his writing.

He applies this standard of helping eliminate suffering to the authors whose individual works he comments on in the other "On Writing" essays. Both Sinclair Lewis and Ralph Ellison come off rather well, as Johnson praises them for their efforts to meaningfully represent the richness of twentieth-century American life and the completeness of their vision. He takes a rather different view of Stowe—one that demonstrates both the complexities of his intellectual position on race and his resolution of that apparent conflict. Although Johnson does acknowledge some of Stowe's successes in *Uncle Tom's Cabin*, he primarily emphasizes the novel as an "ineluctably racist" portrayal of African-American life (98). I do not dispute that characterization; I would, however, suggest that in many ways Stowe is no worse (and arguably, somewhat better) than many of her abolitionist colleagues, who sought the freedom of enslaved blacks but held no brief for their achieving anything like social equality.

What I find interesting about Johnson's essay is that he omits that crucial piece of history while turning much of the rest of his introduction to a lesson on the realities of slave life. He ends that discussion with the assertion that, despite some "admirable attempts," white people cannot meaningfully and effectively "portray a black person *in his own terms*" with "compelling . . . fidelity and veracity" (103). On the surface, this seems to raise once again the specter of the "black experience" issue. And yet, on closer examination, this statement reveals a concern with a different level of awareness, one that actually conveys some sense of hope and that in many ways fulfills the larger mission of *Turning the Wheel*. The call for describing "the racial Other" on his (or her) own terms is a plea for understanding; and what Johnson says makes Stowe's work so useful is that it reminds us of the need for such understanding between racial groups. Here, as in the Buddhist essays, Johnson emphasizes the steps of the Eightfold Path, the Perfect Thought and Perfect Conduct that will ultimately help heal the racial divide in America.

That emphasis on Perfect Conduct and Perfect Thought, as defined in "Reading the Eightfold Path," perfectly characterizes Johnson's position as the author of this series of essays. As he pursues his householder's *svadharma*, giving himself fully and freely that which he is given to do (writing and teaching), he illuminates the Way for readers and seekers struggling to overcome the suffering associated with a narrow view of American racial being. As Johnson himself has said, "over the last three decades, I . . . had to acknowledge and explore the central questions in Eastern religions" as part of his creative effort "to develop black (and thereby American) philosophical fiction." In other words, "the life of the spirit" has been "something I could not—and did not want to—ignore" (Boccia, 205). In *Turning the Wheel*, he brings the life of the spirit to the forefront, emphasizing in the process how mindfulness and sensitivity bring liberation to both black letters and black life.

NOTES

1. For a concise discussion of this, see Johnson's "Accepting the Invitation," first published in *Tricycle* (X.1, Fall, 2000: 63–64) and reprinted in *Turning the Wheel*, 42–45.

2. It is perhaps useful in this context to note Emerson's familiarity with key texts and ideas of Buddhist philosophy. For further discussion of Emerson's debt to Eastern thought, see Richardson.

3. For my more complete discussion of *Dreamer*, and more particularly for my assessment of the importance of "doing well" in Johnson's evolving world view, see *Charles Johnson's Fiction*, 162–95, esp. 174–77, 181–82, and 194–95.

4. Johnson notes the difficulty of organizing the steps of the Eightfold Path in his essay, stating, "this is not a linear movement. . . . Naturally, all the steps presuppose, depend upon, complement, and complete each other; they are not taken one at a time, but worked on simultaneously, and as one matures with them, understanding of the steps deepens" ("Reading," 6–7).

5. For a discussion of Johnson's similarities to Thich Nhat Hahn, see Storhoff, *Understanding Charles Johnson*, especially 9–10.

6. In myriad interviews and essays appearing throughout his career, Johnson disavows any interest in activism or being a spokesperson. And yet, despite that public stance, his novels demonstrate an increasingly strong impulse towards collective action. This, in brief, is one of the guiding arguments of my *Charles Johnson's Fiction*.

7. Thich Nhat Hanh coined the term "interbeing" to describe this state of mutual connection, as Johnson notes in several of his published essays on Buddhism. In earlier interviews, Johnson tends to use a philosophical term from Husserlian phenomenology— "intersubjectivity"—to refer to this same notion.

8. As I argue in *Charles Johnson's Fiction*, 138, 165–69, this pernicious, destructive formulation derives from a deliberate misreading of the original Hebrew. Johnson explores the impact of this idea of blackness as "stain" at length in *Dreamer*.

9. One might think, for example, of Henry Louis Gates. Jr.'s 1990 defense of Luke Skywalker and the other members of the hip hop group 2 Live Crew, who faced obscenity charges and public reprimand for the content of their best-selling album *As Nasty As They Wanna Be*. Although I see some merit in Gates's *New York Times* piece, "2 Live Crew, Decoded," his commentary on the issue speaks most strongly to me of his having been anointed as *the* public authority on African-American vernacular cultural by virtue of his authoring *The Signifyin(g) Monkey* in 1988.

WORKS CITED

A Dictionary of Buddhism. Introduction by T. O. Ling. NY: Scribners, 1972.

African American Perspectives and Philosophical Traditions. Edited and with an introduction by John P. Pittman. New York: Routledge, 1997.

Alter, Robert. *Genesis: Translation and Commentary.* NY: Norton, 1996.

Aristotle. *Aristotle: Poetics.* Translated by Malcolm Heath. NY: Penguin, 1996.

———. *Aristotle's Metaphysics: A Revised Text and Commentary, volume I.* Edited by W. D. Ross. Oxford: Clarendon Press, 1924.

Atherton, James. *The Books at the Wake: A Study of Literary Allusions in James Joyce's Finnegans Wake.* NY: Viking, 1960.

Bagwell, Orlando. "Preface" to *Africans in America: America's Journey through Slavery.* Edited by Patricia White. Fictional material by Charles Johnson. NY: Harcourt Brace & Company, 1998.

Barber, Michael. *Guardian of Dialogue: Max Scheler's Phenomenology, Sociology of Knowledge, and Philosophy of Love.* Lewisburg: Bucknell University Press, 1993.

Bloom, Harold. "Introduction." *Poets of Sensibility and the Sublime.* Edited and with an introduction by Harold Bloom. NY: Chelsea House, 1986.

Blue, Marian. "An Interview with Charles Johnson" in McWilliams 123–41.

Boccia, Michael. "An Interview with Charles Johnson" in McWilliams 192–205.

Boler, Megan, and Michalinos Zembylas. "Discomforting Truths: The Emotional Terrain of Understanding Difference." Trifonas, Peter Pericles, ed. *Pedagogies of Difference: Rethinking Education for Social Change.* New York: Routledge, 2003: 110–36.

Bosche, Phoebe. "An Interview with Charles Johnson" in McWilliams 78–92.

Brightman, Edgar Sheffield. *Person and Reality: An Introduction to Metaphysics.* NY: Ronald Press, 1958.

Brown, Alexandra. *The Cross and Human Transformation: Paul's Apocalyptic Word in 1 Corinthians.* Minneapolis: Fortress Press, 1995.

Bultmann, Rudolf. *New Testament and Mythology, and Other Writings.* Edited and translated by Schubert M. Ogden. Philadelphia: Fortress Press, 1984.

Byrd, Rudolph P. *Charles Johnson's Novels: Writing the American Palimpsest.* Indiana: Indiana University Press, 2005.

———., ed. *I Call Myself an Artist: Writings By and About Charles Johnson.* Bloomington and Indianapolis: Indiana University Press, 1999.

———. "*Oxherding Tale* and *Siddhartha*: Philosophy, Fiction, and the Emergence of a Hidden Tradition." *African American Review,* 30.4 (Winter 1996): 549–58.

Callahan, John F. "Frequencies of Eloquence: The Performance and Composition of *Invisible Man.*" *New Essays on* Invisible Man. Edited by Robert O'Meally. Cambridge: Cambridge University Press, 1988: 55–94.

Campbell, Joseph, and Henry Morton Robinson. *A Skeleton Key to* Finnegans Wake. NY: Harcourt, Brace, and Company, 1944.

Chaundry, Bob. "Damien Hirst: Shockaholic." *BBC Newsmakers*. BBC News. 20 September 2002. http://news.bbc.co.uk/1/hi/in_depth/uk/2000/newsmakers/2268841.stm

Coleman, James W. "Charles Johnson's Quest for Black Freedom in *Oxherding Tale*." *African American Review*. 29.4 (1995): 631–44.

Conner, Marc C. Review of *Charles Johnson's Fiction*, by William R. Nash. *South Atlantic Review* 69:2 (2004): 124–28.

———. "The Litany of Things: Sacrament and History in *Invisible Man*." *Ralph Ellison and the Raft of Hope: A Political Companion to Invisible Man*. Edited by Lucas E. Morel. Lexington, KY: University Press of Kentucky, 2004: 171–92.

———. "Wild Women and Graceful Girls: Toni Morrison's *Winter's Tale*." *Nature, Woman, and the Art of Politics*. Edited by Eduardo A. Velasquez. NY: Rowman & Littlefield, 2000.

———. E-mail to John Whalen-Bridge. 1 December 2004.

Cowper, William. *The Poems of William Cowper*, volume III. Edited by John D. Baird and Charles Ryskamp. Oxford: Clarendon Press, 1980.

Cozzens, Lisa. "The Civil Rights Movement 1955–1965." *African American History*. http://fledge.watson.org/~lisa/blackhistory/civilrights-55-65 (26 September 2004).

Cuomo, Chris J., and Kim Q. Hall, Eds. and Introduction. *Whiteness: Feminist Philosophical Reflections* Lanham, Md: Rowland & Littlefield, 1999.

Davies, A. Powell. "Fact and Fable: A Problem for Scholars." *Perspectives on Old Testament Literature*, edited by Woodrow Ohlsen. NY: Harcourt, Brace, Jovanovich, 1978: 14–20.

Defoe, Daniel. *Robinson Crusoe*. New York: Norton, 1975, rpt. 1994.

Dermot, Moran. *Introduction to Phenomenology*. London: Routledge, 2000.

Dharma, Color, and Culture: New Voices in Western Buddhism. Edited by Hilda Gutierrez Baldoquin. Berkely, CA: Parallax Press, 2004.

Dillon, M. C. *Merleau-Ponty's Ontology*. Bloomington: Indiana University Press, 1988.

Dixon, Melvin. "Mutiny on the Republic." *The Washington Post* 15 July 1990: X6.

Du Bois, W. E. B. "Criteria of Negro Art." *W. E. B. Du Bois: Writings*. Edited by Nathan Irvin Huggins. NY: Library of America, 1986: 993–1002.

———. *The Souls of Black Folk*. NY: Vintage / Library of America, 1990.

Dunbar, Paul Laurence. *The Collected Poetry of Paul Laurence Dunbar*. Edited by Joanne M. Braxton. Charlottesville: University Press of Virginia, 1993.

Eldridge, Richard. *An Introduction to the Philosophy of Art*. Cambridge: Cambridge University Press, 2003.

Eliade, Mircea. *The Sacred and the Profane: The Nature of Religion*. Translated by Willard R. Trask. NY: Harcourt, 1959.

Ellison, Ralph. *Invisible Man*. NY: Vintage, 1980.

———. *The Collected Essays of Ralph Ellison*. Edited by John F. Callahan. New York: Modern Library, 1995.

Emerson, Ralph Waldo. "Self-Reliance." *Essays and Poems*. NY: Library of America, 1996: 257–82.

Frankena, William K. *Ethics*, 2nd ed. Englewood Cliffs, N.J.: Prentice-Hall, 1973.

Franklin, John Hope, and Alfred A. Moss, Jr. *From Slavery to Freedom: A History of African-Americans*. 8th ed. NY: Alfred A. Knopf, 2005.

Freedman, David Noel, Editor-in-Chief. *Eerdman's Dictionary of the Bible*. Grand Rapids, Michigan and Cambridge, U.K.: Wm. B. Eerdmans Publishing Co., 2000.

Freud, Sigmund. *Civilization and Its Discontents*. Translated and edited by James Strachey. NY: W. W. Norton and Co., 1961.

Friere, Paolo. *Pedagogy of the Oppressed*. New York: Continuum, 1975.

Frings, Manfred S. *Max Scheler*. Milwaukee: Marquette University Press, 1996.

Frye, Northrop. *The Anatomy of Criticism: Four Essays*. Princeton: Princeton University Press, 1957.

———. "Cycle and Apocalypse in *Finnegans Wake*." *Myth and Metaphor: Selected Essays 1974–1988*. Edited by Robert D. Denham. Charlottesville: University of Virginia Press, 1990. 356–74.

Gates, Henry Louis, Jr. "2 Live Crew, Decoded." *New York Times*, June 19, 1990: A23.

———. *The Signifying Monkey: A Theory of African-American Literary Criticism*. New York: Oxford University Press, 1988.

Giroux, Henry. *Border Crossings: Cultural Workers and the Politics of Education*. New York: Routledge, 1994.

Gleason, William. "The Liberation of Perception: Charles Johnson's *Oxherding Tale*." *Black American Literature Forum* 25:4 (Winter 1991): 705–28.

Ghosh, Nibir K. "From Narrow Complaint to Broad Celebration: A Conversation with Charles Johnson." *Melus* 29 (2004). 359–75.

Gunn, Giles. *Thinking Across the Grain: Ideology, Intellect, and the New Pragmatism*. Chicago: University of Chicago Press, 1992.

Hayward, Jennifer. "Something to Serve: Constructs of the Feminine in Charles Johnson's *Oxherding Tale*." *Black American Literature Forum* 25 (1991), 689–703.

Hanh, Thich Nhat. *Peace Is Every Step*. Berkeley: Parallax Press, 1991.

———. *Being Peace*. Edited by Arnold Kotler. Berkeley: Parallax Press, 1987.

Heath, Malcolm. "Introduction to Aristotle's *Poetics*." *Aristotle: Poetics*. Translated by Malcolm Heath. NY: Penguin, 1996. vii–lxxi.

Hegel, G. W. E. "Introduction." *The Philosophy of History*. New York: Dover Pub, 1956. 91–99.

Heidegger, Martin. *Being and Time*. Translated by John Macquarrie and Edward Robinson. San Francisco: Harper and Collins, rpt. 1962.

———. *Poetry, Language, Thought*. Translated and with an introduction by Albert Hofstadter. NY: Harper and Row, 1971.

———. *What Is Philosophy?* Translated and with an introduction by William Kluback and Jean T. Wilde. New Haven: College and University Press, 1956.

Herberg, Will. *Four Existentialist Theologians*. NY: Doubleday, 1958.

hooks, bell. "An Aesthetic of Blackness: Strange and Oppositional." *Yearning: Race, Gender, and Cultural Politics*. Boston: South End Press, 1990. 103–13.

Hume, David. "Of National Characters." *The Philosophical Works of David Hume*, Vol. 3. Boston: Little, Brown, and Co, 1854. 217–36.

Hutchinson, George. "Jean Toomer and American Racial Discourse." *Texas Studies in Language and Literature* 35:2 (Summer 1993): 227–51.

Husserl, Edmund. *The Crisis of European Sciences and Transcendental Phenomenology: An Introduction to Phenomenological Philosophy.* Translated by David Carr. Evanston: Northwestern University Press, 1970.

Jackson, Lawrence. *Ralph Ellison: Emergence of Genius.* NY: John Wiley and Sons, 2002.

Johnson, Charles. "A Boot Camp for Creative Writers." *Chronicle of Higher Education* 31 Oct. 2003: B7+.

———. "Alethia." *The Sorcerer's Apprentice: Tales and Conjurations.* New York: Penguin Books, 1986. 97–112.

———. "An Appreciation of Ralph Ellison" *Washington Post* 1994.

———. "And if peace is their goal, they will in the field of politics be themselves peace embodied & other principles of enlightened politics." *Shambhala Sun* 12:6 (July 2004): 28–33.

———. "An Ever-Lifting Song of Black America." *New York Times* 14 February 1999, AR1, 34.

———. "A Phenomenology of the Black Body" in Byrd 1999, 109–22.

———. "A Symposium on Contemporary American Fiction." *Michigan Quarterly Review* (1987).

———. *Being and Race: Black Writing Since 1970.* Bloomington: Indiana University Press, 1988.

———. *Black Humor.* Chicago: Johnson Publishing Co., 1970.

———. *Dr. King's Refrigerator and Other Bedtime Stories.* NY: Scribner, 2005.

———. *Dreamer.* NY: Simon & Schuster, 1998.

———. E-mail to John Whalen-Bridge. 26 September 2004.

———. E-mail to Marc C. Conner. 17 May 2003.

———. E-mail to Marc C. Conner. 29 May 2003.

———. E-mail to Marc C. Conner. 16 February 2006.

———. "Emerson." Introduction to *The Selected Writings of Ralph Waldo Emerson.* New York: Signet, 2003.

———. *Faith and the Good Thing.* NY: Viking, 1974.

———. "Foreword." James McWilliams. *Passing the Three Gates: Interviews with Charles Johnson.* Seattle: University of Washington Press, 2004: ix–xvi.

———. "I Call Myself an Artist" in Byrd, 3–30.

———. "Introduction." *Oxherding Tale, With a New Introduction by the Author.* NY: Penguin, 1995: ix–xix.

———. "Inventing Africa," review of *In My Father's House: Africa in the Philosophy of Culture*, by Kwame Anthony Appiah (Oxford University Press, 1992), *New York Times Book Review*, 21 July 1992.

———. "Keeping the Blues Away," review of Albert Murray's *The Blue Devils of Nada* and *The Seven League Boots. New York Times Book Review*, 10 March 1996, 4.

———. *Middle Passage.* NY: Atheneum, 1990.

———. "National Book Award Acceptance Speech." *TriQuarterly* 82 (fall 1991): 208–9.

———. "Novelists of Memory" in Byrd 1999, 97–107.

———. *Oxherding Tale.* New York: Grove Press, 1983.

———. "Philosophy and Black Fiction" in Byrd 1999, 79–84.

———. "Race, Politics and Ralph Ellison," review of Jerry Gaffo Watts's *Heroism and the Black Intellectual: Ralph Ellison, Politics, and Afro-American Intellectual Life* (University of North Carolina Press). *New York Times Book Review*, 5 February 1995, 15.

———. "Ralph Ellison: Novel Genius." *Crisis* (March/April 2002).

———. Reply to Norman Podhoretz's critique of *Invisible Man* in *Commentary* (October 1999).

———. Review of *American Hunger*, by Richard Wright. *The American Book Review* 1.1 (December 1977): 6–7.

———. Review of *How I Wrote Certain of My Books*, by Raymond Roussel. *The American Book Review* 1.2 (April/May 1978): 11.

———. Review of *The European Tribe*, by Caryl Phillips. *Los Angeles Times Book Review*, 19 July 1987, 3.

———. *Soulcatcher and Other Stories*. New York: Harcourt, 1998.

———. "The King We Left Behind" in Byrd 1999, 193–99.

———. "The King We Need: Teachings for a Nation in Search of Itself." *Shambhala Sun* 13:3 (January 2005): 42–50.

———. "The Lesson of the Mau Mau." Review of Robert B. Edgerton's *Mau Mau: An African Crucible* (The Free Press, 1989). *Los Angeles Times Book Review*. 7 January 1990.

———. "The Philosopher and the American Novel." *California State Library Foundation Bulletin* 35 (April 1991): 1–16.

———. "The Prophet of Black Arts." Review of *Visions of a Liberated Future: Black Arts Movement Writings*, by Larry Neal, edited by Michael Schwartz (Thunder's Mouth Press, 1989). *Los Angeles Times Book Review*, 20 August 1989.

———. "*The Second Front*: A Reflection on Milk Bottles, Male Elders, the Enemy Within, Bar Mitzvahs, and Martin Luther King Jr." *Black Men Speaking*. Edited by Charles Johnson and Jonathan McCluskey. Bloomington: Indiana University Press, 1997.

———. *The Sorcerer's Apprentice: Tales and Conjurations*. New York: Atheneum, 1986, rpt. 1987.

———. "The Twenty-Sixth Paul Tillich Lecture." Harvard Divinity School, Cambridge, MA, 10 April 2003. n.p.

———. *Turning the Wheel: Essays on Buddhism and Writing*. NY: Scribner, 2003.

———. "Where Philosophy and Fiction Meet" in Byrd 1999, 91–95.

———. "White Bandits of the West," review of *The Silent Brotherhood: Inside America's Racist Underground*, by Kevin Flynn and Gary Gerhardt (The Free Press, 1989). *Los Angeles Times Book Review*, 2 July 1989.

———. "Whole Sight: Notes on New Black Fiction" in Byrd 1999, 85–90.

Jones, John. *On Aristotle and Greek Tragedy*. Stanford: Stanford University Press, 1962.

Joyce, James. *Finnegans Wake*. NY: Viking, 1967.

Kakubayashi, Fumio. "An Historical Study of Harakiri." *Australian Journal of Politics and History*. 39:2 (1993). 217–25.

Kant, Immanuel. *Anthropology from a Pragmatic Point of View*. Translated by Victor Lyle Dowdell. Carbondale: Southern Illinois University Press, 1978.

———. *Foundations of the Metaphysics of Morals*. Translated by Lewis White Beck. Indiana: Bobbs Merill, 1959.

———. *The Critique of Judgement*. Translated by James Creed Meredith. Oxford: Oxford University Press, 1952.

———. "What Is Enlightenment?" *Kant's Political Writings*. Edited by Hans Reiss and translated by H. B. Nisbet. Cambridge: Cambridge University Press, 1970. 54–60.

Kass, Leon R. *The Beginning of Wisdom: Reading Genesis*. NY: Simon & Schuster, 2003.

Keneally, Thomas. "Misadventures in the Slave Trade." *New York Times* 1 July 1990: 8.

Kermode, Frank. "Introduction to the New Testament." *The Literary Guide to the Bible*. Edited by Robert Alter and Frank Kermode. Cambridge: Harvard University Press, 1987: 375–86.

King, Martin Luther, Jr. "Antidotes for Fear." *Testament of Hope: The Essential Writings and Speeches of Martin Luther King, Jr.* Edited by James M. Washington. San Francisco: HarperCollins, 1986.

———. "Letter from Birmingham Jail." *I Have a Dream: Writings and Speeches That Changed the World*. Edited by James Melvin Washington. New York: HarperCollins, 1986, 1992.

Kirk, G. S., J. E. Raven, and M. Schofield. *The Presocratic Philosophers: A Critical History with a Selection of Texts*. 2nd edition. Cambridge: Cambridge University Press, 1957, 1983.

Levasseur, Jennifer, and Kevin Rabalais. "An Interview with Charles Johnson" in McWilliams, 246–70.

Levinas, Emmanuel. *Totality and Infinity: An Essay on Interiority*. Translated by Alphonso Lingis. Pittsburgh: Duquesne University Press, 1969.

Little, Jonathan. *Charles Johnson's Spiritual Imagination*. Columbia: University of Missouri, 1997.

———. "An Interview with Charles Johnson" in McWilliams 97–122.

Lyke, M. L. "Author Navigates Uncharted Waters: *Middle Passage* Takes Readers on a Spirited Journey" in McWilliams 42–47.

Macquarrie, John. *An Existentialist Theology: A Comparison of Heidegger and Bultmann*. London: SCM Press, Ltd., 1955.

McKullough, Ken. "Reflections on Film, Philosophy, and Fiction: An Interview with Charles Johnson" in McWilliams 3–15.

McWilliams, Jim. "An Interview with Charles Johnson" in McWilliams 271–99.

———. ed. *Passing the Three Gates: Interviews with Charles Johnson*. Seattle: University of Washington Press, 2004.

Melville, Herman. *Moby-Dick*. NY: W. W. Norton and Company, 1967.

Merleau-Ponty, Maurice. *Phenomenology of Perception*. Translated by Colin Smith. New York: Routledge & Kegan Paul, 1962.

———. *The Visible and the Invisible*. Edited by Claude Lefort and translated by Alphonso Lingis. Evanston: Northwestern University Press, 1968.

Merton, Thomas. *The Way of Chaung-Tsu*. New York: New Directions, 1969.

Mills, Charles W. *Blackness Visible: Essays on Philosophy and Race*. Ithaca: Cornell University Press, 1998.

Morrison, Toni. *Beloved*. NY: Alfred A. Knopf, 1987.

———. *Sula*. New York: Plume, 1982.

———. "Unspeakable Things Unspoken: The Afro-American Presence in American Literature." *Michigan Quarterly Review*. 28:1 (Winter 1989): 1–34.

Moses, Greg. *Revolution of Conscience*. New York: Guilford Press, 1997.

Muther, Elizabeth. "Isadora at Sea: Misogyny as Comic Capital in Charles Johnson's *Middle Passage*." *African American Review* 30.4 (1996): 649–58.

Mudede, Charles. "The Human Dimension: An Interview with Writer-Philosopher Charles Johnson" in McWilliams 236–45.

Myers, George. "Being and Race: An Interview with Charles Johnson" in McWilliams 34–41.

Nash, William. *Charles Johnson's Fiction*. Urbana: University of Illinois, 2003.

———. "A Conversation with Charles Johnson" in McWilliams 214–35.

Neil, William. *Harper's Bible Commentary*. NY: Harper and Row, 1962.

Nietzsche, Friedrich. *The Birth of Tragedy*. Translated by Walter Kaufmann. NY: Random House, 1967.

New American Bible. NY: Catholic Book Publishing, Inc. 1992, 1987, 1980, 1970.

O'Connell, Nicholas. "Charles Johnson" in McWilliams 16–33.

O'Keefe, Vincent A. "Reading Rigor Mortis: Offstage Violence and Excluded Middles 'in' Johnson's *Middle Passage* and Morrison's *Beloved*." *African American Review* 30:4 (Winter 1996): 635–48.

Otto, Rudolf. *The Idea of the Holy*. Translated by John W. Harvey. Oxford: Oxford University Press, 1950, 2nd edition.

Ouimet, Lorraine. "Freedom through Contamination: Collapsed Boundaries in Charles Johnson's *Oxherding Tale* and *Middle Passage*." *Canadian Review of American Studies* 30.1 (2000): 33–51.

Parrish, Timothy. "Imagining Slavery: Toni Morrison and Charles Johnson." *Studies in American Fiction* 25:1 (Spring 1997): 81–100.

Partridge, Jeff. Private communication to John Whalen-Bridge. 26 May 2005.

Patterson, Orlando. *Freedom: Vol. 1: Freedom in the Making of Western Culture*. New York: Basic Books, 1991.

Pittman, John P. *African-American Perspectives and Philosophical Traditions*. NY: Routledge, 1997.

Plato. *Meno*. Translated by Benjamin Jowett. New York: Bantam, 1986.

Plutarch. *The Lives of the Noble Grecians and Romans*. Translated by John Dryden and revised by Arthur Hugh Clough. NY: Modern Library, 1932.

Posnock, Ross. *Color and Culture: Black Writers and the Making of the Modern Intellectual*. Cambridge, Mass.: Harvard University Press, 1998.

Quinones, Ricardo. *The Changes of Cain: Violence and the Lost Brother in Cain and Abel Literature*. Princeton, NJ: Princeton University Press, 1991.

Rahner, Karl. "Unity of the Love of Neighbor and Love of God." *A Rahner Reader*. Edited by Gerald A. McCool. NY: Crossroad, 1975: 239–44.

Richardson, Robert. *Emerson: The Mind on Fire*. Berkeley, CA: University of California Press, 1995.

Ricoeur, Paul. "Ethical and Theological Considerations on the Golden Rule." *Figuring the Sacred: Religion, Narrative, and Imagination*. Translated by David Pellauer and edited by Mark I. Wallace. Minneapolis: Fortress Press, 1995: 293–302.

———. *Oneself as Another*. Translated by Kathleen Blamey. Chicago: University of Chicago Press, 1992.

Rowell, Charles H. "An Interview with Charles Johnson." *Callaloo* 20.3 (1998): 531–47.

Rushdy, Ashraf H. A. "Phenomenology of the Allmuseri: Charles Johnson and the Subject of the Narrative of Slavery." *African American Review*. 26.3 (Autumn 1992): 373–94.

———. "Serving the Form, Conserving the Order: Charles Johnson's *Oxherding Tale*." *Neo-Slave Narratives: Studies in the Social Logic of a Literary Form*. New York: Oxford University Press, 1999.

———. "The Properties of Desire: Forms of Slave Identity in Charles Johnson's *Middle Passage*." *Arizona Quarterly* 50:2 (Summer 1994): 73–108.

Sartre, Jean-Paul. *Existentialism and Human Emotions*. NJ: Citadel Press, 1957, 1985.

Schott, Robin May. *Cognition and Eros: A Critique of the Kantian Paradigm*. University Park, PA: Pennsylvania State University Press, 1998.

———. "Gender and the Enlightenment." *Feminist Interpretations of Immanuel Kant*. Edited by Robin May Schott. University Park, Pa: Pennsylvania State University Press, 1997, 319–37.

Shakespeare, William. *The Tempest*. Edited by Virginia Mason Vaughan and Alden T. Vaughan. The Arden Shakespeare, Third Series. Surrey: Thomas Nelson and Sons, Ltd. 1999.

Sincere, Richard E., Jr. "High-Seas Adventure for a Freedman Stowaway on a Slaver's Ship." *The Washington Times* 23 July 1990: F1.

Smith, Patricia, Charles Johnson, and the WBGH Series Research Team. *Africans in America: America's Journey through Slavery*. New York: Harcourt Brace, 1998.

Spiegelberg, Herbert. *The Phenomenological Movement*. Vol. 1. The Hague, Netherlands: Martinus Nijhoff, 1978.

Staude, John Raphael. *Max Scheler: An Intellectual Portrait*. New York: The Free Press, 1967.

Steeves, James B. *Imagining Bodies: Merleau-Ponty's Philosophy of Imagination*. Pittsburgh, Pennsylvania: Duquesne University Press, 2004.

Storhoff, Gary. *Understanding Charles Johnson*. Columbia: University of South Carolina Press, 2004.

Streng, Frederick J. *Emptiness: A Study in Religious Meaning*. New York: Abingdon Press, 1967.

Sullivan, Roger J. *Immanuel Kant's Moral Theory*. Cambridge: Cambridge University Press, 1989.

Tanahashi, Kazuaki, Ed. *Moon in a Dewdrop: Writings of Zen Master Dogen*. Translated by Tanahashi *et alia*. San Francisco: North Point Press, 1985.

Taussig, Michael. *Mimesis and Alterity: A Particular History of the Senses*. New York: Routledge, 1993.

Thaden, Barbara Z. "Charles Johnson's *Middle Passage* as Historiographic Metafiction." *College English* 59.7 (1997): 753–66.

"The Art of Controversy." Narr. Kwame Holman. *Newshour with Jim Lehrer*. PBS. 8 Oct. 1999. Transcript. 4 May 2006. http://www.pbs.org/newshour/bb/entertainment/july-dec99/art_10-8.html.

The New Catholic Encyclopedia, 2nd ed. Thomson/Gale, 2003.

Travis, Molly Abel. "*Beloved* and *Middle Passage*: Race, Narrative, and the Critic's Essentialism." *Narrative* 2:3 (1994): 179–200.

Trifonias, Peter Pericles, ed. *Pedagogies of Difference: Rethinking Education for Social Change*. New York: Routledge, 2003.

Trucks, Rob. "A Conversation with Charles Johnson." *Triquarterly* 107/108 (Winter 2000).

Tsunetomo, Yamamoto. *Hagakure: The Book of the Samurai*. Translated by William Scott Wilson. Tokyo and New York: Kodansha, 1979.

Walker, Alice. "Everyday Use." *The Norton Anthology of American Literature, Volume E*, 6th ed. Edited by Jerome Klinkowitz and William H. Pritchard. NY: Norton, 2003.

Wanner, Irene. "Interviews with Northwest Writers: Charles Johnson," in McWilliams 159–91.

Watson, Burton, translator. *The Zen Teachings of Master Lin-chi: a Translation of the Lin-chi Lu*. Boston: Shambhala Press, 1993.

West, Cornel. *The American Evasion of Philosophy: A Genealogy of Pragmatism*. Madison: University of Wisconsin Press, 1989.

———. *The Cornel West Reader*. New York: Basic Books, 1999.

———. "The Dilemma of the Black Intellectual," *Critical Inquiry* 29 (4): 39–52.

Whalen-Bridge, John. "Charles Johnson." *Dictionary of Literary Biography, Volume 278: American Novelists Since World War II, Seventh Series*. Edited by James R. Giles and Wanda H. Giles. Detroit: Gale, 2003. 201–11.

———. "Shoulder to the Wheel: An Interview with Charles Johnson" in McWilliams 300–315.

———. *Political Fiction and the American Self*. Urbana: University of Illinois Press, 1998.

———. "Waking Cain: The Poetics of Integration in Charles Johnson's *Dreamer*." *Calalloo* 26:2 (2003): 504–21.

Williams. Angel Kyodo. *Being Black: Zen and the Art of Living with Fearlessness and Grace*. New York: Diane Publishing, 2000.

Willis, Jan. *Dreaming Me: From Baptist to Buddhist, One Woman's Spiritual Journey*. New York: Riverhead Books, 2001.

Wood, Philip. *Understanding Jean-Paul Sartre*. Columbia: University of South Carolina Press, 1990.

Wild, John. "Introduction" to Emmanuel Levinas, *Totality and Infinity: An Essay on Interiority*. Translated by Alphonso Lingis. Pittsburgh: Duquesne University Press, 1969: 11–20.

Wright, Dale S. *Philosophical Meditations on Zen Buddhism*. NY: Cambridge University Press, 1998.

Wright, Richard. "How Bigger Was Born." *Native Son*. New York: Harper Perennial Modern Classics, 2005.

Yeats, William Butler. "The Second Coming." *The Collected Poems of W. B. Yeats*, revised 2nd ed., edited by Richard Finneran. NY: Scribners, 1996.

"Yes . . . but is it Art?" Narr. Morley Safer. *60 Minutes*. CBS. WCBS, New York. 19 Sept. 1993.

CONTRIBUTORS

HERMAN BEAVERS is an associate professor of English at the University of Pennsylvania. He has published poetry and is the author of *Wrestling Angels into Song: The Fictions of Ernest J. Gaines and James Alan McPherson* (University of Pennsylvania Press, 1995).

GENA CHANDLER is an assistant professor of English at Virginia Tech where she teaches critical literary theory and nineteenth- and twentieth-century American and African American literature. She does research on modern and contemporary African American narrative.

MARC C. CONNER is an associate professor of English at Washington and Lee University in Lexington, Virginia. He edited *The Aesthetic Dimensions of Toni Morrison: Speaking the Unspeakable* (University Press of Mississippi, 2000) and has published essays, interviews, and reviews on numerous figures in American and Irish Modernism.

WILLIAM GLEASON is an associate professor of English at Princeton University. He is the author of *The Leisure Ethic: Work and Play in American Literature, 1840–1940* (Stanford University Press, 1999), as well as multiple essays and reviews on nineteenth- and twentieth-century American and African American literature and culture.

WILLIAM R. NASH is an associate professor of American studies at Middlebury College. The author of *Charles Johnson's Fiction* (University of Illinois Press, 2002), his articles and reviews have appeared in *Callaloo*, *African American Review*, and the *New England Review*.

LINDA SELZER is an assistant professor of English at Pennsylvania State University in University Park, Pennsylvania. She is the author of several articles on African American and American literature, and her "Master-Slave Dialectics in Charles Johnson's 'The Education of Mingo'" received the 2003 Darwin T. Turner Award for best article of the year in *African*

American Review. Currently she is completing a book-length study of Johnson's fiction.

GARY STORHOFF is an associate professor of English at the University of Connecticut (Stamford). He has published widely on American and African American literature in such journals as the *African American Review, Style, MELUS,* and the *Faulkner Journal.* He is the author of *Understanding Charles Johnson* (University of South Carolina Press, 2004).

JOHN WHALEN-BRIDGE is an associate professor in the Department of English Language and Literature at the National University of Singapore. He has written *Political Fiction and the American Self* (University of Illinois Press, 1998), as well as articles on Charles Johnson, Norman Mailer, Gary Snyder, and Christopher Isherwood. He is currently co-editing, with Gary Storhoff, a series of books about Buddhism and American culture.

INDEX